R. S. Thomas

MANCHESTER
UNIVERSITY PRESS

*To
Mary Margaret,
Jane, and John*

R. S. Thomas

Identity, environment, and deity

CHRISTOPHER MORGAN

Manchester University Press

Manchester and New York

distributed exclusively in the USA by Palgrave

Published by Manchester University Press
Oxford Road, Manchester M13 9NR, UK
and Room 400, 175 Fifth Avenue, New York, NY 10010, USA
www.manchesteruniversitypress.co.uk

Distributed exclusively in the USA by
Palgrave, 175 Fifth Avenue, New York,
NY 10010, USA

Distributed exclusively in Canada by
UBC Press, University of British Columbia, 2029 West Mall,
Vancouver, BC, Canada V6T 1Z2

British Library Cataloguing-in-Publication Data
A catalogue record for this book is available from the British Library

Library of Congress Cataloging-in-Publication Data applied for

ISBN   0 7190 6248 9 *hardback*

First published 2003

11 10 09 08 07 06 05 04 03   10 9 8 7 6 5 4 3 2 1

Typeset in Galliard by
D R Bungay Associates, Burghfield, Berks

Printed in Great Britain
by Bell & Bain Ltd, Glasgow

Contents

Illustrations

Preface

Who are we? Where are we going? At what cost? R. S. Thomas poses such questions so repeatedly and in such earnest that they have become the cornerstone of the edifice of his life's work. In answer to the questions one discovers the life of the man, rife with tensions, straddling paradox: a priest grappling with despair, a pacifist-nationalist, an activist-poet ardent for his second tongue. Thomas has been the quiet man embroiled in public controversy, the private man of outspoken causes, the shy man feared for the heat of his convictions. The passions that sent out the green probes of his work also animated his long life.

My first impressions of Thomas's work were of a direness, an anger, a metaphysical weight, a certain grief. Even now I cannot discredit these first impressions as false. But pursuing the poetry and the man over an ocean and years, I discovered that such impressions were merely the chronic symptoms of his deep regard. Behind the strenuous veil of rage and tears one discovers poignant sources: a profound reverence for the wild earth, a deep concern with creation's fate at the hands of humankind, a compassion for the broken and the lost, a vigorous wrestling with the possibility of a spiritual life, an insistence on the dignity of the individual reality, the individual identity, the individual language, culture, nation. Thomas repeatedly dares to imagine a more perfect world, and that daring inevitably forces him into the more dangerous dark of his pursuit until, in the end, the questions and their attendant muse appear to pursue him at least as much as he pursues them. Thomas is haunted by the dark precisely because of his heightened awareness, his keener consciousness of what might have been possible, of what might still be possible. One senses his powerful intelligence fused to a human heart; and his greatness lies partially for me in his uncompromised trueness to the accepted life as it is held up in tension against the dream. His despair is not merely despair but the duskier fruit of his hope.

It was a great privilege for me to live in Wales and write this book. Indeed, I am certain that I could not have written it without my life in Wales. I still get the distinctly palpable sense of Thomas's poems as a part of that earth, those hills, the rain, the sea, and the birds, which together form the substance and subject of their fierce celebrations. I am grateful for the strange good fortune that our separate paths crossed in the manner and at the time that they did; that we were thrown together as it were; and that Thomas's questions became my own. I hope this book succeeds in sharing some of that sense.

Acknowledgements

There are a number of organisations and individuals who have helped to bring this book to completion. I must first thank David Townsend for introducing me to the poetry of R. S. Thomas and for encouraging me to pursue my research in Wales. I must also thank the Rotary International Foundation for the Rotary International Ambassadorial Scholarship 1996–97 which first made it possible for me to undertake a study of R. S. Thomas in Wales. Equally my thanks go to the Committee of Vice-Chancellors and Principals of the Universities of the United Kingdom for the Overseas Research Student Award 1998–99 without which I could not have completed my work in Wales.

I would like to thank the English Department at the University of Wales Aberystwyth. I owe the greatest debt of thanks to Professor Peter Barry. Without his most generous gifts of time and conversation, his meticulous consideration and editing of countless drafts, and, not least, his kindness, wisdom, and friendship, this book could not have been completed. I must also thank the staffs of the Hugh Owen Library and the National Library of Wales. In particular I need to acknowledge my debt to the late Richard Brinkley for his continual help in locating materials, as well as for his ongoing support and friendship, both of which contributed toward the completion of my research.

In the field of Welsh writing in English, my heartfelt thanks go to members of The Association of Welsh Writing in English for their interest in, and support of, my work, and for their own important work which continues to enlighten and excite.

I must also thank John Pugh-Jones whose knowledge and love of Welsh language, people, and places proved contagious and, along with his personal warmth and long-standing devotion, continually fuelled my work.

Finally, my thanks go to R. S. Thomas himself for, on every occasion, his warm regard and honest concern, as well as, of course, for the poems themselves.

Portions of Chapter 1 of this book were presented in a paper to the Annual Conference of the Association of Welsh Writing in English,

March 1998. Portions of Chapter 4 were presented as a paper to the Department of English, University of Wales, Aberystwyth, October 1998. The final section of Chapter 5 was previously published as an article in *Welsh Writing in English* 4 (1998).

Introduction

Overview

The themes of identity, environment, and deity treated in this book reflect the major preoccupations of R. S. Thomas's life and work. My intention in the book has been to set out a detailed and comprehensive examination of these major themes as they occur across Thomas's substantial oeuvre, while at the same time providing an expanded frame within which the considerable complexity of Thomas's work can be more profitably explored. However, I want to stress throughout the book that these 'categories', while necessary to a practical exploration of the subtlety and interrelation of Thomas's work as a whole, are, ultimately, heuristic constructs. Like the individual poems, the 'categories' explored here are never strictly divisive or exclusive but, rather, fluid, very often reflecting, expanding, and qualifying one another. Thomas's search for identity cannot be divorced from his theological probings. His reflections on nature and science are equally the important settings and occasions for these 'other' questions of identity and deity. Thus, Thomas's work, viewed as a whole, forms a highly wrought mosaic. In its radical adherence to the truth of experienced life, both exterior and interior, it depicts an intricate, intimate, and ultimately inextricable reciprocity and tension across these broader categories. Finally, in each of the 'categories' examined, I have argued that Thomas's poetry is uniquely expansive in its effect, broadening each category intellectually while simultaneously relating all three to one another, making the oeuvre an organic whole with a life greater than the sum of its parts. This effect is what Thomas, quoting Wallace Stevens's 'Chocorua to Its Neighbor', refers to as 'acutest speech', the creation of a poetry of being, a speaking 'humanly from the height or from the depth / Of human things' (Stevens 1955: 300). It is this quality of 'acutest speech' in Thomas's work which I want to suggest, in the end, is the force which underpins its 'categories' and the deepening complexity and paradox explored within those categories, and which raises it, finally, to stand among the finest English poetry of the twentieth century.

Chapters 1 and 2 of the book argue that underpinning Thomas's oeuvre is a 'project' in autobiography which is rooted in the question of the poet's own elusive identities. I want to suggest that such poetic explorations and revelations of identity provide the *prima materia* of the poetry and form an underlying foundation to Thomas's poetry viewed as a single body of work. I will also suggest that, over the course of his many collections, a gradual development can be seen in Thomas's approach to this 'project' in autobiography, from a strenuous interior exploration of 'lost' or 'wounded' selves, towards a deepening philosophical acceptance and what he calls 'turning aside'.

Chapter 3 explores Thomas's treatment of the natural world, in particular the theology of nature mysticism vital to much of his work. I will argue for the importance of the natural world not only as revelatory for Thomas but also as distinctly violent and discompassionate, a paradox central to his understanding and his poetry.

Chapters 4 and 5 look closely at Thomas's increasing preoccupation with science: his long-standing philosophical concern with a scientific register for poetry, his own increasing experimentation with that register, his subtle ambivalence with regard to applied technology, his ongoing critique of 'the machine', and his view of modern physics as a branch of pure science potentially reconstructive in its employment of imagination and intuition. Although the significance of these topics is generally recognised by critics, that significance has, as yet, received scant detailed attention. My treatment in this chapter is aimed to reveal an often-underestimated intellectual breadth and sophistication in Thomas's philosophical grounding and poetic experimentation.

Finally, Chapters 6 and 7 examine Thomas's 'religious poetry'. I will look not only at the more exact nature of his re-configuring of Christian theology through a close consideration of his collections *H'm* (1972), *Frequencies* (1978), and *Destinations* (1985) but equally at his radical expansion of the category 'religious poetry', and at what he sees as the function of that poetry. My aim here is to *expand* discussion of Thomas by re-focusing more sharply on the exact nature of his poetic approach to a 'theology of experience' as reflected in his 'mythic' and '*via negativa*' modes. It is also my aim to highlight, again, the considerable intellectual breadth and sophistication of Thomas's thought and work in this regard. In addition to this expansion and re-focusing, however, I will argue, in concluding Chapter 7, for a movement in the general emphasis of Thomas's later 'religious poetry' away from the predominating experience of spiritual absence, fragmentation, and despair, towards, increasingly, apprehensions of presence, unity, and hope. I will suggest in the final section of the chapter not only the definite existence of a shift in this direction, but also that Thomas's 1985 collection *Destinations* represents the most concentrated expression of that shift, an expression which can be seen as emerging intermittently prior to *Destinations*, but which is most concentrated *within* the collection, and which continues to make itself felt throughout Thomas's later poetry to his final collection *No Truce with the Furies* (1995).

Of course this book is not intended to be exhaustive. At a time when R. S. Thomas is becoming widely recognised as among the finest poets and most penetrating thinkers of the twentieth century, rich seams in his work remain to be more thoroughly explored. Among these are the Prytherch cycle, the 'portrait-poems', the painting-poems, the love lyrics and, not least, his consistently surprising and powerful employment of metaphor. What I *have* intended is to bring Thomas's most important preoccupations into sharper focus, to deepen and broaden discussion of his large body of work, and to update and expand critical awareness of his significant achievements.

'Biculturality' and 'the wound' as source

Considering not only the sheer size of Thomas's twenty-seven-volume oeuvre but also its sustained vigour, urgency, and often angst, it is important to establish, briefly, the possible sources which underlie such a prodigious poetic energy. In addition to further highlighting the links underlying the categories of self, nature, science, and God, an examination of 'source' can serve both to ground an understanding of Thomas's work in the personal and simultaneously to provide access to a wider understanding of that work as reaching beyond the personal, as defeating a solipsistic isolation, and as becoming potentially representative in its wider significance.

In a 1990 interview for *Planet* magazine entitled 'Probings' Thomas remarks: 'I complained once to Saunders [Lewis] about the tension of writing in one language and wanting to speak another and his reply was that out of such tensions art was born' (35). The tension which Thomas complains of in this quotation between 'writing in one language and wanting to speak another' is more far-reaching and fundamental than the passing nature of his remark might at first indicate. As Lewis's reply indicates, the question of language for Thomas was and is not merely the utilitarian consideration of an appropriate medium for communication but the significantly deeper and ultimately more important question of personal *identity*. As Thomas knew, Saunders Lewis was able to answer that question by devoting his considerable energies and talents to the continued development of the

specifically Welsh-language culture which formed him. He simultaneously existed and expressed himself from a position wholly within the
linguistic parameters of such a culture and ultimately became its leading proponent. By contrast, Thomas's reported 'complaint' to Lewis
indicates a painful awareness of his own strenuous existence *between*
two cultures – the anglicised culture of his upbringing, education, and
profession as priest and poet, and the Welsh-language culture to which
he, as a young man, aspires, but outside of which he ultimately feels
himself to exist. Lewis's reply to Thomas's complaint indicates the older
writer's sensitive understanding of, and sympathy for, Thomas's existence between these two cultures and, most importantly, his reply neither denies the existence of such tension in Thomas nor encourages
any strenuous resolution towards one or the other cultural-linguistic
pole. Instead, Lewis affirms in Thomas the tension itself as the vital
source of art. What I am suggesting here, and throughout the chapters that follow, is that this reply by Lewis proves, in retrospect, to have
been of singular vital importance to the young Thomas by pointing to
the source and method of his future life's work. Thomas's poetry can
be viewed as an ongoing excavation of that tension of 'inbetweenness',
most often not as a reaching after resolution but as an embracing and
straddling of the frequently dire tensions of a divided identity, an exploration of 'woundedness', what he refers to in the poem 'Petition' from
H'm (1972) as 'Seeking the poem / In the pain' or, in 'The Porch'
from *Frequencies* (1978), as keeping his place 'on that lean / threshold, neither outside nor in' (2, 10). Indeed, despite his hard-won
Welsh-language fluency, and later what some have seen as his inheri-
tance of cultural leadership from Saunders Lewis, Thomas referred to
what he felt was his necessary restriction to English-language poetic
composition as 'the scar on my personality', a comment which, in its
graphic metaphorical power, indicates not only the existence of such a
wound but equally its depth and visible aftermath (*South Bank Show*,
1991). Indeed, that aftermath is apparent even as late as Thomas's
1995 collection *No Truce with the Furies* in which he writes, in the
poem 'Reflections', of the mirror as

> a chalice

> held out to you in
> silent communion, where graspingly
> you partake of a shifting
> identity never your own. (31)

In these lines, as across the oeuvre as a whole, the scrutiny of self becomes a primary and even sacred poetic act for Thomas, but one resulting characteristically in the uncomfortable perception or experience of a shifting identity.

While this 'inbetweenness' or 'wounding' in Thomas may be the result primarily of a linguistic, and therefore cultural, exclusion, a wide variety of additional tensions can be seen as contributory. It is possible that Lewis was himself somehow aware of this deeper complexity, stating in his reply to Thomas not that out of *this one linguistic tension* but that 'out of *such tensions*' (my italics) art is born. A plurality of tensions come into play here and include, for example, a political yearning by Thomas for a predominantly agricultural, pre-industrialised, independent Welsh nation, as against the factual weight of a history which has often eroded the possibility of either linguistic or political autonomy. There is, as well, the matter of Thomas as a priest of the Church in Wales, an Anglican vicar ministering amongst a native community traditionally non conformist.

Beneath the surface of these more obvious linguistic, political, and religious hauntings are still other tensions, less overt, more obscure and even obscured, but none the less central and potent. For example, the first prose-poem from his autobiographical collection *The Echoes Return Slow* (1988) describes, in a shocking way, what Thomas, at that time past seventy years old, imagines to have been the experience of his caesarean birth. It is not primarily his mother who is 'wounded' in the operation but, rather, in a fundamental way, the infant poet is 'marked out' for life as a creature doomed to suffer and search:

> Pain's climate. The weather unstable. Blood rather than rain fell. The woman was opened and sewed up, relieved of the trash that had accumulated nine months in the man's absence. Time would have its work cut out in smoothing the birth-marks in the flesh. The marks in the spirit would not heal. The dream would recur, groping his way up to the light, coming to the crack too narrow to squeeze through. (2)

The quotation places a finger squarely on the pulse of Thomas's poetic sources: emotional pain; a perception of the self as insubstantial and devalued or 'trash'; spiritual wounding; the dream of healing, of a unity and wholeness to be regained; grief over loss; anxiety at the inability to 'squeeze through', to belong wholly to one world or another.[1] If the poem reveals a generalised view of existence as primarily a matter of unrelieved pain and anxiety, other poems by Thomas such as, for example,

'Ap Huw's Testament', 'Welsh', 'The Boy's Tale', 'In Memory', 'Album', 'Salt', 'Roles', and even certain prose remarks, indicate, in a much more specific, though still at times veiled way, the sources of such pain to be rooted equally in the young Thomas's early experiences of family relationship. There are suggestions by the poet of a needy and oppressive mother, of an absent and later distant father, of the sense of that father's independent masculinity being brought ultimately to bay by a dominant matriarchy, and, as a part and direct consequence of all this, of the sensitive and inward boy's own significant bewilderment to the point of wounding.

Although this book is not an attempt at biography, I do want to suggest that Thomas's life-experience, as he repeatedly expresses it in his work, seems to revolve significantly around painfully complex issues of identity and belonging that can be traced to a multiplicity of causes, and that such interior divisions are, indeed, as Saunders Lewis suggests, the powerful wellsprings not only of difficulty and suffering but, potentially, of construction and art. The themes treated here are, as we shall see, on various levels and in different ways, all similarly grounded by and shot through with the fact of that multiply fragmented experience, the pain entailed in its necessary confrontation, and the recurrent, although often frustrated, dream of its healing. Thomas himself seems to accept this view of fragmentation, inbetweenness, wounding, and its attendant suffering as the ultimate source of his work by his identification with Kierkegaard's description of the poet, with which the Danish philosopher opens his *Either/Or*:

> What is a poet? An unhappy man who hides deep anguish in his heart, but whose lips are so formed that when the sigh and cry pass through them, it sounds like lovely music. His fate is like that of those unfortunates who were slowly tortured by a gentle fire in Phalaris's bull; their cries could not reach the tyrant's ears to cause him dismay, to him they sounded like sweet music. And people flock around the poet and say: 'Sing again soon' – that is, 'May new sufferings torment your soul but your lips be fashioned as before, for the cry would only frighten us, but the music, that is blissful.' (43)

Thomas cites a portion of this description in his 1978 article for *Planet* entitled 'The Creative Writer's Suicide' where he discusses 'the question of pressure on the creative writer, pressure which has been experienced down the centuries' (178). What Kierkegaard, and Thomas in turn, seems to be suggesting is that the poet by his or her very nature must

suffer, and furthermore that such suffering is the most important source
of art, that the poet's natural function is and always has been to trans-
pose emotion into the substance of 'lovely music'.² The poet's lot is 'deep
anguish', 'slow torture', 'gentle fire', but because the poet's 'lips are so
formed', the experience of such pain is to be heard only as 'blissful song'.
Indeed, Thomas asks in the poem 'Probing' from his 1975 collection
Laboratories of the Spirit:

> Where are the instruments
> of your music, the pipe of hazel, the
> bull's horn, the interpreters
> of your loneliness on this
> ferocious planet? (23)

These lines indicate what Thomas, like Kierkegaard, sees as the singularity of the poet: his or her peculiar designation in and isolation from
the wider world. The interpretation of that loneliness through music
or poetry becomes the special province of the poet. But while
Kierkegaard and Thomas may share this view of the poet as a kind of
wounded singer, it should be noted too that both men suggest a simultaneous exploration and veiling of personal suffering. Kierkegaard, in
the quotation above, writes of the poet as 'an unhappy man who *hides*
deep anguish in his heart' (my italics). Similarly, J. P. Ward, in his book
R. S. Thomas (1987), writes that the poetry often 'indicates a strong
character covering a deep hurt' (8). Thomas himself seems to confirm
that suggestion, writing in 'To a Young Poet' from the 1963 collection *The Bread of Truth* that 'From forty on ... time fosters / A new
impulse to conceal your wounds' (11). Although poetic explorations
of woundedness are central to Thomas's work, there is a sense in which
the more exact sources of that pain do become consciously obscured
by the poet. Thomas, like Kierkegaard's poet, opens his mouth, and
the sound which issues forth is the transposition of anguish into song.
But there is an added subtlety and nuance to the song as its more particular origins are blurred over, as, for example, in the above quotation from *The Echoes Return Slow*. The reader experiences not so much
a clear vision along revealed lines, as in some 'confessional' verse, but
the sensation of a leashed, subterranean grief, its continually rising pressure, a simultaneous capping of that pressure, and, as a result, a tightly
controlled poetic atmosphere often electric with plangency. Thomas
repeatedly exhibits a kind of dual compulsion toward the exploration
and masking of wounds, towards a kind of nakedness and vulnerability on the one hand and towards armour and concealment on the other.

Some of Thomas's most powerful poems indulge both tendencies, revealing an often warm and delicate humanity at the centre of more strenuous exteriors. Thomas declares, for example, in 'Evening' from *No Truce with the Furies* (1995):

> Let us stand, then, in the interval
> of our wounding, till the silence
> turn golden and love is
> a moment eternally overflowing. (19)

We find in these lines the narrator's reaching out in simple acknowledgement and acceptance of his own individual pain as somehow representative of a wider, universal pain. The lines are 'confessional' not by any meticulous tracing to exact personal sources but by their branching beyond the ego to touch a wider, human experience.

This brings me to my final point in this introduction, which is that Thomas's intense, if veiled, scrutiny of his own inbetweenness does not, paradoxically, narrow or parochialise his relevance but, on the contrary, ultimately broadens it. Anthony Thwaite, in his 'Introduction' to a selection of Thomas's work, calls the poems 'an embodiment of Robert Frost's dictum: "You can't be universal without being provincial"' (1996: ix). I want to suggest that R. S. Thomas's 'provincialism' – that is his close, intimate, even at times microscopic attention to and scrutiny of his own immediate localities, both exterior and interior – ultimately branches into a broader relevance, the reason for this being not only the depth of his poetic or philosophical probings, the pressing ever farther and deeper in a quest for understanding and meaning but, equally and in conjunction with this drive, the relentless demand by Thomas for the real, the actual, for poetic renderings which reflect the truths of physical and spiritual experience. Together these compulsions discover a shared human ground which ultimately transcends the personal. These requirements often confront and even explode Thomas's own romantic penchant for ideal states of being. But my point here is that such demands, for meaning and for truth, according to their urgency for Thomas, effectively broaden his most private explorations into wider representations. Thomas becomes not only a Welsh poet writing in English from the edge of Western Europe, but a poet who, by way of pursuing and exploring these 'fated particulars', has, paradoxically, broadened or even mythologised them into a wider human context and connection. In his poem 'The Word' from *Laboratories of the Spirit* (1975) Thomas writes:

> A pen appeared, and the god said:
> 'Write what it is to be
> man.' And my hand hovered
> long over the bare page,
> until there, like footprints
> of the lost traveller, letters
> took shape on the page's
> blankness. (3)

According to these lines Thomas's poetic project involves not only what he elsewhere calls the 'illumination of the self', but, according to that illumination, also 'what it is to be / man' (*Echoes*, 1988: 103).

In terms of criticism of Thomas's work this has not always been the predominant view. W. Moelwyn Merchant acknowledges that, concerning Thomas's poems, 'They have appeared to many readers and critics to have a direct, even disarming simplicity and to compass a very limited and readily available range of themes' (1990. 1). More recent and notorious is Ian Gregson's 1994 article for *New Welsh Review* entitled 'An Exhausted Tradition' in which he implies that Thomas's work is lacking in 'its alertness to issues currently concerning Western culture in general' and in which he argues that Thomas and Seamus Heaney are both 'products of comparatively static rural cultures whose preoccupations are largely irrelevant to anyone brought up with television' (23, 22). In contrast to Gregson and others, and central to my overall argument in the chapters which follow, is my contention that the poetry of R. S. Thomas is in fact *distinctly* alert 'to issues currently concerning Western culture' and that, as such, it is uniquely relevant; that his preoccupations, the most important of which I will take up in these pages, are significantly more complex and sophisticated than is often acknowledged, reflecting not only a quite cosmopolitan multiplicity of classical and contemporary sources and influences but also some of the major preoccupations of a post-industrial West.

Finally, in his 1990 interview for *Planet* magazine which I have already referred to, Thomas defines poetry as 'the communication of thought and emotion at the highest and most articulate level. It is the supreme human statement' (1990b: 40). He then refers to Wallace Stevens's 'Chocorua to Its Neighbor' and quotes the following lines from section XIX:

> To say more than human things with human voice,
> That cannot be; to say human things with more
> Than human voice, that, also cannot be;
> To speak humanly from the height or from the depth
> Of human things, that is acutest speech.

It is precisely Stevens's idea of 'acutest speech' as speaking humanly from
the heights and depths of human things which ultimately underpins R.
S. Thomas's oeuvre, and therefore also the various subjects and argu-
ments which I present in the following chapters. What I have undertaken
in this book is a closer and fuller examination of Thomas's most important themes in order to disseminate and highlight not only the significant intellectual breadth and linguistic sophistication of his work but also
its 'acutest speech', its speaking humanly from the height and depth of
human things which effectively expands its parameters from a poetry
highly individual, local, and in time, to a poetry more widely human, representative, outside of time and yet *for* time. It is, I think, primarily this
quality of acutest speech in Thomas's poetry which elicits Ted Hughes's
tribute to Thomas's *Collected Poems 1945–1990*: 'Lorca said: "The poem
that pierces the heart like a knife has yet to be written". But has anybody
come closer to it than R. S. Thomas? And not merely once, in his case,
but again and again.' It is, in part, with an academic examination of this
heartfelt judgement by Hughes that this book is concerned.

Notes

1 Thomas's poem 'The Son' from his 1975 collection *Laboratories of the Spirit* posits a
   similar pain and grief as befalling his own new born son.
2 Dylan Thomas's work would likewise seem to support this idea of 'the wound' as poetic
   source. In his 'Poem on his Birthday', for example, he describes the poet as one who
   'Toils towards the ambush of his wounds', who 'sings towards anguish', and for whom
   'Dark is a way and light is a place' (1993: 145–6).

Part I
Elusive identities

1 Poetry as autobiography

Introduction

'This To Do' is a frequently overlooked poem in R. S. Thomas's 1966 collection *Pieta*. Although appearing twenty years into Thomas's career as a published poet, *Pieta* effectively ends the early periods of work at Manafon (1942–54) and Eglwysfach (1954–67) and simultaneously initiates the succeeding periods at Aberdaron (1967–78) and Rhiw (1978–94) on the Llŷn peninsula in north Wales. The collection falls not only within a geographical transition for the poet but at a major thematic cross-roads as well. The move to Aberdaron in 1967 marks in Thomas's work a gradual letting go of his long absorption and wrestling with the life of the upland farm communities and, if not his actual insistence, at least his poetic insistence on a personal and national Welsh identity.[1] The poetry of Aberdaron and later Rhiw is conspicuously 'ingrowing'. It depicts an altogether inward and downward metaphysical probing of the nature of deity and of the individual self. Of course in one sense Thomas has always been a poet of interiors, and yet it seems clear that the poems of the Aberdaron period contribute increasingly toward a sustained project in autobiography. My suggestion here is not that Thomas begins a project in poetic autobiography after moving to Aberdaron, but more that, for Thomas, poetry, by its very definition, *is* autobiography. The poems written after the move to Aberdaron illustrate a significant acceleration and intensification of that autobiographical instinct.

In this first chapter my technique will be to explore the idea of poetry as autobiography using Thomas's poem 'This To Do', but also introducing the work of a fairly wide range of other major writers who, while perhaps not directly influential on Thomas's work, have nevertheless undertaken similar projects in their own writing and thus become a loose context in the light of which Thomas's work in this area becomes more clear. I rely most heavily here upon Montaigne's writings in his *Essays* and on much of the prose work of Seamus Heaney. I also suggest specific parallels in the theoretical work of Charles Olson and Wallace Stevens, and in the poetry of Derek Walcott. In addition to these parallels I want also to suggest that Thomas's 'project' in autobiography has much in common with Carl Jung's theories of the subconscious and unconscious as he writes of them in his *Memories, Dreams, Reflections* (1961). Chapter 2 is devoted almost exclusively to a detailed investigation of Thomas's poems as a guide to the crucial aspects of his own project of poetic auto-biography.

'The door to myself'

'This To Do' (*Pieta*, 1966) is a good place to start, not only because it falls 'on the cusp', as it were, of Thomas's geographical move and a cor-responding intensification of the autobiographical instinct but because it says something about what poetry as autobiography is for R. S. Thomas. Despite its forward-looking title, the poem functions as a kind of anchor and pivot in the oeuvre, echoing a process which underlies the prior work while consciously reaffirming a purpose in writing which may have been more or less unconscious up to this point. Thus the poem consolidates, foregrounds, and, in some ways, reinitiates the ongoing project of auto-biography in Thomas's work, what I refer to here as the 'project of the self'. The poem begins:

> I have this that I must do
> One day: overdraw on my balance
> Of air, and breaking the surface
> Of water go down into the green
> Darkness to search for the door
> To myself. (12)

Underpinning the poem as a whole is an experience of dislocation or alienation in which a 'surface self' is clearly conscious of an alternate hidden or 'buried self', the recovery of which is fraught with difficulty and danger. The opening phrase 'I have this that I must do / One day' is at once direct, determined, and yet tinged with vague misgiv-ing, with dread and with an actual *in*determinacy. Thomas accepts the search as both uniquely his own and imperative, and yet the enjambment of 'one day' creates a doubling back effect, a recoil from the bold approach of the opening line so that a reader is presented with knowledge and purpose as well as, in Kierkegaard's words, fear and trembling. The final lines of the poem reiterate this ambiva-lent opening and add to it an acknowledgement of the courage and sacrifice necessary for the discovery of the hidden door to the self:

> I must go down with the poor
> Purse of my body and buy courage,
> Paying for it with the coins of my breath.

This project of the self is not a literary rendering of the ego, an aim
asserted by Pound and Eliot as the hallmark failure of the Romantic
period. It is precisely the wounded ego here which recognises its alienation, its incompletion. Thomas's project is one which seeks a reversal of
the birth sequence, a passage back to the womb. Comfortable balances
of air are disrupted in the process, the light abandoned. According to the
poem the passage back to the door of the self requires a negation of the
air-element natural to the poet. He ceases to breathe and must live on
gulped reserves of oxygen in the green dark. In this sense the state of
original alienation is not wholly one of discomfort: the poet lived at the
surface of life, breathing, balanced, hearing and seeing. The descent to
search for the door to the self entails a forfeiture of such normal 'com-
forts', an initiation into 'dumbness and blindness / And uproar of scared
blood / At the eardrums'.

Thomas's metaphor of submersion and underwater exploration
implies not only a surface alienation but a revisiting of lost sources in the
self which can, if only temporarily, counteract that alienation. The search
is essentially hopeful and aimed at a reunification of the divided self. The
poet's perilous descent into the land of the dead where 'the slow corpses
/ Swag' is also a descent toward some life-giving force.[2] Though the poet
is 'dumb' in the process of the dive, he must still return to his surface
life, to air, light, and speech. Thus the poems become a narrative of these
repeated forays into the self; brief illuminations of lost sources. Poetry in
this manner becomes both the product of search and the search itself. It
becomes the breathing space, as the American poet Charles Olson would
claim, the breath itself, the respiration of the poet.[3]

If Thomas's poetry is an underwater archaeological excavation of the
self, the unity he achieves over alienation, though repeatable, can only be
temporary. The fragments of the divided self remain touchstones for each
other but can enjoy no permanent reunion such as that anticipated in
Derek Walcott's 'Love after Love' from his 1976 collection *Sea Grapes*:

> The time will come
> when, with elation,
> you will greet yourself arriving
> at your own door, in your own mirror,
> and each will smile at the other's welcome
>
> and say, sit here. Eat. (328)

Walcott implies a dislocation and search clearly similar to Thomas's. The difference however lies in Thomas's lack of closure and 'elation' as the self and the other re-adhere. Walcott ends 'Love after Love' with the line: 'Sit. Feast on your life.' For Thomas the comfort afforded by this kind of epiphany is never realised. Thomas's project of the self is achieved in endless returns, in 'spending the coins of the breath from the body's poor purse', in revisiting the lost sources at cost, over and over again.[4]

This idea of poetry as the product of endless returns to the door of the self is approached from a slightly different angle in Thomas's 'Introduction' to the *Penguin Book of Religious Verse* (1963). There Thomas 'roughly' defines religion as 'embracing an experience of ultimate reality', and poetry as 'the imaginative presentation of such' (64). According to these qualifications poetry becomes, for Thomas, the imaginative presentation of an experience of ultimate reality. In the light of Christ's declaration that 'the Kingdom of God is within you', it becomes natural to equate Thomas's experiences of ultimate reality with the sub-aqua encounters at the door of the self. This is not something new to poetry. It is essentially a harking back to the words of the Oracle of Apollo at Delphi: '*Gnothi seauton*', know thyself, which later became the Socratic dictum and the seed of the notion of the *daimon* as teacher and guide. In sixteenth-century France '*gnothi seauton*' becomes, for Montaigne, the leading principle of his *Essays*:

> What does Socrates treat more amply than himself? And what does he most often lead his pupils to do, if not to talk about themselves – not about what they have read in their books but about the being and movement of their souls? (1991: 425)

This talking about the being and movement of the soul is not something put forth as stored knowledge, not a series of careful revelations. The being and the movement are those things which poetry, like the Socratic dialogues, discovers as poetry happens. In his 1978 lecture 'The Makings of a Music' Seamus Heaney describes this as

> a version of composition as listening, as a wise passiveness, a surrender to energies that spring within the centre of the mind, not composition as an active pursuit by the mind's circumference of something already at the centre. (1980: 63)

Heaney's use of the words 'surrender' and 'spring' points to a delicate immediacy, a simultaneous cause and effect in the process of poetry as autobiography. Though the poem recounts, in Thomas's words, an experience of ultimate reality, the poem is, simultaneously, an integral part of the experience itself. For all three writers, Montaigne, Heaney, and Thomas, that experience becomes not only central but religious in significance, requiring a conscious turning away from the emptiness of exteriors in order to be realised. In his essay 'On Vanity' Montaigne makes his most emphatic discourse on this idea. One can hear in the essay the same chords Thomas strikes in 'This To Do':

> We are swept on downstream, but to struggle back towards our self against the current is a painful movement; thus does the sea, when driven against itself, swirl back in confusion. Everyone says: 'Look at the motions of the heavens, look at society, at this man's quarrel, that man's pulse, this other man's will and testament' – in other words always look upwards or downwards or sideways, or before or behind you. That commandment given us in ancient times by that god at Delphi was contrary to all expectation: 'Look back into your self; get to know your self; hold on to your self'. Bring back to your self your mind and your will which are being squandered elsewhere; you are draining and frittering yourself away. Consolidate your self; rein your self back. They are cheating you, distracting you, robbing you of your self. (1991: 1132)

Montaigne suggests the distinguishing characteristic and natural inclination of humanity to be a capacity for self-division or alienation. Also in keeping with Thomas, Montaigne claims that the process of reunification, of healing of such fragmentation, entails a 'painful movement' against such tides. But where Montaigne proves particularly helpful is in his articulation of why such a painful movement toward reunification of the divided self is important. The verbs Montaigne uses to describe the man who refuses to know himself are translated as 'squander', 'fritter', and 'drain', verbs of dispersal and of lessening which imply that the alienated self is being spent in a gradual thinning of powers. Not knowing its centre, the self achieves a splintering process which can end only in annihilation. The project of the self as a counter-activity to such inertia is a search and discovery, a grappling with sources of being and identity which, while painful, is ultimately a matter of self-preservation. For Thomas and Montaigne it is only in this way that one achieves any sense of one's proper place and purpose in life. It is only in this way that one comes to know the authentic identity on which human happiness is continually predicated.[5]

Neither Montaigne nor Heaney underestimates the difficulties involved in the project of the self. Montaigne writes of these difficulties

in a passage from his 'On Practice' which becomes an excellent portrait
of the poet's work and life:

> It is a thorny undertaking – more than it looks – to follow so roam-
> ing a course as that of our mind's, to penetrate its dark depths and
> its inner recesses, to pick out and pin down the innumerable char-
> acteristics of its emotions. It is a new pastime, outside the common
> order; it withdraws us from the usual occupations of people – yes
> even from the most commendable ones. (424)

Unlike Montaigne, Heaney writes in his 1974 lecture 'Feeling into
Words' of the project of autobiography more specifically in terms of
poetry and its exploration of a buried life:

> poetry as divination, poetry as revelation of the self to the self, as
> restoration of the culture to itself; poems as elements of continu-
> ity, with the aura and authenticity of archaeological finds, where the
> buried shard has an importance that is not diminished by the
> importance of the buried city; poetry as a dig, a dig for finds that
> end up being plants. (1980: 41)

While this reiterates much of what Thomas describes in 'This To Do',
Heaney refers here to 'elements of continuity'. The kind of intense struggle evidenced in Montaigne and more acutely in Thomas is, I think, conspicuously absent in Heaney. Like Wordsworth, Heaney not only seems
capable of easier reconnections with 'sources', but the selves in Heaney
appear fewer and more grounded, less shifting and elusive than the often
myriad selves which emerge in Thomas's poems. For example, Heaney,
in his 1966 poem 'The Diviner' from his first volume *Death of a
Naturalist*, likens the poet's rediscovery of such sources to the water
diviner's gift with the forked hazel, 'circling the terrain, hunting the
pluck / Of water', feeling in his veins and flesh its course under the earth
(1966: 48). Subsequently, in 'Feeling into Words', Heaney calls this the
'gift for being in touch with what is there, hidden and real' (1980: 47).
Using slightly different imagery Heaney also 'finds' himself in texture of
the felt earth and the action of digging.[6] In 'Bogland', from his collection *Door into the Dark* (1969) he writes: 'Our pioneers keep striking /
Inwards and downwards' (41). The element here is earth, bog, and the
movement is through layers of the sedimentary self. Again, in 'Feeling
into Words' (1974) Heaney admits: 'When I called my second book *Door
into the Dark* I intended to gesture towards this idea of poetry as a point
of entry into the buried life of the feelings' (1991: 52). But in con-
tradistinction to Heaney's images of accessing the 'buried life', Thomas's

images are characteristically fluid and shifting: the murky sea, the clouded sky, the shifting mirror.[7] For example, Thomas writes in 'Reflections' from *No Truce with the Furies* (1995) that

> The furies are at home
> in the mirror; it is their address.
> Even the clearest water,
> if deep enough can drown. (31)

This kind of resignation to a confrontation with the furies in the mirror, the many selves all seemingly pitted against the poet, is typical in Thomas's work, not a vocalisation of the Romantic first-person stance but a more Modernist grappling with multiple elusive identities. While he writes in the final stanza of the poem of the mirror as a chalice, significantly it is one

> held out to you in
> silent communion, where graspingly
> you partake of a shifting
> identity never your own.

One feels that Thomas's discoveries of an inner identity or source, when they do occur, are won by bitter toil rather than received as gift, as in Heaney. Wallace Stevens writes in his 1942 lecture 'The Noble Rider and the Sound of Words' that nobility in poetry is not artifice of the mind but is

> a violence from within that protects us from a violence without. It is the imagination pressing back against the pressure of reality. It seems, in the last analysis, to have something to do with our self-preservation; and that, no doubt, is why the expression of it, the sound of its words, helps us to live our lives. (1951: 36)

And though Heaney, in his 1989 lecture 'The Redress of Poetry', refers to this selection from Stevens, the ideas seem characteristic more of Thomas's project than of Heaney's: the violence within, the pressing back, the self-preservation.[8] Montaigne writes in 'On Practice', 'I can think of no state more horrifying or more intolerable for me than to have my Soul alive and afflicted but with no means of expressing herself' (1991: 421). Such a statement foregrounds one of the differences between Heaney's project and Thomas's. Thomas's poetry grows out of the intolerability of mute affliction. It seems that his soul, suffering a chronic fragmentation and alienation, strives towards discovery through expression.[9] Conversely, Heaney's project grows out of the hidden spring that swells in gift, and accordingly his work is more the celebration of discovery than the dire angst of often frustrated pursuit.

Two final distinctions and one final note will help distinguish this notion of poetry as autobiography in R. S. Thomas, the first a distinction between craft and technique, the second a distinction between will and waiting, and the note an effort to locate the project of the self in its significantly wider context.

In 'Feeling into Words' (1974) Heaney offers a subtle insight into the nature of the poetic project of the self by distinguishing between definitions of craft and technique. He defines craft as

> what you can learn from other verse. Craft is the skill of making. It wins competitions in the *Irish Times* or the *New Statesman*. It can be deployed without reference to the feelings or the self. It knows how to keep up a capable verbal athletic display. (1980: 47)

Craft is formal skill in the expression of poetry, without reference to the project of the self. And yet earlier I suggested that poetry as autobiography consists in a kind of instantaneous, simultaneous listening, discovery and expression; that the listening and the discovery are inherent in and inseparable from the expression. Thus while craft is a vital force brought to bear primarily in the expression of poetry, it remains, in Heaney's holistic view, equally dependent upon the hearing and the finding as well. Without craft the poetic project of the self is certainly not impossible but is, for Heaney, significantly crippled. Conversely, technique, Heaney suggests, is the experience of the well bucket caught when 'the chain draws unexpectedly tight and you have dipped into waters that will continue to entice you back. You'll have broken the skin on the pool of yourself' (1991: 47). Technique is an experience at the hidden door to the self. Heaney claims it involves for the poet 'a definition of his own reality … a dynamic alertness that mediates between the origins of feeling in memory and experience and the formal ploys that express these in a work of art' (1991: 47). It becomes possible of course that either side of such an equation might prove weak, that is, that one might understand and utilise formal ploys but lack an alertness to 'the origins of feeling in memory and experience'. In the same way one might lack understanding and use of formal ploys but demonstrate an acute alertness to origins of feeling. While affirming Heaney's view of the ultimate interdependence of craft and technique, what these first two chapters examine specifically is Thomas's poetic technique, his habitual 'breaking the skin on the pool of himself', the process of unveiling 'his own reality'.

In his 1972 article 'Belfast' Heaney also differentiates between the passivity and the activity required by the poet in pursuit of the self. He refers to his own listening for poems, to waiting and to hearing, much as Wordsworth did, but he also writes of seeking, of journeying, of dredging up, of overmastering, as he claims Yeats did. His conclusion is that poems

> involve craft and determination, but chance and instinct have a role in the thing too. I think the process is a kind of somnambulist encounter between masculine will and intelligence and feminine clusters of image and emotion. (1980: 34)

This dichotomy is vital to an understanding of R. S. Thomas's poetry as autobiography. What Heaney refers to as the active masculine will and the passive feminine image are characteristics which recur in Thomas's poetry. And yet Thomas's poems are full of images of waiting as well. A reference to Keats can help here. In his famous 'Negative Capability' letter to his brothers in December 1817 Keats claims that the 'Man of Achievement' is able to suffer in partial knowledge, able to accept that he cannot, in this life, know himself fully, but has learned contentment with partial knowledge, with listening and waiting for what is yielded up from outside of his conscious power (1954: 53). Paradoxically, that apparent passivity, that listening in half-light is, for Keats, the key to literary achievement. The impulses at work are towards polar opposites, towards definitiveness and solidity as much as toward the darkness of unknowing. It is precisely according to these kinds of tensions and through these joined channels that I am suggesting Thomas approaches himself in poetry.

There is a paradoxically universal application of the project of the self in which the limitation necessary to the project is also the gateway to a kind of transcendence. Again, Charles Olson, while differing from Thomas in most aspects of theory and content, is closely in tune with this idea of a transcendence made available through the recognition of natural limits. In his 1950 essay 'Projective Verse' Olson asserts that

> the use of a man, by himself and thus by others, lies in how he conceives his relation to nature, that force to which he owes his somewhat small existence. If he sprawl, he shall find little to sing but himself, and shall sing, nature has such paradoxical ways, by way of artificial forms outside himself. But if he stays inside himself, if he is contained within his nature as he is participant in the larger force, he will be able to listen, and his hearing through himself will give him secrets objects share. (1967: 60)

Interestingly, Olson's singing by way of 'artificial forms' outside of the
self is akin here to the overweighting of craft, the lack of technique
pointed up by Heaney. But most importantly here, according to Olson,
to have the ability to remain contained within one's individual nature and
to express that nature within its boundaries is to achieve a transcendence
into the larger world, is to receive 'the secrets objects share'. Similarly,
the attempt on the part of the poet to achieve transcendence not only
shatters that more proper containment but results in a dislocation, an
artificiality, a dispersal of powers towards impotence and ultimately annihilation. W. B. Yeats reiterates the idea with great clarity in his 'Samhain:
1905':

> If I had written to convince others I would have asked myself, not
> 'Is that exactly what I think and feel?' but 'How would that strike
> so-and-so? How will they think and feel when they have read it?'
> … If we understand our own minds, and the things that are striv-
> ing to utter themselves through our minds, we move others, not
> because we have understood or thought about those others, but
> because all life has the same root. Coventry Patmore has said, 'The
> end of art is peace', and the following of art is little different from
> the following of religion in the intense preoccupation it demands.
> (1962: 199)

'The things that are trying to utter themselves through our minds', and
which address the one root of all life, are loosed, according to Yeats, not
by an active pursuit of transcendence but by an almost religious attention to the ground falling within the more humble parameters of the self,
what Thomas has referred to as his playing 'on a small pipe, a little aside
from the main road' (Merchant 1990: 4). Thomas writes in his
'Autobiographical Essay' originally published in the *Contemporary
Authors: Autobiographical Series*:

> Was it a slight gift of Keats's negative capability that made it often
> so difficult for me to believe in my separate, individual existence?
> Certainly it has come to me many times with a catch in the breath
> that I don't know who I am. (1986: 20)

And yet a gift for Keats's negative capability does not imply a complete
lack of self-knowledge so much as a partial and incomplete self-knowledge, a knowing and a not knowing. This is what characterises Thomas's
project of the self: a knowing and a not knowing, an aggressive pursuit
and standing off, a rage to master and a humble waiting, all finally resolv-
ing themselves into a quest inwards and downwards in which, as we shall

"Poetry as autobiography" 23

see, the strenuous, active journey eventually gives way to a gentler turning aside.

The title of Barbara Prys-Williams's article '"A consciousness in quest of its own truth": Some Aspects of R. S. Thomas's *The Echoes Return Slow* as Autobiography' itself indicates this antipathy between knowing and unknowing which underlies Thomas's poetic project. In particular, Prys-Williams's use of the term 'quest' (originally by G. Gusdorf from whom the phrase in the title originates) is highly appropriate here. Prys-Williams writes that

> Boundaries of the genre have expanded considerably beyond the limiting supposition that autobiography is coterminous with self-written biography. Theorists now allow that good autobiography may as fully communicate the sense of a life as the events of a life and that 'self-enacting, self-reflexive verbal structures' may be important means of communicating the feel of a life from inside, in areas in which discursive prose might be inherently inadequate. (1996: 98)

Prys-Williams asserts that

> the poetic medium ... enables Thomas to explore fully his own sense of self, partly through allowing privileged access to the unconsciousness (and image-producing) part of his psyche, so important a determinant of the unique nature of his whole being.

What she so rightly points to in all of this is a poetic act that is autobiographical not in the sense of depiction of the 'finished' or 'unified' self but rather as exploration and discovery of the many, often contradictory selves of the individual as they reside within and, indeed, play between the conscious and unconscious layers of the poet's psyche. I would suggest that this exploration and discovery of an interior and often subconscious complexity is rooted in Jungian psychology. In the 'Prologue' to his autobiographical *Memories, Dreams, Reflections* (1961), composed when he was eighty-three, Jung writes:

> My life is a story of the self-realisation of the unconscious. Everything in the unconscious seeks outward manifestation, and the personality too desires to evolve out of its unconscious conditions and to experience itself as a whole ... In the end the only events in my life worth telling are those when the imperishable world irrupted into this transitory one. That is why I speak chiefly

of inner experiences, amongst which I include my dreams and
visions ... All other memories of travels, people and my surround-
ings have paled beside these interior happenings ... But encounters
with the 'other' reality, my bouts with the unconscious, are indeli-
bly engraved upon my memory. In that realm there has always been
wealth in abundance, and everything else has lost importance by
comparison ... I can understand myself only in the light of inner
happenings. It is these that make up the singularity of my life, and
with these my autobiography deals. (1963: 17–19)

I would argue that this is precisely the project of the self that Thomas
undertakes in poetry, the gradual self-realisation of the unconscious, the
strenuous evolution towards wholeness, encounters or even 'bouts' with
the 'other' reality. In this sense Thomas crosses a bridge as it were from
an early affinity with Wordsworth and Tennyson to a more complicated
project in keeping with ideas of Yeats's *daimon* and Pound's personae.
What one finds in Thomas's poetry is increasingly a portrait of 'inner
happenings' next to which the outward circumstances and more traditionally 'autobiographical' details of the poet's life become the mere setting of a more interior drama. Though Prys-Williams never suggests this
link to Jung, she does write that 'For Thomas, then, autobiographical
writing can be seen as an aid to consolidation of a self' and cites Paul J.
Eakin's view of 'autobiography not merely as the passive, transparent
record of an already completed self but rather as an integral and often
decisive phase of the drama of self-definition' (1996: 101). Interestingly,
Prys-Williams refers in this capacity to Sartre's *The Words*, in which the
philosopher claims to have not rendered but *discovered* his identity
through the very act of writing:

I was born of writing. Before that, there was only a play of mirrors.
With my first novel, I knew that a child had got into the hall of mirrors. By writing I was existing ... I existed only in order to write and
if I said 'I', that meant 'I who write'. (1996: 99)

In this wider light we can reassess what is commonly referred to as R.
S. Thomas's 'autobiographical proseworks'.[10] Although interesting and
informative, the prosework is largely a record of the poet's exterior
rather than interior life. As traditional autobiography it can be thought
of as forming something of a shell, a definite and sometimes protective
covering which houses the softer flesh of the poems within. Again, it
must be kept in mind that while Thomas's identity clearly incorporates
the important external factors of race, family, culture and geographic

locations, and while those externals are very much reflected in the early poetry of the Manafon and Eglwysfach periods, it is the quest for a deeper sense of identity and belonging, for understanding of the interior and ultimate components of being, beyond those of the physical and exterior, which the project of the self in Thomas's poetry takes up. It is in the poems that he achieves his transparency of being, his complex display of the search for identity. The prosework forms mostly the solid framework of what Montaigne calls 'Fortune', within which the transparency of the poems has been achieved. None the less, as we shall see, the prosework can reveal important clues to the project of the self which Thomas undertakes in the poetry.

Notes

1 Speaking to the Conference of Library Authorities in Wales and Monmouthshire in 1968 in a lecture titled 'The Making of a Poem' Thomas said: 'I became rather tired of the themes about nationalism and the decay of the rural structure in Wales … I can now think more about poetry and remember all the wonderful poems which I might have written and never will write if I had concentrated more on pure poetry and on the technique of poetry without pushing these themes and propagandas; without strutting and beating my chest and saying I am Welsh' (1969: 110).

2 Such descent into the land of the dead has a pertinent classical parallel in Virgil's *The Aeneid*, Book VI, in which Aeneas plucks the golden bough and descends into Hades to reunite with his dead father Anchises. The reunion can be seen as a touching of his source by Aeneas which fires him with resolve in his continuing journey on upper earth. The allusion is made use of by both Heaney and Thomas. See Heaney's 1991 collection *Seeing Things* and Thomas's poem 'First Person' in *Mass for Hard Times* (1992).

3 Breath plays a central role in Olson's theory of projective verse. In particular he argues that poetry must take up the 'possibilities of the breath, of the breathing of the man who writes as well as of his listenings' (1967: 51).

4 Also see Thomas's 'The Wood' from *Experimenting with an Amen* (1986) in which the man enters the labyrinthine wood of himself in search of his lost identity. The poem concludes: 'How many times / over must he begin again?' (16). Similarly, in *The Echoes Return Slow* (1988) Thomas refers to 'the slowness / of the illumination of the self' (103).

5 Note Thomas's allusion to the function of the Oracle at Delphi in 'The Reason' from *Mass for Hard Times* (1992). The poem is discussed in the final portion of the present chapter.

6 See 'Digging' from Heaney's first collection *Death of a Naturalist* (1966).

7 Even in 'Inside' from his *Later Poems* (1983), though Thomas describes himself as a geological phenomenon, the solidity and availability created by such an image is effectively counteracted by simultaneous use of opposing images of obscurity and transience.

8 Thomas clearly echoes these sentiments in 'After Jericho' from *Frequencies* (1978):
>   There is an aggression of fact
>   to be resisted successfully
>   only in verse. (43).

9 This idea seems clearly related to the theory of masks one finds in Wilde and Yeats in which both protection and renewal can be achieved through the struggle towards connections with multiple identities. See Carol Christ's excellent treat ment of this idea in her *Victorian and Modern Poetics* (1984).

10 *Y Llwybrau Gynt* (1972); an essay for *Contemporary Authors: Autobiographical Series* (1986); *Neb* (1985); *Blwyddyn yn Lleyn* (1990); *ABC Neb* (1995).

2 'No-one with a crown of light'

Introduction

In his autobiography, *No-one* (1985), R. S. Thomas recounts his reaction to the sight of his shadow falling on the pre-Cambrian rocks at Braich y Pwll on the Llŷn peninsula:

> On seeing his shadow fall on such ancient rocks, he had to question himself in a different context and ask the same old question as before, 'Who am I?', and the answer now came more emphatically than ever before, 'No-one.'
>
> But a no-one with a crown of light about his head. He would remember a verse from Pindar: 'Man is a dream about a shadow. But when some splendour falls upon him from God, a glory comes to him and his life is sweet.' (78)

The quotation briefly highlights, in a three-part progression, the project of the self which, for R. S. Thomas, is integral to the project of poetry. In its first phase the experience raises the recurring question of identity for the poet: 'Who am I?' Immediately following that question, in phase two of the progression, comes the equally emphatic and recurring answer to the question: 'No-one'. Phase three begins the new paragraph and qualifies the original answer, expanding its single dimension into a wider paradox. A no-one with a crown of light about his head is clearly not merely someone, but someone of importance, a glorified someone, a saint or a god.[1] The quotation, from Pindar's eighth Pythian Ode, which forms the latter half of phase three, brings the experience back to its origins in shadow and at the same time restates the entire progression: '"Man is a dream about a shadow. But when some splendour falls upon him from God, a glory comes to him and his life is sweet."' Thomas's answer to the question 'who am I?' has two parts: I am no-one; I am someone. Pindar's answer echoes the poet's, but with one significant difference: man is a dream about a shadow, and yet in the favour of God he *becomes* something more, something characterised by glory and sweetness. Pindar's transformation of man from dream and shadow to glory and sweetness is directly contingent upon the splendour falling from

God. Thomas's no-one and someone are, by contrast, simultaneous real-
ities apparently independent of any such contingency.

It is important to isolate and retain this discrepancy without attempting to resolve it down into a unity. Much of Thomas's poetry can be seen
as flowing out of the single recurring question 'who am I?' The poems
which spring from that root are sometimes characterised by the paradoxical answer of no-one *and* someone, and at other times characterised by the
answer of no-one who *becomes* someone through a recognition of divine
grace. In the first case the conjunction is important. Thomas is not claim-
ing to be no-one *or* someone, but rather these things together, no-one *and*
someone. The poet is not charting fluctuations between options which
occur across time, but investigating how the emotional experience of
being no-one and someone can coexist, how the insubstantiality of the
dream and shadow he feels himself to be can partake equally of the characteristics of glory and sweetness which he also feels himself to be.
Ultimately this becomes an investigation into the pain of non-being and
the pleasure of actual being. It is his repeated attempts to reconcile this no-
one and this glorified someone, to realise them alone and together, which
creates the sense of a personal *agon* in much of Thomas's work.

But the search for Pindar's transformer, the splendour of God, the
acceptance by God of the no-one, is equally vital to Thomas's project.
Thomas becomes increasingly aware that the search for the self *is* the
search for God; that the discovery of God *is* the discovery of the hidden
or lost self. This search for and waiting on grace or acceptance can be
seen as the driving force behind the poet's metaphysical probings into
the being and nature of God which become so prominent in the collections of the 1970s. In those collections Thomas can be found searching for positive evidence of God, for response and vocalisation from
God, for the words or even for the sense of the words 'you are
accepted'.

What the prose passage from *No-one* reveals then, upon this closer
inspection, are three foundations of Thomas's project of the self. First, the
search for the self is rooted in the recurring question of identity. Second,
the answer to that question 'who am I?' entails the paradoxical possibility
of being at once no-one and someone. Third, the discovery of the someone is contingent upon grace, that is, upon divine communication of
acceptance of the no-one. These ideas comprise the points of departure in
a study of Thomas's poetry as autobiography. The six points which I will
now explore in the remainder of this chapter, with reference to Thomas's
actual poems, are more particular and subtle elements which can be seen
to arise from these three foundations.

Although this chapter treats these six points in a generally chrono-logical order, and while the points themselves may seem to indicate a kind of linear development in Thomas's work, it would be a simplification of the idea, and of the poetry, to categorise the project in this way. Thomas's poetic movements are often circular and involve a scrupulous reworking of themes. Although some linear developments might be tracked, the ideas of return, variation and even contradiction are of equal importance to the expression of a whole and reality-based experience upon which the poet insists. Keeping in mind, then, that they are not intended as a chronological mapping, the six points to be treated are as follows.

1. The poetic project of self-discovery as an interior journey through obscurity toward contact with the lost self. This idea foregrounds the del-icate, paradoxical nature of the relationship between the seeker and the lost self for Thomas.

2. The spiritual evolution of the seeker which, for Thomas, is inte-gral to and dependent upon the search for the self. Thomas's assertion of this evolutionary process introduces his notion of the multiplicity of interior selves. In particular he makes the important link between the receptivity of the seeker to the multiple voices within and the continued spiritual evolution of the seeker.

3. The interior wound as the source of poetry and the issue of its possible healing. This leads naturally into Thomas's view of the poet's role in society.

4. The appropriateness of the poet's inner journey, powers assisting in that journey, and the mystical, supernatural context of which that jour-ney becomes a part.

5. The inseparability of the search for the self and the search for God.

6. The questioning of the journey image in favour of the seeker's turning aside as a means of reunification or arrival. This turning aside for Thomas enables a temporary defeat of time and healing of the wound, while itself becoming a source of poetry. Thomas's stance can be seen to turn gradually from one of active pursuit to one of contemplative silence.

In all this we can see as well that, for Thomas, poetry does not merely function as tool in the work toward realisation of the self and God, but that poetry, its process, *is* the exploration and discovery of that self.

'Long torture of delayed birth'

If 'This To Do' seems to indicate a project yet to be undertaken by the poet, 'A Person From Porlock' from *Song at the Year's Turning* (1955) is evidence that the project has been ongoing since the beginning of

Thomas's poetic career. The poem is about an interruption in the poet's writing by a 'caller at the door' and reveals some important aspects of Thomas's idea of poetry as autobiography. The poem inverts our first point above by considering first the relationship of the seeker to the self before taking up the motif of the journey.

The poem's central metaphor is that of birth. The narrator is inter-rupted while his mind is

> big with the poem
> Soon to be born, his nerves tense to endure
> The long torture of delayed birth. (103)

But as early as line 2 Thomas reveals that the caller is 'eternal, nameless', not a particular person from Porlock, as in Coleridge's footnote to 'Kubla Khan', but the perpetual diversion and division which threatens to abort the poem's safe passage into light. We are reminded of this again in stanza 2 when Thomas relates that the caller is 'casual', a 'chance cipher that jogs / The poet's elbow, spilling the cupped dream'. Thomas is highlighting two aspects of his own poetic process here: the concentration and suffer-ing required of the poet to bring the poem safely to birth, and the extreme delicacy of the whole undertaking. In the first case the poet, with 'the still-ness about his brain', is 'tense to endure / The long torture of delayed birth'. In the second case the poem is referred to as both 'the embryo' and 'the cupped dream'. But as a result of the chance interruption the embryo is 'maimed', the cupped dream 'spilled'. Already what we see here is not the poet exhuming the preserved carcass of the poem in its entirety from the bog-preserve of memory, as in Heaney, but a much more interior process involving the poet's own physiology and calling up ideas of con-ception, gestation, development. Thomas is suggesting here an interior growth of a living creature whose survival is by no means assured, precar-ious as a cupped dream, vulnerable to the chance ciphers which divert the poet's intent. But something of equal importance here is that we do not perceive the poet so much as the maker, the word-smith of the poem, as the feminine vessel, the womb within which the poem is nurtured to matu-rity. Thomas portrays at once a strange remove as well as a deep intimacy between the poet and the poem. They are one, the poem wholly depen-dent on the poet, and yet they are also distinct, the poem developing out of a force paradoxically beyond and within the poet which 'uses' the poet. We lack here the sense of the poem as something achieved, except in its being brought successfully to birth by the poet.[2]

In the last stanza of the poem the narrator, having been called away from the poem's birth at its critical moment, must make his long return:

> The encounter over, he came, seeking his room;
> Seeking the contact with his lost self;
> Groping his way endlessly back
> On the poem's path, calling by name
> The foetus stifling in the mind's gloom.

These lines foreground the whole idea of interior journeying which is central to 'This To Do' and, indeed, to Thomas's poetic project as a whole. 'His room' here is, of course, not only the poet's actual room but the inner room of the mind as a womb 'big with the poem / Soon to be born'. Isolating the verb sequence in the sentence out of which the stanza is composed both highlights this motif of the inward journey and underscores the opacity of that journey, its characteristic obscurity: seeking, seeking, groping, calling, stifling. What the narrator is seeking is the embryo, the cupped dream. But, significantly, not only has the embryo become a foetus, having grown in the narrator's absence; it is also referred to as the 'lost self' with which the narrator seeks contact. Here again we can sense the poet's intimacy with 'the other' as well as his detachment. The narrator is able to call the foetus by name, but that he is calling at all is indication of their separation. The poem becomes not merely the expression of a search for contact with the lost self but a map, a path 'endlessly back' to where the child lies 'stifling in the mind's gloom'. Here again is the straining of poetic sight in the mind's dark on a journey toward the lost self.[3]

'The Letter', from Thomas's *Poetry for Supper* (1958) is also a poem about the process of poetic composition. The letter of the title may as readily be a poem as a correspondence. And though Thomas makes reference to geographical locations, those names become metaphors for places

> That the spirit recalls from earlier journeys
> Through the dark wood, seeking the path
> To the bright mansions. (26)

In these images one can see again the interior journeying and attendant visual obscurity which characterise, for Thomas, the project of the self. 'The Letter' is not, however, simply a reiteration of the philosophy of composition we find in 'A Person from Porlock'. Thomas adds two significant variations here. First, in stanza 2 Thomas writes of man's 'long growth / From seed to flesh, flesh to spirit', suggesting that man's journey into the 'dark wood' of himself, while primarily at this stage a search for contact with the lost self, is not merely a symptom of his earthly life but functions on another level as a catalyst in his larger evolutionary movement from non-being (seed) to physical being (flesh) to spiritual being (spirit). The letter is both a record of, and an instrument in, this movement from flesh to spirit, thus adding to the search for the lost self a wider spiritual dimension which, as we shall see, becomes important in the later poems. Second, we learn in the final stanza of the poem that the pen with which the letter is written is dipped 'in black ink of the heart's well'. But while we are led to assume that the narrator has composed the letter himself, we find, in the concluding lines, that it is the hand that 'has written / To the many voices' quiet dictation'. Here again are the simultaneous intimacy and distance which the poet experiences in relation to the inner self. But significantly in this case it is not the inner self but the inner *selves*. The dictation is by the 'many voices'. Once again the narrator has come seeking through darkness for the lost self, the hidden self, but when that self is discovered it is not only other than the seeking self but is many rather than one. As in 'A Person From Porlock' the successful birth of the poem or letter requires the poet's strict attentiveness to these inner selves. The narrator must agree to become, in part, an instrument of the many selves in order to continue in his 'long growth / From seed to flesh, flesh to spirit'. Thus we find in 'The Letter', in conjunction with our second point above, an expansion of the context within which the search for the self takes place, a multiplication of the inner selves and a necessary receptivity to those selves as significant additions to the project of poetry as autobiography in R. S. Thomas.

Another crucial aspect of Thomas's project of poetry as a form of autobiography, our third in the list above, is highlighted in his first collection of the Aberdaron period, *Not that He Brought Flowers* (1968), in the short and somewhat inconspicuous 'No'. For Thomas poetry seems frequently to be the product of an interior pain, a sustained wound, a deep sense of grief over the broken condition of humankind and its inability to heal itself. The first prose sequence in the autobiographical collection *The Echoes Return Slow* (1988), examined briefly in the Introduction, traces this sense of the wound to the remembered moment of birth:

> Time would have its work cut out in smoothing the birth-marks in the flesh. The marks in the spirit would not heal. The dream would recur, groping his way up to the light, coming to the crack too narrow to squeeze through. (2)

Here we have both the marking of flesh and spirit at birth and the poet's helplessness to remedy either. Time may smooth the flesh but Thomas is adamant that 'the marks in the spirit would not heal'. Coupled with this sense of crippling and inadequacy is the recurrent dream of 'the light', here not only the light after the darkness of the womb, but the light as healing, as spiritual wholeness and resurrection from the brokenness Thomas seems to feel is endemic to human existence. Thus the project of poetry becomes, for R. S. Thomas, an exploration of the wound, a searching of it partly, but not merely, because it hurts, but primarily because, if understood rightly, the wound may provide an access to the light which Thomas envisions as always just beyond reach.

The poem 'No', while in some ways enigmatic, is clear in its depiction of poetry as the product of this examination of the wound. In the poem the nameless man is a singer approached by the 'Thing', here evil and sin, which causes him to retch. Significantly, none of the onlookers knows why the Thing has caused such a reaction in the man. And though the Thing allows the man a short respite, eventually it touches him with its raw hand. At that touch, Thomas tells us,

> the wound took
> Over, and the nurses wiped off
> The poetry from his cracked lips. (10)

Not only is this a graphic portrayal of the wound as the source of poetry but it highlights what, for Thomas, is one of the essential roles of the poet in society. As he relates in the phrase 'none knew why', the poet exists emotionally 'outside of' the masses in his highly developed sensitivity to the Thing. This sensitivity and consequent wounding effectively isolate him from the others who never fully understand it. For Thomas the creative artist is set apart, privileged even, to suffer more deeply than others, an idea which, as I have suggested already in the Introduction, he shares with Kierkegaard. For both men the creative artist becomes a kind of wounded icon doomed by his very nature to a suffering which, paradoxically, is the key to his art: his wound is, simultaneously, his gift. This is depicted equally powerfully in the picture-poem 'Guernica' which accompanies Picasso's painting of the same name in the collection *Ingrowing Thoughts* (1985). Thomas claims that

> The painter
> has been down at the root
>   of the scream and surfaced
> again to prepare the affections
>   for the atrocity of its flowers. (9)

In these lines the poet is clearly writing about his own project as much as Picasso's. In an image reminiscent of 'This To Do' the painter goes down to the root of the scream and surfaces again. The root is here both the door to the lost self and the door to the wound. The atrocious flowers in the poem's final line are, of course, the product of the visited root. The image is strangely appropriate. The flowers/paintings/poems are a natural exhalation of the root, screams emanating from a buried source with which the artist comes into contact. The results of that contact, the flowering of art, are often as frightening as they are beautiful.

Thomas's volume *Frequencies* (1978) is the last in the Aberdaron period before his retirement to nearby Sarn Rhiw. We find two things highlighted in *Frequencies* which expand our understanding of Thomas's project of poetic autobiography. These expansions refer to my fourth point of inquiry. The first is an affirmation that the journey inwards and downwards to make contact with the lost self and explore the wound is not always one characterised by fear and foreboding, as images up to this point tend to indicate. The second expansion is one in which the search for the lost self becomes contextualised in a wider and somewhat mystical spiritual dimension.

In the poem from sequence 35 of *The Echoes Return Slow* (1988) Thomas refers to his mind as 'this dark pool I / lean over' and writes of probing that dark pool in the disturbing image of

> putting my hand
> down, groping with bleeding
> fingers for truths too
> frightening to be brought up. (71)

And yet in *Frequencies*, in the poems 'Groping', 'In Context', and 'Night Sky' we find evidence of the appropriateness and the pleasures of the poet's inward journey. 'Groping' does not merely indicate the darkness of the journey, but includes hands, voices, lights without shadow which become for the poet guiding, reassuring spirits:

> Moving away is only to the boundaries
> of the self. Better to stay here,
> I said, leaving the horizons
> clear. The best journey to make
> is inward. It is the interior
> that calls. Eliot heard it.
> Wordsworth turned from the great hills

> of the north to the precipice
> of his own mind, and let himself
> down for the poetry stranded
> on the bare ledges.
>   For some
> it is all darkness; for me, too,
> it is dark. But there are hands
> there I can take, voices to hear
> solider than the echoes
> without. And sometimes a strange light
> shines, purer than the moon,
> casting no shadow, that is
> the halo upon the bones
> of the pioneers who died for truth. (12)

In the first stanza Thomas rejects an exterior 'moving away' as essentially superficial, as merely an escape to 'the boundaries / of the self'. The poet also affirms in stanza one the interior call and places himself in a tradition of poetic responses to that interior call. Even Wordsworth, Thomas claims, turned from his cherished exteriors in nature in order to scale an inner landscape where poetry resided.[4] The final stanza of the poem begins by affirming the darkness up to this point so characteristic of the poet's journey. But central to the poem is Thomas's insistence that the hands to take and the voices to hear are both more substantial than the dark and 'solider than the echoes / without'. By this Thomas indicates both the appropriateness of the poetic response to the interior call and the succour, and even pleasure, which that response can elicit. The contemplative life of interiors becomes here, for Thomas, a more substantial reality than the exterior life of the senses.

In the final five lines of 'Groping' Thomas describes a 'strange light' that is 'purer than the moon' and which casts no shadow as it becomes a 'halo upon the bones of the pioneers who died for truth'. This strange light that sometimes falls is the ultimate confirmation for Thomas that his interior journeying is of the highest calling and that, while at times perilous and difficult, it is no less than divinely ordained. It also points to a widening of the context of the poet's search from the merely personal to the supernatural or cosmic. This opening out of the context of the search is developed more fully, though still vaguely, in 'In Context', the poem which directly follows 'Groping'. 'In Context' depicts the narrator as being acted upon by those same cosmic, 'unseen forces'. There is considerable disproportion in the co-operation of the narrator with these unseen forces:

> There was a larger pattern
> we worked at: they on a big
> loom, I with a small needle. (13)

What one senses here is the poet's expanding vision of his project in which he plays a minor role in a larger, more mysterious plan. Thomas writes that

> a power guided
> my hand. If an invisible company
> waited to see what I would do,
> I in my own way asked for
> direction, so we should journey together
> a little nearer the accomplishment
> of the design.

And again:

> It was not
> I who lived, but life rather
> that lived me.

What we are seeing in both of these poems is that, for Thomas, the journey within is the response to a definite call. While that response is both difficult and frightening, it also yields art to the extent that the conscious will is subsumed into the voice of the other, the lost self or selves which somehow partake of the supernatural world. Such a forfeiture of will appears to make possible an assistance in the journey by inner forces previously unknown, as well as to involve the poet increasingly in a significantly wider supernatural context.

This sense of being caught up into the larger elemental life of the universe is dramatically illustrated in 'Night Sky', also from *Frequencies*. Thomas writes that

> Every night
> is a rinsing myself of the darkness
>
> that is in my veins. I let the stars inject me
> with fire, silent as it is far,
> but certain in its cauterising
> of my despair. (18)

The words 'I let' suggest that this connection to higher power is, to some extent at least, an act of the will. We should also note how the narrator's partaking in this higher life is a rinsing of the darkness within and affords

a cauterising of the wound. The final lines of the poem describe a meditative state in which the journey inward has produced a unity with the
supernatural and ubiquitous power without:

> Resting in the intervals
> of my breathing, I pick up the signals
> relayed to me from a periphery I comprehend.

The rhythmic breath and rest of the narrator and the ease with which he
receives the supernatural signals, even his mere comprehension of the
periphery, all stand in stark contrast to the angst-ridden explorations of
obscurity typical of Thomas's journeying.

Two final aspects of Thomas's project of poetry as autobiography
remain to be explored here, corresponding to points five and six above.
Both of these aspects appear (though not for the first time) in *Frequencies*
and become prominent in the poems of the Rhiw period. As we have
seen, Thomas's search for the self becomes grounded in a larger and
somewhat mysterious spiritual context almost Whitmanesque in its
dimensions.[5] But we can also see developing in Thomas's search for the
self a unification with the more particular search for God. God becomes
relocated in these poems as a being not so much 'out there', as he, she
or it is typically portrayed in Thomas's collections from the 1970s, as a
God 'in here', whose discovery by the poet is increasingly a part of the
self-discovery undertaken in poetry. The first stanza of 'Pilgrimages' is
typical in its portrayal of search after the elusive God. Thomas writes that

> He is such a fast
> God, always before us and
> leaving as we arrive. (51)

Here is the image of the search for the anthropomorphised God as a journey outward from the self, with God forever moving off ahead of the
poet's constantly outward probing. But in the final lines of the poem
Thomas poses a rhetorical question that effectively reverses that older
image, replacing it with a new realisation:

> Was the pilgrimage
> I made to come to my own
> self, to learn that in times
> like these and for one like me
> God will never be plain and
> out there, but dark rather and
> inexplicable, as though he were in here?

The journey outward becomes a return to the self, and not only to the self but specifically to a God of interiors who is dark and inexplicable, in much the same way as the self. The poem 'Perhaps', also from *Frequencies*, reinforces this idea in a more complex way. Here the narrator looks into the mirror of his own intellect for God, that is, he looks into himself, but finds, at first, only God's absence there. The poet tells us that

> Looking in that mirror was a journey
> through hill mist where, the higher
> one ascends, the poorer the visibility
> becomes. (39)

Here is the search of the mirrored self for God characterised as a journey through obscurity.[6] But although Thomas asserts God's absence from the mirror in the beginning of the poem, he goes on to state in lines 11–13 that the journey

> could have led to despair
> but for the consciousness of a presence
> behind him, whose breath clouding
> that looking-glass proved that it was alive.

While God is never clearly delineated in the looking glass of the self the narrator is none the less distinctly conscious of his presence and finds for proof of his existence the very cloud that obscures him.[7] Further, it is in the search for the self that God's presence is finally discerned. Indeed, for Thomas the search for the self *becomes* the search for God.

The final aspect we must turn to here is point six, Thomas's own challenging, in the later poetry, of the adequacy of the journey as an image. Does the journey ever end? Are the self and God fully realisable in this life? Does one proceed to a terminus, to the end of a stage, only to begin a new stage? Does the wound heal? Is the interior pressure of seeking relieved? And if the wound is healed and the terminus reached, what then?

Thomas suggests in the poem 'Travels', from *Frequencies*, that his journeying has been in error to the extent that it has led him away from what he calls 'the smooth pupil / of water' (38). That water is a stationary stillness requiring one to turn aside from movement in order to contemplate its depths. Thomas rejects his previous journeying in this poem as a kind of self-deceit, a movement away from the self which might have been approached in the stillness of the pool that was always available to him. In the poem the narrator feels

> the coldness
> of unplumbed depths I should have
> stayed here to fathom.

Water here, the still pool of water, is the element in which the self and
God can finally be realised. In disregarding the still pool Thomas claims
to be doomed to watch

> the running
> away of the resources
> of water to form those far
> seas that men must endeavour
> to navigate on their voyage home.

Thus, once the pool is forsaken, the voyage home becomes a return to
beginnings. The element and resource of still water in which the self and
God reside run out to become obstacles, 'far seas' that must now be nav-
igated in order to recover the still pool. This turning aside to an acceptance of the spiritual plenitude at hand becomes increasingly, for
Thomas, an overturning of the corrupting influence of time and a corresponding realisation of eternity. Thus journeying for the poet is juxtaposed to an acceptance in which can be found the elusive self, the elusive
God, the healing of the wound, the terminus of the search and which is
also, for Thomas, the proper end of human existence.[8]

   This pausing by the still pool is the subject of the painting-poem
'Cézanne: The Bridge at Maincy' from *Between Here and Now* (1981).
Thomas writes that the empty bridge is

> awaiting
> the traveller's return
>
> from the outside
> world to his place
> at the handrail to
> watch for the face's
> water-lily to emerge
> from the dark depths. (49)

The still pool waits for the traveller's return from a journeying outside
of or beyond himself. It is only upon his return and by way of his watching of the dark depths that the water-lily of his face will finally emerge.
This image of flowers is of course reminiscent of the other painting-
poem, 'Guernica', in which flowers emerge from contact with the roots
of the hidden self. But it is ultimately the turning aside that is important

here. The traveller returns 'to his place / at the handrail to / watch'. It
is precisely this finding of one's place at the still pool to watch for the self
to emerge that the poem seeks to highlight.[9]

Another example of this halting in the journey and turning aside to
a revelation of eternity in the present moment is Thomas's 'The Bright
Field' from the 1975 collection *Laboratories of the Spirit*, a poem I will
examine more closely in Chapter 3. Thomas writes that

> Life is not hurrying
>
> on to a receding future, nor hankering after
> an imagined past. It is the turning
> aside like Moses to the miracle
> of the lit bush, to a brightness
> that seemed as transitory as your youth
> once, but is the eternity that awaits you.

In these lines the ephemeral moment becomes an occasion for the poet's
perception of the eternal. Clearly the emphasis here is not on journeying, but precisely on a withdrawal from the journeying, both its backward probing of the 'imagined past' and its forward anticipations of the
'receding future', in favour of a present-tense waiting which becomes
expanded into what might be called, for Thomas, a sacramental experience of the eternal in time.

Thomas writes powerfully about this possibility of a transcendence
of time in the 1990 volume *Counterpoint* as well:

> But the silence in the mind
> is when we live best, within
> listening distance of the silence
> we call God. This is the deep
> calling to deep of the psalm
> writer ...
>
> It is a presence, then,
> whose margins are our margins;
> that calls us out over our
> own fathoms. What to do
> but draw a little nearer to
> such ubiquity by remaining still. (50)

Paradoxically in these lines, we 'draw a little nearer' to God 'by remaining still'. Here also is the finding of the self in a God who 'calls us out
over our own fathoms'. Instead of God at a far remove, disappearing
upon one's arrival, we find here a ubiquitous presence 'whose margins

are our margins'. The seemingly disparate elements of time and eternity achieve a conflation to unity here that becomes the defeat of time and alienation and a temporary healing of the wound. Although the wound for Thomas continues to be a primary source of poetry, never fully healing in this life, this turning aside to eternity and healing itself becomes, simultaneously and paradoxically in his work, a source of poetry as well. Together the two sources, the wound and its healing, time and eternity, form a kind of dialectic between the reality of the lost self and the dream of its rediscovery.[10]

The opening lines of 'The Reason' from *Mass for Hard Times* (1992) begin with characteristic angst:

> I gird myself for the agon.
> And there at the beginning
> is the word. (27)

Here the word at the beginning is both the poem and Christ, destinations which, while obscured, are also at hand, which are both in time and out of time. In the poem the journey progresses:

> Nearer the sound,
> neither animal nor human,
> drawn out through the wrenched
> mouth of the oracle at Delphi.
> Nearer the cipher the Christ
> wrote on the ground, with no one
> without sin to peer at it
> over his shoulder.

Slowly the *agon* of the journey is relieved for the poet. The poem's final image is not one of underwater probing or of the pangs of birth or of dredging up with bloody hands the frightening truth but, through a turning aside, the blind man's discovery of the word, the momentary realisation not only of the self but of the eternal nature of that self as it exists in God. That discovery and realisation are a place for the poet to rest finally, sitting down in the 'mysterious presence' that is the warmth of a heart beating:

> my place, perhaps,
> is to sit down in a mysterious
> presence, leaving the vocabularies
> to toil, the machine to eviscerate
> its resources; learning we are here

> not necessarily to read on,
> but to explore with blind
> fingers the word in the cold,
> until the snow turn to feathers
> and somewhere far down we come
> upon warmth and a heart beating.

The task which Thomas sets down for himself in 'This To Do' turns out to be the project of poetry itself, an ongoing exploration of often murky interiors and pain which reveals not only the deep and often paradoxical complexity of identity for Thomas but equally his discovery, as here, of sudden transformations, arrivals, intimations of immortality as a part of identity. *Gnothi seauton* entails, for Thomas, not only the poetic journey 'far down' in the cold but repeated discoveries there of 'warmth and a heart beating'.

Part I has highlighted a particular *interiority* in R. S. Thomas's poetry, an instinct towards introspection as a primary action of self-discovery. It is important to remember, however, that Thomas is not merely self-referential in his meditations on identity. The natural world and its struggle with an emerging scientific mastery become the settings for Thomas's ongoing probes. Thomas is simultaneously a poet of *exteriors*, exploring identity not only as the product of individual isolation but as inseparable from context and contextual strife. It is to Thomas's deepening preoccupation with environment, with a mystical connection to the natural world and the challenges posed by science, that we now turn in Part II.

Notes

1 The title of the autobiography itself points up the paradox one is forced to grapple with here. The Welsh *neb* translates into English as no-one or nobody, an ironic title in the genre of autobiography which finds its entire grounding and justification in the idea of a substantial *someone*.

2 Contrast Thomas's explicitly feminine imagery here with a more masculine and aggressive image of the poet in 'The Maker' from the collection *Tares* (1961).

3 See also the poem 'Navigation' from *No Truce with the Furies* (1995).

4 Although this assertion by Thomas seems true of the late Wordsworth, it is clearly descriptive of a shift in Thomas himself, indicating more of a departure from Wordsworth than a parallel with him.

5 See Whitman's 'Song of Myself' as perhaps the fullest expression of his achieved oneness with both the flesh of the earth and the supernatural powers which he perceives as infusing the wider universe.

6 The image of the mirror is a major one for Thomas, especially in relation to exploration of the self and God. Compare the poem 'Looking Glass' from

Experimenting with an Amen (1986) to the prose passage in sequence 54 of the 1988 *The Echoes Return Slow* (108). See also the poems beginning 'I waited upon' and 'It is one of those faces', from the 1990 collection *Counterpoint* (45–6).

7 See Chapter 7 for a discussion of the *via negativa* in Thomas's religious poetry.

8 See the poems 'Aside' and 'Stations' in the collection *Mass for Hard Times* (1992) as further examples of this. Thomas writes in these poems of 'a turning aside, / a bending over a still pool' in order 'to hold the position / assigned to us' (34, 16).

9 See Thomas's poem 'Bequest' from *Destinations* (1985). See also 'Fathoms' in *No Truce with the Furies* (1995) and 'Sea Watching' from *Laboratories of the Spirit* (1975).

10 For more on this see my article 'Reality and the Dream in the Recent Poetry of R. S. Thomas', *New Welsh Review*, 44 (spring 1999).

1 St Michael and All Angels church, Manafon, Montgomeryshire.
Thomas took up his post as vicar here in 1942 at the age of twenty-nine.

2 The Rectory at Manafon where Thomas lived from 1942 to 1954.

3 R. S. Thomas during a private reading at St Michael's church, Manafon in August 1998.

4 St Michael's church, Eglwysfach, between Aberystwyth and Machynlleth. Thomas lived in the Rectory at Eglwysfach from 1954 to 1967.

5 St Hywyn's churchyard, Aberdaron on Penrhyn Lleyn where Thomas was vicar from 1967 to 1978.

6 The cottage at Sarn-y-Rhiw overlooking Porth Neigwl (Hell's Mouth) on Lleyn. Thomas retired to the cottage in 1978.

Part II

A poetics of environment

3 'Green asylum': the natural world

Introduction

William Scammell, in the 'Introduction' to his anthology *This Green Earth: A Celebration of Nature Poetry* (1992), writes that

> For the earliest men and women, and perhaps for some remote tribes still today, nature was not so much an environment (a word that didn't get itself invented until the nineteenth century, and grew tall with the advent of Darwinism) as the ground of being. Consequently ideas of appreciating, loving, conserving or exploiting it hardly arose. It was simply there, omnipresent and all-powerful, to be propitiated, thanked, obeyed, and co-operated with. (13–14)

While Scammell, in this quotation, seems to create an historical then/now dichotomy, he goes on in succeeding lines to defeat that dichotomy by reference to the poetry of Dylan Thomas. He writes that, for those early humans, '"The force that through the green fuse drives the flower" … was no more detachable from existence than birth or death, and certainly not an object of study' (13–14). Scammell is using Thomas here to indicate a modern consciousness towards nature at odds with a more primitive and unconscious relation. And yet it is precisely a poet like Dylan Thomas who reflects a contemporary *link* with that more ancient sensibility, proving that, ultimately, a strict historical dichotomy is untenable. It is not that Scammell's delineation is not valuable academically. His suggestion that there are two 'types' of nature poetry, a primitive type in which nature forms a 'ground of being' in the subconscious or unconscious, and a more contemporary type in which nature functions as an altogether more conscious 'object of study', seems true, if not strictly so. According to such a view it might be argued that the foremost distinguishing characteristic of modern civilisation is its expanded consciousness of itself, both of the inner workings of its own 'mind' and of its place within the wider natural world. It would seem that humanity has achieved, by the early twenty-first century, the ability to stand apart from itself, to view itself in detachment, looking on, as it were, dispassionately. It might be argued further that just as infants at birth view themselves to be the centre of a small universe to which they are physically attached, only later developing a sense of detachment and decentralisation, so human cultures, through oral traditions and eventually early drama, reflect a developing self-conscious detachment from, and subtle contextualisation within, the natural world. According to such an argument contemporary post-industrial society might be seen as having proceeded so far in this process of detachment as to have superseded a conscious contextualisation in the natural world and achieved, through science and technology, an actual alienation from it. Civilisations could be viewed as passing through three 'stages', the first an early innocence in which they form a physical and largely unconscious part and parcel of nature, the second a state of increasing detachment and contextualisation in which they form a more conscious part of nature while simultaneously becoming its stewards, and the third a so-called advanced state of complete detachment and alienation, a form of mastery or tyranny over the natural world as 'other'. Scammell's argument for two types of nature poetry could be used to corroborate such a hypothesis and its associated stages, with so called 'primitive' cultures representing a 'ground of being' relation and the more 'advanced' cultures writing of nature as an 'object of study'.

A problem with this theory recurs however. 'Nature poetry', as actually encountered, often seems very much a subtle combination of the two types Scammell proposes. For example, much of the power of Dylan Thomas's 'The force that through the green fuse drives the flower' resides in its very consciousness of *un*consciousness. It is precisely by way of his *detachment* that the poet becomes aware of his deep *attachment* to primal forces in the natural world, and eager, despite that rational detachment, to celebrate the mystery of those deeper ties. In the same way the American painter Jackson Pollock is reputed to have asserted: 'I do not paint nature, I am nature.' Pollock's declaration is a staunch refusal to separate himself from nature, to make nature an object, and by it he seems to suggest that art might be less a rendering of nature and more an extension of nature itself. Like Dylan Thomas, Pollock vigorously denies the so-called 'advancement' of rational thinking in favour of the more 'primitive' ground of being. And yet, paradoxically, his statement clearly indicates the very understanding of nature as object which it so vigorously rejects. What I am suggesting by this is that 'nature poetry' is consistently underpinned by this difficult complexity of unconscious force and conscious detachment, and that, as we shall see, R. S. Thomas's relation to nature is similarly complex, an amalgam of detachment and attachment, consciousness and unconsciousness, nature as object and nature as ground of being, nature as other and nature as self.

A second point is that R. S. Thomas's work, much like that of Ted Hughes', can be seen to draw upon and depict a 'darker side' of nature.[1] One of my purposes in this chapter, especially in its second half, is to draw more exacting attention to Thomas's poetic engagement with nature in order to reveal him as developing specifically away from the pastoral tradition which Edward Thomas seems to represent, away even from the view often associated with Dylan Thomas of nature as a force primarily benign and embracing of humanity in its cyclic creative energies, and instead towards what I will call a 'romantic-realism', romantic in the sense that R. S. Thomas's experiences and explorations of nature continue, ultimately, to be experiences and explorations of the self and of God (Scammell 1992: 12), and yet realist by his consistent acknowledgement of nature as not merely sublime in its aspect or nurturing in its action, but equally as fierce in its tumult, ruthless in its purpose, deadly in its possibilities, frightening in the harshness of its very discompassion towards itself and its human interpreters.[2] For example, as early as 1952, in his second collection, *An Acre of Land*, Thomas writes:

> Wandering, wandering, hoping to find
> The ring of mushrooms with the wet rind,
> Cold to the touch, but bright with dew,
> A green asylum from time's range. (27)

Here, it seems, is the poet in pursuit of the Romantic pastoral. However, the poem's final stanza is, unequivocally, a realisation by the narrator of a more brutal reality exploding that notion of the romantic pastoral, and the recognition that nature must be accepted on its own harsher terms:

> And finding instead the harsh ways
> Of the ruinous wind and the clawed rain;
> The storm's hysteria in the bush;
> The wild creatures and their pain.

It is in their depictions of these 'harsh ways' that Thomas's poems, like those of Ted Hughes, become suddenly surprising and unique expressions of nature not as tamed and predictable but as harbouring equally a wildness, a fierceness which, while often frightening to confront, can also, ultimately, be freeing as a recognition of beauty which has its source and logic in powers beyond human reason.[3] Thomas, like Hughes, does not insist on the known, does not resist the unknown, but continually opens doors into the real and waits there for its creatures to emerge.[4]

Having set out these preliminary markers I want to suggest that R. S. Thomas's poetic engagement with nature as a 'ground of being' has two major characteristics. The first and most important of these is the poet's view of himself as a 'nature mystic', an intellectual view arising from an emotional conviction which underlies and informs virtually every collection of his poems. In John Ormond's 1972 television broadcast 'R. S. Thomas: Priest and Poet', Thomas states: 'I'm a solitary, I'm a nature mystic; and silence and slowness and bareness have always appealed' (transcript in *Poetry Wales*: 51). A precise understanding of just what Thomas means by the term 'nature mystic' thus becomes a fundamental prerequisite not only to an understanding of his particular outlook but also to an understanding of his particular positions on major topics such as science (Chapters 4 and 5), and God (Chapters 6 and 7). The first half of this chapter defines Thomas's use of the term 'nature mysticism' by distinguishing it both from pure mysticism (treated more closely in Chapter 6) and from pantheism. It goes on to contextualise Thomas's position within a specifically Welsh tradition of nature mysticism by comparing his 'The Moor' with Dafydd ap Gwilym's 'The Woodland Mass' and Euros Bowen's 'Reredos' before turning to examine his little-known essay 'A Thicket in Lleyn' (1984) as perhaps his most candid description and philosophical elucidation of what he means by the term 'nature mysticism'. Finally, I will examine Thomas's 'The Bright Field' and 'Sea Watching', both from the collection *Laboratories of the Spirit* (1975), as important examples of nature mysticism, and, in particular, as examples of how a 'turning aside' to stillness and waiting comes to form a major element in Thomas's theology of nature.

The second major characteristic of Thomas's poetic engagement with nature is a philosophical problem that arises out of that 'theology of nature'. Thomas can often be found wrestling in the poems with the paradox of a Christian God of love having created a natural economy based upon cycles of violence and consumption, what Tennyson in *In Memoriam* refers to as 'Nature, red in tooth and claw'. The second half of this chapter highlights and explores this paradox as it emerges in Thomas's work, examining it first in relation to certain statements by Tennyson in his *In Memoriam,* and then detailing each poet's ultimate response to the problem.

Anthony Conran, in his 1979 article for *Poetry Wales* entitled 'R. S. Thomas as a Mystical Poet', puts his finger exactly on what might be called the 'dual paradox' of nature mysticism with which this chapter is concerned. Commenting on Thomas's 'The Minister' (1953) in which the poet writes, 'God is in the throat of a bird', Conran asks, 'what is infinite and yet "in the throat of a bird", loving and yet willing that bird to die in agony?' (12). In his article Conran does not answer those questions but proceeds rather to an elucidation of the 'five stages of contemplation' as depicted in the writings of St John of the Cross, the sixteenth century Spanish mystic, and to locating parallel poetic expressions of these stages in Thomas's work. But it is precisely with the exploration of this 'dual paradox' that I am concerned in this chapter, first with the intersection of time and eternity in nature, with that which is 'infinite' and yet 'in the throat of a bird', and, second, with the apparent contradiction of divine love and natural violence.

In Welsh woods: nature mysticism

In his autobiography, *No-one* (1985), R. S. Thomas writes that 'Thomas Aquinas believed that God revealed Himself according to the creature's ability to receive Him. If He did this to R. S., He chose to do so through the medium of the world of nature' (106). In the February 1991 *South Bank Show* devoted to his life and work, Thomas reiterates this sentiment, stating that 'God chooses to reveal himself I suppose to people in different ways ... He has evidently chosen to reveal himself to me through the natural world'. These statements by Thomas can be used as a working definition of 'nature mysticism': the experience of deity, or what Thomas elsewhere refers to as 'Ultimate Reality', revealing itself through the natural world that it created. As Hopkins describes it, 'The world is charged with the grandeur of God. / It will flame out, like shining from shook foil' (1990: 139). Or again: 'nature is never spent; / There lives the dearest freshness deep down things'. Echoing these sentiments by Hopkins, Thomas writes in *The Echoes Return Slow* (1988):

> Myself I need the tall woods,
> so church-like, for through their stained
> windows and beneath the sound
> of the spirit's breathing I concede a world. (27)[5]

That 'need', and that conceding of 'a world' through the stained window of nature, are the foundations of Thomas's nature mysticism. Indeed, the 'need' for nature is so predominant in the poet as to become a major characteristic of his perceptions of an afterlife. He writes in *No-one* that

> on a fine day in May, on the moorland extending from Y Migneint as far as Llandewibrefi, when the golden plover was singing enchantingly above the blue lakes, R. S. used to feel that if there

were no places like these in heaven, then he didn't want to go there. (100)

Nature mysticism is, however, a variation, some might say corruption, of 'simple' or 'pure' mysticism, which alleges a personal experience of divinity unmediated by the physical senses. 'Pure mysticism' describes a spiritual encounter in which the outer world of the senses no longer informs the inner experience of the mind/soul, but, rather, gives way to, or is suspended before, the more powerful dimensions of pure spirit. While pure mysticism precedes and is in no way restricted to Christianity, Thomas Aquinas provides its finest description in *Summa Theologiae*, article 4, question 175, where he writes:

> When the intellect of man is raised to the supreme vision of God's essence, it must be that the whole of a mind's intent is borne that way – to the extent that he grasps no other reality from images but is wholly borne to God. Hence it is impossible for a man, in this life, to see God in his essence without abstraction from the senses. (109)

Clearly, the distinction between pure and nature mysticism can be subtle, hinging as it does on this 'abstraction from the senses'. The question arises, for example, whether an experience of nature mysticism might naturally modulate into an experience of pure mysticism, whether the exterior, sensory, and mediating *vehicle* (nature) might give way to the wholly interior and non-sensory or extra-sensory experience of the final *object* and *source* (deity). There are poems by Thomas such as 'The Bright Field', which I shall examine shortly, that seem to point to a complex interplay between the experiences and language of nature mysticism and those of pure mysticism.[6] But this apparent movement by Thomas between nature mysticism and pure mysticism is, at the same time, strangely paradoxical since, traditionally, the experience of pure mysticism, while ultimately considered a divine gift, is said to be encouraged not through sensual participation in the created world but precisely by continued abstention from that world. Such abstentions constitute one of the foundations underlying Christian asceticism and the 'way of negation' or *via negativa,* which I shall examine more closely in Chapter 6. Thomas himself recognises this tradition of abstention, in poems such as 'Sea Watching', which I shall turn to shortly, and his own tension in relation to that tradition when he states that 'The medieval Church feeling was of course that it was a sin to fall in love with created things, and I would have to answer guilty to that sin' (*South Bank Show*).[7] We can see, however, a similar tension in the work of Hopkins and Herbert, both of them, like Thomas, spiritual poets with a deeply sensuous attachment to the natural world. One might compare, for example, Hopkins's 'The Habit of Perfection' in which he silences each of the senses as an approach to the divine, to his 'Pied Beauty', an unbridled celebration of the natural world as 'fathered-forth' by God. Similarly, George Herbert's 'Virtue' is a good example of the seemingly diametrical opposition of nature mysticism and pure mysticism as forms of spiritual apprehension.

It should be remembered too that the paradox which underlies both types of mystical experience is no less than that of the Christian incarnation – the emergence into realms of time and space, that is, into history, of that which, according to its nature, transcends time and space and is uniquely ahistorical. Although the pure mystic may escape the dimensions of sense experience into a higher reality completely removed from those dimensions, the nature mystic experiences *in* and *through* those dimensions of sense experience a similar reality. The prepositions 'in' and 'through' are important here since nature mysticism must be distinguished from pantheism, (the 'sin' referred to by Thomas above), an often subtle variation on nature mysticism which suggests that nature is itself divine. Thomas is emphatic on this point, stating that, while guilty of falling in love with created things, 'it is the word "created" that is the key word. Nature isn't my God. I'm not in love with things and scenes for themselves. They are the creation' (*South Bank Show*).[8] As creation and revelation the natural world becomes, for the nature mystic, a reflection of deity, without itself being deity. Nature, according to this view, is said to be sacred not because it *is* God but, rather, by association, as the creation and revelation of a God which it reflects and to whom it leads back again.[9] Nature, for the nature mystic, is not divinity in and of itself, as it is for the pantheist, but the outward sign of that divinity.

As I turn now to examine more closely the poetry of nature mysticism, it is important to emphasise that Thomas's mystical poetry, as indeed his poetry in general, draws at least as deeply on a Welsh-language tradition as it does on an English-language tradition. Beyond my suggestion in the Introduction that this 'dual affiliation' is just one of the creative tensions which drives Thomas's work, it is not my intention here to explore the exact sources and effects of these separate language traditions in the poetry. But to note this duality is to understand better the kind of complex 'bi-culturality' that Thomas brings to his work.[10] For example, while later in this section I will point up Thomas's contextualisation of himself within the English tradition of Blake and Eliot, I will first examine in some detail Dafydd ap Gwilym's 'The Woodland Mass',

written in the fourteenth century, and the Welsh poet and Anglican priest
Euros Bowen's 'Reredos' written in the twentieth, and compare these to
Thomas's 'The Moor' from his 1966 collection *Pieta*, and to two additional prose selections. The three poems bear striking similarities and
serve to highlight more accurately not only Thomas's position but a long
continuity in the Welsh-language tradition of nature mysticism which is
the more remarkable given the dramatic changes, both physical and
philosophical, which have occurred in the intervening centuries. I will
then go on to examine Thomas's poem 'A Thicket in Lleyn', comparing
it both to his essay of the same title and to another prose selection.
Finally, I will turn to 'The Bright Field', 'That Place', and 'Sea Watching'
as further examples before closing the section with reference to Thomas's
1974 article 'Where Do We Go from Here?' It might also be noted, in
this section, that as elsewhere in Thomas's work, the poetry and prose
can be seen to work together, as co-textual and interactive, that is, as reciprocal in their enrichment of one another and as occupying the same
'textual domain'.

Dafydd ap Gwilym's 'The Woodland Mass' begins as a poem of place
and a simple praise of nature:

> A pleasant place I was at today,
> under mantles of the worthy green hazel,
> listening at day's beginning
> to the skilful cock thrush
> singing a splendid stanza
> of fluent signs and symbols. (Jones 1997: 40–1)

Use of the phrase 'signs and symbols' is the first indication that nature,
in this case the cock thrush, is not only itself but a code or language
fronting a deeper source. In the lines which follow these we discover that
the cock thrush is a stranger to the locale, 'a brown messenger who had
journeyed far'; that 'with no password, / he comes to the sky of this
valley'. I want to suggest a parallel between the visiting narrator and the
visiting cock thrush in the first half of the poem. Both singers are pil-
grims to the wood, and yet while each may be a temporary visitor, an
alien 'with no password', both are simultaneously at home in the wood
and both are capable of 'fluent signs and symbols', that is, of becoming
channels for a power residing there.

The second half of the poem confirms these currents more explicitly. Although lines 1–18 of 'The Woodland Mass' appear to be a leisurely
meditation, lines 19–36 are characterised by a more pointed force as
nature in the poem becomes explicitly sacramental:

> There was here, by the great God,
> nothing but gold in the altar's canopy.
> I heard, in polished language,
> a long and faultless chanting,
> an unhesitant reading to the people
> of a gospel without mumbling;
> the elevation, on the hill for us there,
> of a good leaf for a holy wafer.
> Then the slim eloquent nightingale
> from the corner of a grove nearby,
> poetess of the valley, sings to the many
> the Sanctus bell in lively whistling.
> The sacrifice is raised
> up to the sky above the bush,
> devotion to God the Father,
> the chalice of ecstasy and love.

In these lines nature not only replaces the objects of the Catholic Mass but
enacts its most significant dramatic action as well, so that we have not only
the 'altar's canopy' but the 'faultless chanting' and the 'reading to the
people / of a gospel'; not only 'a good leaf for a holy wafer' but its 'elevation'; not only 'the chalice of ecstasy and love' but 'the Sanctus bell in lively
whistling' and 'The sacrifice ... raised / up to the sky above the bush'. For
the poet nature reflects the Christian incarnation, sacrifice and resurrection or redemption. One might argue that for Dafydd ap Gwilym it is the
'nature of Nature' to reflect eternal truth in time. There is in this reflection
however no artificiality, no pretension, perhaps not even consciousness by
nature of the reflecting act, but rather that innate electric charge which
Hopkins describes as 'the shining from shook foil'. One senses by the
poem's end that this reflection in nature of a creator-God is not imitative
of the orthodox act of the Mass, but precisely the opposite, that the orthodox act of Christian worship is in some way an isolated and consciously
contrived ceremony which seeks to partake in the widespread and instinctual ritual inherent in the natural world. This sense is confirmed in the
poem's closing lines:

> The psalmody contents me;
> it was bred of a birch-grove in the sweet woods.

Euros Bowen's 'Reredos', composed some six centuries later, is similar to 'The Woodland Mass' not only by its portrayal of a tension
between the human ceremony of the Christian Mass and the more pervasive and instinctual reflection of that ritual in the natural world, but

also in its portrayal of the primacy of the latter over the former. Rowan
Williams, in his 'Foreword' to *Euros Bowen: Priest-Poet*, writes of his work
as reflecting an 'awareness of the whole earth, indeed the whole of life,
as being sacramental, letting God's presence and glory through' (Bowen
1993: 11). Here, again, is the core of nature mysticism. Williams goes
on to assert that such a view was 'imbibed' by Bowen 'from the 1400
year long Welsh poetic tradition. It can be described as the genius of
Celtic Spirituality.' Important here is the fact that, unlike Bowen (and
Herbert and Hopkins), Thomas is less a 'devotional' religious poet and
more, like Eliot, a poet of the 'wasteland' journey, declaring with considerable angst and often crippling despair the apparent and frightening
absence of a God-centre according to which humanity might derive its
meaning. And yet, quietly alongside his interrogation of silence and
absence we find surviving in Thomas the kernel of this '1400 year long
Welsh poetic tradition', this 'genius of Celtic Spirituality' according to
which the world of nature retains a sustaining sacramental power.[11] While
we encounter in Thomas a thoroughly contemporary sensibility and an
apprehension of the fragmented modern experience, we find also a constant returning to sources of unity in nature and glimpses of eternity
afforded by this long tradition in poetry of nature as the mysterious
reflection of God. The 'reredos' of Bowen's poem refers to the orna-
mental screen at the back of the altar which, until recent changes, the
priest would have faced as he prepared the sacrifice of bread and wine.
A. M. Allchin, in his *Praise Above All: Discovering the Welsh Tradition*,
writes of the poem's setting as 'the chapel of a house in Anglesey ... looking out across the Menai Strait, into the mountains of Snowdonia'
(1991: 47). Bowen opens the poem, which consists of a single sentence
broken into three free-verse stanzas, by stating that

> The reredos was not
> an ecclesiastical adornment
> of symbols,
> but plain glass,
> with the danger
> of distracting the celebrant
> from
> the properties of the communion table. (75)

This initial declaration, though seemingly straightforward, resonates
with unanswered possibilities. For example, why *was* the reredos formed
of plain glass instead of the traditional ecclesiastical adornment?
Furthermore, use of the word 'danger' seems at first ambiguous. Is the

danger here one of the celebrant falling into a distraction that is sacri-
lege, or a distraction which reveals a broader truth, but which, in doing
so, explodes a protective ceremonial restriction? Both of these questions
are answered in the poem in the second and final stanzas respectively.
Bowen writes in stanza two:

> for
> in the translucence
> the green earth
> budded in the morning view,
> the river was in bloom,
> the air a joyous flight,
> and the sunshine
> set the clouds ablaze.

It would seem, according to this second stanza, that the reredos is
formed of 'plain glass' specifically for translucence, specifically for viewing, during the celebrant's preparation of gifts, the natural landscape
beyond. The reredos becomes a window on a window as it were, directing the celebrant to look from the elements of the Christian mass to the
elements of the natural world, from the particular gifts of the bread and
wine as they are confined in ceremony, toward their unconfined magni-
fication in the wider natural world, and therefore, somehow, into deity
itself. Not only does the translucent reredos point to a Welsh tradition
of nature mysticism going back to Dafydd ap Gwilym and beyond, but
it indicates that the 'danger' of distraction in stanza one is, for the poet,
ironic, since the distraction is toward a fuller realisation of the sacramental nature of the created world. This point is pressed home in the
poem's final lines where Bowen writes:

> I noticed
> the priest's eyes
> as it were unconsciously
> placing his hand
> on these gifts,
> as though these
> were
> the bread and the wine.

The priest here has 'fallen' into the 'danger', into a kind of awe-ecstasy
in which the conscious formula of the church ritual is lifted up or even
exploded outwards into a mystical experience of the sacramental world,
a recognition through nature and in time of a non-physical source and
presence originating outside of time in eternity.

Returning to R. S. Thomas one finds, in a poem from his 1988 collection *The Echoes Return Slow*, a strikingly similar experience to the one
described by Bowen, in which he too interprets the world of nature as
reflective of the Eucharistic drama:

> The breaking of the wave
> outside echoed the breaking
> of the bread in his hands.
>
> The crying of sea-gulls
> was the cry from the Cross:
> Lama Sabachthani. (69)

It is within this tradition of reverencing the natural world as divine creation
and revelation, as a window on the eternal, that R. S. Thomas's work takes
its place. His sonnet 'The Moor', for example, from the 1966 collection
Pieta, is clearly reminiscent of 'The Woodland Mass' and 'Reredos' in its
depiction of nature as sacramental both in its physical attributes and in its
symbolic action. Thomas writes in the octave that the moor

> was like a church to me.
> I entered it on soft foot,
> Breath held like a cap in the hand. (24)

Here is nature as the site of encounter with deity. Although 'The Moor'
was published in 1966 its imagery reappears in a passage from *No-one*,
published some twenty years later in 1986:

> Going into the quiet and beauty of the moorland was like entering
> a more beautiful church than any he had ever seen. And looking on
> morning dew in the sun was like listening to the heavenly choir
> singing glory to God. He was doubtful whether, in an industrial
> town, he could have worshipped and continued to believe. That is,
> the countryside was indispensable to his faith. (84)

In both the poem and the prose the experience described is similarly infor-
mal, unorthodox, intuitive or emotional, as opposed to rational, and continually mediated by the sense experience of nature. Thomas continues in
'The Moor':

> What God was there made himself felt,
> Not listened to, in clean colours
> That brought a moistening of the eye,
> In movement of the wind over grass.

This sense of ubiquitous presence experienced in and through nature is the hallmark of Thomas's nature mysticism. The experience elicits from the poet no action except the simple enjoyment of an attendant stillness and a surrendering of the individual will. Thomas describes these effects in the poem's sestet:

> There were no prayers said. But stillness
> Of the heart's passions – that was praise
> Enough; and the mind's cession
> Of its kingdom.

Central to this experience is an acceptance by the poet which is itself a prayer of praise. And it is precisely that sense of acceptance that makes room for the poem's closing paradox:

> I walked on,
> Simple and poor, while the air crumbled
> And broke on me generously as bread.

As in 'The Woodland Mass' and 'Reredos', it is the narrator's experience in nature which here is sacramental. The consecration and breaking of bread of the Christian Mass become the metaphorical equivalents, the language and symbol, of an action occurring naturally in the wider, created world. For Thomas, the 'stilled passions' of the heart refer to a sense of the self as one and centred, rather than as multiple and scattered, a sense which causes the poet to refer to himself as 'simple'. Similarly, use of the adjective 'poor' signals a recognition by the poet of proper dependence upon forces greater than himself, a dependence joyous for the poet because it permits freedom and rest, 'the mind's cession / Of its kingdom'. The poet seems, in these lines, to have entered a state of humility, which is to say that he see, feels, understands and *is a part of* reality without distortion or alienation. In his *A Year in Llŷn* (1990) Thomas describes this same sense of intense spiritual integration experienced while standing at the edge of Ty Mawr pool, listening to the wind and the sea:

> At moments such as these, every problem concerning the purpose of life, death and morality disappears, and man feels in touch with existence, pure and simple. For a moment he is one with the creation, participating in the genius of life, as every creature in time has done over millions of years. My name for such a rare, but not alien, experience, is nature-mysticism. (122)[12]

It is precisely in this state of clarity, of oneness and dependence or unity and freedom, ultimately of acceptance, that the poet is most able to *receive*, and in which, in 'The Moor', he goes on receiving, becoming suddenly conscious not only of the encompassing air as sacramental substance, as Christ in the Eucharist, but of the breaking of that substance into gift, of the atmosphere itself as crucified and redeemed. In the fullest sense of the words the poet receives, in nature and through nature, communion and inspiration. Of course language here begins to falter as the spiritual experience on the moor begins to transcend physical sensations in time and take on more purely mystical proportions and force. One can sense in these final lines experience outpacing vocabulary, a sudden dropping into spiritual depth which metaphor and symbol must struggle to accommodate.

For Thomas, this reflection of the eternal divine within the confines of time and nature is most often momentary, a flash, a brief revelation, and, as such, it requires a continual turning aside, not only on the exterior, to the physical presence of the natural world, but at the same time, interiorly, to an attitude of stillness and waiting, a poised expectancy which often must remain undiscouraged by inevitable delay and absence. In the poem 'A Thicket in Lleyn' for example, from *Experimenting with an Amen* (1986), Thomas describes his physical, exterior stillness and waiting in a thicket filling with birds and how that stillness eventually permits an experience of their closeness which becomes, briefly, '"A repetition in time of the eternal / I AM"' (45). As the birds in the poem become metaphors for divinity, the narrator's stillness and waiting become as much interior as they are exterior. What I am especially interested in here, however, is that, predating the poem's publication by two years, but co-textual with it, is a little-known essay by Thomas of the same title and concerning the same experience, written for the book *Britain: A World by Itself* (1984). In the essay Thomas significantly expands his reflections on this 'repetition in time of the eternal / I AM' into perhaps the most lucid physical description and philosophically precise analysis of the experience of nature mysticism in all his work, including his other, and more widely known, prose description of the experience in *A Year in Lleyn* (1990). I will examine this prose essay somewhat closely before turning to the poems 'The Bright Field', 'That Place', and 'Sea Watching' as further examples.

Thomas begins the essay 'A Thicket in Lleyn' with the following request and admission:

> Leave it for me: a place in Lleyn, where I may repair to mend my feelings … It is, where I hide, where only the light finds me, filtering through the leaves in summer, and in winter the flash from a blade brandished by the sea nearby. (92)

Slowly, this place to hide becomes a place in which the poet will be 'found', not so much physically as caught up spiritually, contextualised in a wider cosmic world made radically present through nature:

> I approach it warily. It is nervous. Pfft! A sparrow-hawk is plucked from a branch, like an arrow from a bow. A magpie scolds, out of sight. The place sighs and is still. I wait, and tune my breath to its own … So little by little the life of the thicket is resumed and I am forgotten. (95–6)

The thicket here is alive: nervous, sighing, and eventually still. In response to that uneasiness we find the poet patiently turning aside, approaching warily, waiting, tuning, all, for Thomas, essential preliminaries, preparations, ready-making for the possibility, in time, of the eternal I AM. It is very slowly that the poet becomes integrated into the scene and, finally (and most importantly), forgotten.

As suggested earlier, the actual revelation, when it comes, is, in the essay as in the poem, momentary at best, not the shattering surge of an electric divinity but a moment of extraordinarily quiet simplicity in which the migrating goldcrests come to fill the thicket and surround the waiting poet:

> The air purred with their small wings. To look up was to see the twigs re-leafed with their bodies. Everywhere their needle-sharp cries stitched at the silence. Was I invisible? Their seed-bright eyes regarded me from three feet off. Had I put forth an arm, they might have perched on it. I became a tree, part of that bare spinney where silently the light was splintered, and for a timeless moment the birds thronged me, filigreeing me with shadow, moving to an immemorial rhythm on their way south. (96)

In this quotation nearly every sense is filled with the ingathering presence of the goldcrests: the air purrs with the motion of their wings, the twigs are re-leafed with their bodies, their cries stitch the silence, Thomas imagines them perching on his outstretched arm. This presence is simultaneously natural presence and divine presence for Thomas. We are told that 'silently the light was splintered, and for a timeless moment the birds thronged me, filigreeing me with shadow, moving to an immemorial rhythm on their way south'. This splintering of light for a timeless moment is, for Thomas, nothing short of the splintering of time and space, a soft but none the less powerful explosion, in and through nature, of the divine, an opening of sealed portals in the mind, a sudden sight of bridges between two worlds. Thomas seems to be suggesting that in this moment he is thronged by divinity itself, and filigreed with its shadow, taken up bodily into its immemorial rhythm.[13]

It is only later, after the experience has passed, that Thomas is able to examine it more closely and rationally. And it is in that examination that he sets out most candidly his own interpretation of the experience:

> Then suddenly they were gone, leaving other realities to return: the rustle of the making tide, the tick of the moisture, the blinking of the pool's eye as the air flicked it; and lastly myself. Where had I been? Who was I? What did it all mean? While it was happening, I was not. Now that the birds had gone, here I was once again … Had that infinite I announced itself in a thicket in Lleyn, in the serenity of the autumnal sunlight, in the small birds that had taken possession of it, and in the reflection of this in a human being? And had the I in me joined seemingly unconsciously in that announcement; and is that what eternity is? And was the mind that returned to itself but finite mind? (96)

This then, for Thomas, is at the heart of what he calls nature mysticism. First, an announcement, in and through nature, of the 'infinite I'. Second, the unconscious commingling of the individual soul as an intimate part of that announcement, as part of that eternity, in which physical reality is dissipated. Third, the inevitable falling back to time and the 'finite mind', to memory, bewilderment, and wonder.

I will turn now to 'The Bright Field', 'That Place', and 'Sea Watching', all from *Laboratories of the Spirit* (1975), as perhaps the most crystallised poetic renderings of what Thomas has elucidated in 'A Thicket in Lleyn'. Like 'The Moor', all three poems underscore the ongoing necessity, for Thomas, of turning aside to stillness and waiting, both external and internal, as preparation for the possible apprehension of the divine in nature, as well as the ultimately fleeting nature of that apprehension.

'The Bright Field' begins with an experience which the narrator at first takes for granted:

> I have seen the sun break through
> to illuminate a small field
> for a while, and gone my way
> and forgotten it. (60)

There are two things to note here: first, the transitory nature of the experience expressed in the phrase 'for a while' and, second, Thomas's deliberately literal or non-mystical rendering. Though the narrator claims to

have 'seen', one senses, even in these opening lines, that it is with the
outer eye only, that a deeper significance has been missed or ignored. The
narrator's realisation of such blindness is, however, immediate:

> But that was the pearl
> of great price, the one field that had
> the treasure in it. I realise now
> that I must give all that I have
> to possess it.

Here Thomas quickly broadens the implications of the experience by allusion to two gospel parables, 'the pearl of great price' from Matthew 13.45,
and 'the field with the treasure in it' from Matthew 13.44. In the parables
the pearl and the field are symbols of 'the kingdom', a life of the soul in the
presence of the divine. Thomas seems to be suggesting that such a kingdom waits to be glimpsed, experienced, albeit momentarily, in and
through the natural world, but also that it is easily overlooked. Of course
the poem is another example of nature mysticism giving way to pure mysticism since the bright field is both a revelation of, and a metaphor for,
deity. But my point here is that, for Thomas, nature mysticism is a kind of
seeing which is not only momentary but which depends as much on an
internal apprehension as it does on an external sight.

The poem's second stanza becomes didactic, admonishing the
reader to 'turn aside' to the experience as spiritual revelation:

> Life is not hurrying
>
> on to a receding future, nor hankering after
> an imagined past. It is the turning
> aside like Moses to the miracle
> of the lit bush, to a brightness
> that seemed as transitory as your youth
> once, but is the eternity that awaits you.

'Life' here refers to the purpose of life, which, for Thomas, consists in a
spiritual awareness which, he suggests, has everything to do with the present tense. The analogy to Moses and the miracle of the lit bush underscores this 'turning aside' to the immediacy of the present tense. In the
actual story from Exodus 3.1–6 we find that

> the angel of the Lord appeared unto him in a flame of fire out of
> the midst of a bush: and he looked, and, behold, the bush burned
> with fire, and the bush was not consumed. And Moses said, 'I will
> now turn aside, and see this great sight, why the bush is not burnt'.

And when the Lord saw that he turned aside to see, God called unto
him out of the midst of the bush. (Reader's Bible)

While it is the phenomenon of the burning bush which is not consumed
that seems central here, the greater significance of the story, especially
for Thomas in 'The Bright Field', lies, rather, in Moses's response to the
sight, in his action of 'turning aside', and in the subsequent revelation
from God which that turning aside elicits. Moses says, '"I will now turn
aside and see"'. Only then, 'when the Lord saw that he turned aside, to
see', does God call 'unto him out of the midst of the bush'. That calling
by God of Moses by name is, in the Exodus story, a constant possibility,
hinged upon Moses's ability to turn aside. And it is precisely and only his
turning aside which triggers God's further 'self-revelation', his calling of
Moses by name. Divinity here is not elusive but, rather, presses in on
Moses through nature, awaiting his response.

What Thomas seems to be suggesting in 'The Bright Field' is that
the eternal, what Matthew calls 'the pearl of great price' and 'the field
with the treasure in it', exists in the lit bush of creation, and is an enduring *potential*, that is, is perpetually *accessible* to humankind, even awaits
humankind in the life of the natural world. The possessing of that kingdom, which Thomas seems to yearn for in this poem as in so many others,
is, he argues, repeatedly possible to the one who stops and turns and sees,
both exteriorly in nature, but, more importantly, interiorly, within a landscape of the spirit. For Thomas, the landscape of 'The Bright Field' is at
once exterior *and* interior, a physical manifestation and a spiritual revelation. The poem's imagery, both literal and metaphorical, can be said to
contain the tension of this duality, expressing both the physical truth of
what *is* to the 'outer' eye, and the more elusive 'inner' *experience* for
which, ultimately, there can be no words.

What we have seen so far in 'The Moor', 'A Thicket in Lleyn', and
'The Bright Field' is that the experience of eternity or deity in and
through nature, while powerful, is, for Thomas, a fleeting experience,
one that may come regularly, but which, when it does come, is necessarily fragile and temporary. And yet, each experience generates in the poet
an increasingly more fervent desire for its repetition and even perma-
nence. For example, in the poem 'That Place', also from *Laboratories of
the Spirit* (1975), he writes that

> Occasions
> on which a clean air entered our nostrils
> off swept seas were instances
> we sought to recapture. (8)

These 'instances', like 'that place' from the title are, for Thomas, not merely literal but physical manifestations of a spiritual reality. He writes later in the poem that

> One particular
> time after a harsh morning
> of rain, the clouds lifted, the wind
> fell; there was a resurrection
> of nature, and we there to emerge
> with it into the anointed
> air.

Use of the words 'resurrection' and 'anointed' clearly point to an experience of nature as simultaneously an experience of eternity or deity. But my point here is that this experience, while powerful, is necessarily brief for Thomas and results in an increased desire that cannot, ultimately, be satisfied. 'That Place' ends with the realisation not only of having found 'that place' but of having lost it just as quickly. Thomas calls it the place 'that we had found and would spend / the rest of our lives looking for'. Thus the poet is repeatedly faced in these experiences with the cyclical process of waiting, watching, absence, and fleeting presence, all of which together form the subject of the exquisite 'Sea Watching'.

'Sea Watching' is a poem about vigilance in which the sea becomes the empty stage of God's absence. Where in 'The Bright Field' the 'blinded' narrator is being pressed in upon by the revelation of divinity in nature, in 'Sea Watching' it is the searching narrator who is consistently denied that revelation. The sea in the poem becomes interior, 'vast / as an area of prayer / that one enters' (64). Thus, while Thomas establishes again a tension between exteriors and interiors, he seems to be using nature here, and the sea in particular, primarily as a metaphor for an interior landscape of the spirit.[14] The first ten lines of the poem are notable for their description of ongoing watching in the face of ongoing absence. Referring to the vast grey waters of line one Thomas writes that

> Daily
> over a period of years
> I have let the eye rest on them.
> Was I waiting for something?
> Nothing
> but that continuous waving
> that is without meaning
> occurred.

Lines 11–14 attempt to justify the poet's expectant position:

> Ah, but a rare bird is
> rare. It is when one is not looking,
> at times one is not there
>   that it comes.

This appears paradoxical as well as defeating. If one's absence ensures the rare bird's presence, and one's presence ensures the rare bird's absence, there seems little reason to hope for its appearance. Still, Thomas persists, even to the point of becoming a part of nature himself:

> I became the hermit
> of the rocks, habited with the wind
> and the mist.

But a strange thing happens next. Rather than conceding the absence, Thomas claims, in the very experience of the absence and emptiness, an implied presence. If absence is the *lack* of some *thing*, then that thing must exist, that is, must be present, albeit beyond one's more immediate experience. According to this *via negativa* position which I examine closely in Chapter 6, the narrator begins to experience, by implication, a certain presence-in-absence which is characteristic of the experience of the pure mystic:

> There were days,
> so beautiful the emptiness
> it might have filled,
>   its absence
> was as its presence; not to be told
> any more, so single my mind
> after its long fast,
>   my watching from praying.

Indeed, not only is its absence 'as its presence', but that absence and the presence it makes possible are 'not to be told / any more'. There is a cessation of yearning in this phrase, a rediscovery of 'that place' which comes not through the experience of a presence, as in 'The Moor', 'A Thicket in Lleyn', 'The Bright Field', and 'That Place', but, paradoxically, in absence and waiting, in fasting and the 'single mind' which that abstinence creates. We are close here to an inner landscape that is wholly separate from the natural world in which Thomas must forsake indulgence in nature as revelatory and make instead an ascetic's approach to a more interior world.

I will end this first half of the chapter with a description of nature mysticism used by Thomas to close his 1974 talk for *The Listener* titled 'Where Do We Go from Here?'. He prefaces the description by stating: 'I must end this talk, surely, by telling you how he [God] has revealed himself to me, if that is the right way to describe the knowledge – half hope, half intuition – by which I live' (159).

Not only is the description which follows this a fascinating encapsulation of Thomas's ideas on nature as revelatory, and on the necessity of 'turning aside' to that revelation, but, also, his reference here to such ideas as 'the knowledge – half hope, half intuition – by which I live' places nature mysticism firmly at the very centre of the poet's philosophy or theology. The description begins, significantly, with a quotation from Blake's *A Vision of the Last Judgement:*

> 'When the sun rises, do you not see a round disc of fire somewhat like a guinea?' 'O no no, I see an innumerable company of the heavenly host crying, "Holy, Holy, Holy is the Lord God Almighty!" I question not my corporeal or vegetative eye any more than I would question a window concerning sight. I look through it and not with it.' So said William Blake and, similarly, in my humbler way, say I. With our greatest modern telescope we look out into the depths of space, but there is no heaven there. With our supersonic aircraft we annihilate time, but are no nearer eternity. May it not be that alongside us, made invisible by the thinnest of veils, is the heaven we seek? The immortality we must put on? Some of us, like Francis Thompson, know moments when 'Those shaken mists a space unsettle'. To a countryman it is the small field suddenly lit up by a ray of sunlight. It is T. S. Eliot's 'still point, there the dance is', Wordsworth's 'central peace, subsisting at the heart of endless agitation'. It is even closer. It is within us, as Jesus said. That is why there is no need to go anywhere from here. (159–60)

Although this quotation does not reveal any new aspects to Thomas's nature mysticism, it is none the less remarkable not merely for placing the poet within a specific tradition of English literary mysticism, but also for the power of its conviction, and for its advocacy of a nature mysticism which, as we have seen in the poems, gives way ultimately to the experience of pure mysticism. Again we find that divinity is, for Thomas, made manifest primarily in and through the natural world; that it emerges from behind 'the thinnest of veils' and out of eternity into time and space; but also, and no less important, we can see again Thomas's stress on the need to turn inward, away from exterior, physical journeying to 'the depths of space', away from the annihilation of time by science, not only towards a realisation of the divine mediated through nature but also towards a distinctly pure form of mysticism, towards what, for him, is a stillness, a waiting, an eternity within.

'Nature, red in tooth and claw': Tennyson's anti-pastoral

The second major characteristic of Thomas's poetic engagement with nature, and the one that I will highlight and explore in this final section of the chapter, concerns what he refers to as 'the problem of killing as part of the economy of the God of love' (*No-one*, 1985: 107). This 'problem' becomes, in the poems, a kind of persisting dark underside to the poet's view of the natural world as reflective of a benign divinity. The difficulty, for Thomas, is essentially this: If the creation is viewed as divine revelation by a Christian God of love, how is one to understand the natural economy of that creation, founded, as, for Thomas, it so evidently is, not upon the New Testament model of self-sacrificing love but, rather, upon an instinctual aggression and violence according to which the weak are doomed to suffer, die, and be consumed at the hands of the ruthless and the strong? Even in the 1984 essay 'A Thicket in Lleyn', discussed above as perhaps his most poignant depiction of the experience of the divine in nature, Thomas is driven to lament:

> What talons and beaks were not in waiting for the goldcrests on their way south, to be themselves devoured later by the huge maw of the sea over which other goldcrests would return north in the spring passage? (101)

Here, the cyclic movements of nature take on a more sinister hue. Two years later Thomas writes in *No-one* of his early realisation of this paradox:

> The young rector would himself see the birds of prey hunting and the weasel and the stoat going about their bloody work ... One of the unfailing rules of that world is that life has to die in the cause of life. If there is any other way on this earth, God has not seen fit to follow it. This is a doctrine that plays straight into the hands of the strong. As far as this world is concerned, Isaiah's vision of the wolf dwelling with the lamb, and the leopard lying down with the kid, is a myth. The economy doesn't work like that. And too often in this world, the race is to the swift, the battle to the strong. (95–6)

In this quotation Thomas isolates the paradox, calling it 'one of the unfailing rules' of existence 'that life has to die in the cause of life'. His obvious frustration, even anger, over that stark necessity stems primarily from its neglect of the weak. 'Survival of the fittest', for Thomas, stands in blatant contradiction not only to Isaiah's vision but also, and perhaps more powerfully, to Christ's promise in the New Testament of the meek inheriting the earth. The deep frustration and philosophical scrutiny engendered in Thomas by this paradox remains unallayed some five years later. In the final pages of his *A Year in Lleyn* (1990) Thomas muses over the sparrowhawk 'mewing in the wood at Ty'n Parc, as if it were sharpening its beak for the feast that will come its way in the new year':

> This is how it was before man appeared here. That is nature. Is that God's economy? Life depends on the ability to obtain sufficient sustenance. The weak go to oblivion. In some ways, and at times, it is quite terrifying. Couldn't God have done better than to make the earth some giant mouth which devours, devours unceasingly in order to sustain itself? (170)

Here, again, Thomas attains no rational synthesis to the perceived contradiction and is forced to face a world that is, for him, disconcertingly *discompassionate,* which favours the strong and sacrifices the weak.

His reference to Isaiah's vision in the quotation from *No-one* underscores the depth of his concern. In the actual text from Isaiah 11.6–9, the prophet imagines a fundamental re-ordering of relations in nature in which

> The wolf also shall dwell with the lamb,
> And the leopard shall lie down with the kid;
> And the calf and the young lion and the fatling together; ...
>
> And the cow and the bear shall feed;
> Their young ones shall lie down together:
> And the lion shall eat straw like the ox ...
>
> They shall not hurt nor destroy in all my holy mountain:
> For the earth shall be full of the knowledge of the Lord.

Here, the cycles of natural violence have been broken, replaced by peace and compatibility between previously natural and mortal enemies. The difference between these states of existence, between the 'old' order based upon the relation of predator and prey and the new, non-violent order proclaimed by Isaiah, hinges on what the prophet refers to as 'the knowledge of the Lord'. For Isaiah, the new order will be brought about by an infusion of divine knowledge or presence, which will finally eradicate the old cycles of violence and consumption. The

vast ecosystem of the natural world and the natural law which governs
it will be replaced, according to this view, by a kind of harmony which
Thomas finds difficult to fathom. For example, he asks in his 1992
Mass for Hard Times

> How will the lion remain a lion
> if it eat straw like the ox? (22)

These lines question Isaiah's vision as a challenge to the very foundations
of our understanding of the natural world, our very definitions of things
as they are in that world, and therefore as a kind of incomprehensible
transformation. Still, St Paul, in chapter 8 of his Letter to the Romans,
reiterates Isaiah's vision, suggesting as well that the old order, the unre-
deemed creation, positively yearns for that transformation:

> the creation itself also shall be delivered from the bondage of cor-
> ruption into the glorious liberty of the children of God. For we
> know that the whole creation groaneth and travaileth in pain
> together until now.

From what we have so far examined, it would seem that Thomas agrees
with St Paul here that 'the whole creation groaneth and travaileth in pain
together until now'. But while St Paul and Isaiah both favour a vision of
future redemption or transformation as the answer to that pain, Thomas
underscores again and again in the poetry how that 'fallen state' in nature
can be, simultaneously, reflective of a divine fullness and glory. Isaiah in
the Old Testament and St Paul in the New both raise the important question whether a creation denied the 'knowledge of the Lord', as Isaiah
describes it, or under 'bondage' as St Paul describes it, can at the same
time remain a revelatory creation. This is a paradox which seems fundamental to Christianity: the realisation of deep separation, even alienation,
in the 'fallen' creation, and yet the affirmation of that creation as
uniquely good, as a manifestation of divine presence and divine love. And
it is precisely this paradox which Thomas, as an Anglican priest and a
nature mystic, explores in his work: the distance, the disturbing absence,
of divinity in a 'fallen' creation and, yet, simultaneously, its somehow radical proximity, its revelation of presence. One of the best examples of this
paradoxical duality can be found in 'The Parish' from Thomas's 1961
collection *Tares*, where he writes of a townspeople's ignorance of the
darker side of the natural world,

> how with its old violence
> Grass raged under the floor. (15)

Thomas seems to find in this grass a hidden aggression, a violence and rage that threaten the very foundations, as it were, of civilisation. An awareness of that aggression is reserved in the poem for the farmer and the narrator. Thomas writes:

> But you knew it, farmer; your hand
> Had felt its power, if not your heart
> Its loveliness. Somewhere among
> Its green aisles you had watched like me
> The sharp tooth tearing its prey,
> While a bird sang from a tall tree.

Here the violence and rage of nature become transposed not only into 'power' but into 'loveliness' as well. The paradox which emerges in these lines is the paradox central to Thomas's writing on nature: destructive, consuming power in league with transcendent beauty. We find in this poem both the dire culpability of nature and its perfect innocence. The poem's final lines clearly reiterate this paradox. The narrator and the farmer are differentiated from the townspeople by a certain vigilance, as they view not only the bird singing but also the 'tooth tearing its prey'. Thomas is not concerned here so much with a vision of redemption or transformation as he is with the riddle of things as they are. And yet there is no attempt in the poem to resolve these seeming opposites into any rational context. Thomas allows the paradox to stand up, and, as we shall see, this becomes an important aspect of his 'answer' to the 'problem of nature'.

I will turn now to make a brief comparison between Thomas's philosophical concern and agitation over this 'natural violence' and a similar concern and agitation expressed by Tennyson in his *In Memoriam*. Following that comparison I will go on to examine closely Thomas's own concern with and depictions of such natural violence in the poems. Finally, I will close the chapter by assessing Thomas's ultimate response to the paradox, to see whether, finally, he is able to locate the phenomenon of natural violence within any wider context. Although Tennyson can be seen to locate the paradox of natural violence and an allegedly loving God rationally within a philosophical schema anticipatory of Darwin's theory of evolution, Thomas, on the other hand, holds to the original paradox, preserving and balancing its tensions and, ultimately, moving toward a deeper acceptance of what he seems to view as the fundamentally paradoxical nature of existence itself.

In his autobiography, *No-one* (1985), Thomas is explicit about Tennyson's early influence:

Was he [Thomas] preparing himself to be a poet? ... From where
did the desire to write verses come from? ... How did Tennyson
become his favourite poet? After winning a school prize and having
to choose a book, he asked for a biography of the poet. Tennyson's
early poems were full of references to the countryside, even though
it was the countryside of England. The boy doted on the descriptions in 'The Lady of Shalott'. (32)

In addition to this early enthusiasm for Tennyson that clearly influenced
his poetic development, Thomas writes of him again, later in the autobiography, as his precursor in taking up the philosophical dilemma of a
violent creation which is the product of a God of love. Commenting
on his realisation of such natural violence Thomas writes: 'What kind
of God created such a world? A God of love? The question was formerly
asked by Tennyson in his long poem *In Memoriam*'" (78). In these quo-
tations Thomas places himself within a distinctly English tradition of
nature poetry, the other side of his 'dual-affiliation'. His alarm over the
observation that 'life has to die in the cause of life', is clearly an echo
of Tennyson's own alarm (and that of his age). Like Thomas, Tennyson
asks:

> Are God and Nature then at strife,
>   That Nature lends such evil dreams? (1973: 34)

It is worth citing the lines that follow these in section 55 of *In Memoriam*
in order to highlight the exact nature of their affinity with Thomas's sentiments. Referring to Nature as 'she', he continues:

> So careful of the type she seems,
> So careless of the single life;
>
> That I, considering everywhere
>   Her secret meaning in her deeds,
>   And finding that of fifty seeds
> She often brings but one to bear,
>
> I falter where I firmly trod,
>   And falling with my weight of cares
>   Upon the great world's altar-stairs
> That slope thro' darkness up to God,
>
> I stretch lame hands of faith, and grope,
>   And gather dust and chaff, and call
>   To what I feel is Lord of all,
> And faintly trust the larger hope. (1973: 35)

Phrases such as 'Her secret meaning' and 'the great world's altar-stairs' hint at a nature mysticism in Tennyson quite similar to Thomas's as we have seen it in the first half of this chapter. The poem's ethos, however, is primarily lament over nature's peculiar discompassion for the individual, her 'careless[ness] of the single life', which causes the poet to 'falter' and 'fall' in his faith. By the poem's final stanza the narrator is reduced by his realisation of nature's discompassion from an implied experience of former presence through nature to 'lame hands of faith', to groping, and faintly trusting. The experience of a natural world inflated, infused, animated and electric with divine presence, gives way here to a disappointment bordering on despair. This sense of an apparent divide between divinity and its creation reaches its oft-cited climax in section 56, in which Tennyson writes of humankind as those

> Who trusted God was love indeed
> And love Creation's final law–
> Tho' Nature, red in tooth and claw
> With ravine, shriek'd against his creed. (35–6)

Here, in famously dramatic terms, Tennyson encapsulates the dilemma faced by Thomas, and indeed by every mystic working from a Christian framework. The supposition that God is love is overcome in these lines by the ravine shriek of nature against such a creed. The law of creation becomes not love but cycles of violence in which the weak are consumed by the strong.

Turning to examine Thomas's probing of such cycles of violence in the poems one finds that 'January', from the 'Later Poems' section of *Song at the Year's Turning* (1955), is an excellent example of what Tennyson sees as this radical discompassion of nature towards individual suffering, of 'nature, red in tooth and claw'. In the poem the fox, traditionally imaged as predator rather than prey,

> drags its wounded belly
> Over the snow, the crimson seeds
> Of blood burst with a mild explosion,
> Soft as excrement, bold as roses. (107)

The image in these lines derives much of its startling power from the effects of rhythm and metaphor. For example, repetition of the hard 'd' in 'drags', 'wounded', 'blood', 'bold' combines and overlaps with a modulating assonantal repetition of the 'o' in 'wounded', 'over', 'snow', 'crimson', 'of', 'blood', 'explosion', 'soft', 'bold', 'roses' to create not only a rhythmic thread as it were, loosely tying the lines,

but also a darkening mood. That shadow effect is simultaneously countered by a peculiar lightness derived from other sounds, as well as from
Thomas's use of metaphor. The hard 'd' and the darkly chiming 'o'
are countered, first, by repetition of the soft 'b' in 'belly', 'blood',
burst', 'bold' and, second, by the repetition of the hushed 's' of 'drags',
'its', 'crimson', 'seeds', 'burst', 'soft', 'as', 'roses'. Combining with
these sound effects are the excruciating images: the blood, the seep-
ing life-force, becomes in line 2 the 'crimson seeds', as if this suffering and imminent death were also a planting of new life in the January
snow. Furthermore, that blood *bursts*, not violently but as quietly as it
does vividly, in a 'mild explosion / Soft as excrement, bold as roses'.
All of this gives to the dark thrum of the lines a hushed lift and resignation, the sense, in sound and image, of a brutality and futility that,
while painfully real, are somehow serene in their very inexorability.[15]

    The second and final stanza of 'January' is three lines long and
depicts nature's response to the wounded fox:

> Over the snow that feels no pity,
> Whose white hands can give no healing,
> The fox drags its wounded belly.

Part of the power of these closing lines lies, of course, in their very simplicity, their brevity and their repetition, in the final line, of the poem's
first line. But in addition to these elements one notices that Thomas has
anthropomorphised the snow, giving it feelings and hands, while simultaneously declaring its lack of any pity and denial of any healing. This
intensifies the discompassion that is the real subject of the poem, as well
as underscoring the paradox with which Thomas, as a nature mystic, is
faced. It is not that nature is void of presence and therefore of pity and
love. The whole problem, for Thomas, is precisely that nature is *big* with
presence, *pregnant* with meanings, reflective, in the end, of a Christian
God of love. And yet that presence, while seemingly capable, 'feels no
pity' and 'can give no healing'. Through nature the divine presses in on
humanity, and yet not in the alleviation of suffering as humanity might
see fit. This is, philosophically, the problem of pain. Thomas's poem
'Aim', from *Experimenting with an Amen* (1986), is an exquisite depiction of the ethos residing behind the realisation of that problem:

> A voice out of the land –
> animal, vegetable, mineral –
> 'The pain, the beauty – Why, why, why?
> Tell me the truth, give me
> understanding.' (64)

This is at once Thomas's cry and the cry of creation, but also the cry of Christ from the cross: '*Eli, Eli, lema sabachthani?*', 'my God, my God, why hast thou forsaken me?'. All of them, Thomas, creation, Christ, presuppose in this cry a divine presence and therefore the real possibility of an answer. And yet the answer Thomas perceives through nature in the poem is silence and continuation, *discompassion*:

> And the rose
> wastes its syllables; the rock fixes
> its stare; the stoat sips
> at the brimmed rabbit.

This awareness of a natural economy based on the relation of predator to prey forms a kind of sub-song in Thomas's nature mysticism. While, as we have seen, he often locates divinity and eternity as emerging specifically through nature, he continually probes and explores this darker side of nature as well. For example, in 'Pisces', also from *Song at the Year's Turning*, Thomas asks:

> Who said to the trout,
> You shall die on Good Friday
> To be food for a man
> And his pretty lady? (110)

Implied in the question here, behind the mere 'who' is the deeper question for Thomas of what *kind* of God has ordained this cycle of violence and consumption upon which the earth appears to turn? Thomas's use of the term 'Good Friday' also raises the question from the specific and natural to the universal and supernatural: not only why is nature grounded in cycles of violence, but why the ultimate sacrifice which forms the foundation of the Christian religion?[16] Although God speaks in the final stanza of 'Pisces,' he, she or it answers only the original question 'who' and none of these deeper 'whys' which underlie the poem:

> It was I, said God,
> Who formed the roses
> In the delicate flesh
> And the tooth that bruises.

Such an answer, while asserting a kind of divine supremacy, is merely a repetition of the original paradox for Thomas of a natural world reflective of divinity and yet predicated on 'the tooth that bruises'. Thomas reiterates that paradox again and again in the poems, as if in an effort to accept, finally, its mysterious necessity without explanation. I have already examined, in 'The Parish' from *Tares* (1961),

> The sharp tooth tearing its prey,
> While a bird sang from a tall tree. (15)

Similarly, in 'Then' from *Pieta* (1966) Thomas writes:

> Nothing that nature
> Did was a contradiction
> That time, and the prey hung
> Jewels of blood round the day's throat. (35)

Thomas's use of the word 'contradiction' here to indicate an absence of contradiction, as well as the adornment with 'Jewels of blood' create in these lines an ironic tension. If there is, in fact, a lack of contradiction in nature's violence, it is a lack which, it seems, must be accepted rather than rationally understood. In the poem 'Ah', also from *Pieta*, Thomas declares:

> But the God
> We worship fashions the world
> From such torment, and every creature
> Decorates it with its tribute of blood. (45)

Here, again, the lack of contradiction that these lines imply seems intended not to assuage the dilemma of a God of love and the suffering of its creation, but in fact to underscore that alarming contradiction further. Similarly, the poem 'Earth' from *H'm* (1972) seems to assert violence and bloodshed as the 'signature' characteristic of the creator-God:

> What made us think
> It was yours? Because it was signed
> With your blood, God of battles? (28)

Here blood, the very sign of violence, becomes proof of divine ownership. Finally, in 'Rough', from *Laboratories of the Spirit* (1975), Thomas's use of irony becomes embittered, signalling the depth of his distress, what he sees as the paradox of an omnipotence in which love is continually overshadowed by violence:

> God looked at the eagle that looked at
> the wolf that watched the jack-rabbit
> cropping the grass, green and curling
> as God's beard. He stepped back;
> it was perfect, a self-regulating machine
> of blood and faeces. (36)

The referent of 'it' in the penultimate line of this quotation is, of course, the 'self-regulating machine', the natural ecosystem. God emerges here as distinctly sinister, not as loving or protecting but 'stepping back' to approve that natural system based upon suffering, death, and the survival of the fittest. Underlying such bitter irony is an ongoing attempt by Thomas to integrate an awareness of such natural ferocity into a rational understanding of the Christian God. Unlike Tennyson, Thomas consistently resists the lure of any easy or artificial 'answer' to that paradox and is willing to face, finally, no answer, absence, acceptance of the mystery of these cycles of natural violence older than humankind, not as evil but as simply mysterious.

In a sense, such acceptance has always formed a significant part of Thomas's position. Even in his first collection, *The Stones of the Field* (1946), Thomas writes in 'The Airy Tomb' of how Tomos, the poem's protagonist, has

> seen sheep rotting in the wind and sun,
> And a hawk floating in a bubbling pool,
> Its weedy entrails mocking the breast
> Laced with bright water. (43)

And yet we are told that, for Tomos, as for Thomas (perhaps significantly equivalent names in Welsh and English),

> the dead and living
> Moved hand in hand on the mountain crest
> In the calm circle of taking and giving.

In these lines the cycles of violence in nature are not troubling rationally, but accepted as a unity, a harmony moving 'hand in hand ... / In the calm circle of taking and giving'. Here, suffering and death in nature are given no rational explanation by the poet, are afforded no pity or compassion, and yet these lines seem to exude a beauty and even a serenity in their depiction of the cyclic motion of the natural world.

I will end this chapter by looking briefly at the little-known poem 'Islandmen', from Thomas's 1972 collection *Young and Old*. The poem depicts neither a revelatory moment in nature nor an instance of natural violence, but is none the less highly representative of Thomas's stance on nature, both the romantic idealisation he brings to nature and the factual realism to which he seems determined to remain faithful.[17] He writes:

> And they come sailing
> From the island through the flocks
> Of the sea with the boat full
> Of their own flocks, brimming fleeces
> And whelk eyes, with the bleating
> Sea-birds and the tide races
> Snarling. And the dark hull bites
> At the water, crunching it
> To small glass, as the men chew
> Their tobacco, cleaning their mind
> On wind, trusting the horizon's
> Logic. (15)

It is the close integration of the men in nature that I am interested in here, their actuality as an equal part of nature itself no less than the wind, the island, the sheep, the boat, the sea, the birds. Thomas's commentary in the second and final stanza consolidates this effect of unity, of man *as* nature:

> These are the crusted men
> Of the sea, measuring time
> By tide-fall, knowing the changeless
> Seasons, the lasting honeysuckle
> Of the sea. They are lean and hard
> And alert, and while our subjects
> Increase, burdening us
> With their detail, these keep to the one
> Fact of the sea, its pitilessness, its beauty.

These lines seem not merely bucolic. Like so many of Thomas's farmers, the men in this portrait are worn and weathered, creatures not resigned to, but actively absorbed in, their particular fate without, it seems, ever noticing it *to be* their particular fate. It is this quality of unselfconscious integration into nature and participation *as* nature which constitute the underlying power of the portrait. Their leanness, hardness, alertness, is distinctly satisfactory, even saintly, contrasted here to an implied fatness, a softness, a sluggishness and distinct *dis*satisfaction bred by the divorce from nature, by a growing separation from nature and a self-consciousness giving way to alienation. In this sense the portrait is pointedly political as well, its message being that, for Thomas at least, such satisfaction comes from keeping to the 'fact' of the natural world, 'its pitilessness, its beauty'.

What we have seen in this chapter is that the natural world for Thomas can be viewed as an important 'occasion' of the self and of deity, repeatedly becoming the context and the wellspring both of a personal identity and of a ubiquitous deity. Nature is equally for Thomas, however, the occasion of deity as other – as unknowable, awesome, all-powerful, and threatening. Thomas refuses to resolve this apparent paradox, instead building his startling perceptions of it into questions that are let to stand. What remains to be examined is Thomas's perception of science as a major threat to this unifying force of the natural world and even as a threat to the fierce otherness of deity. One of the critically neglected foundations of Thomas's later work is the deepening preoccupation with science, and it is to his sometimes complicated ambivalence over scientific potential and endeavour that I now turn in Chapters 4 and 5.

Notes

1   I am thinking in particular of Hughes's *The Hawk in the Rain* (1957), *Lupercal* (1960), and *Crow* (1970), but also of Paul Bentley's description of Hughes as 'a poet who celebrates the amoral and often violent energies of nature' (1998: 117).

2   Thomas's 1968 essay 'The Mountains' is a good example of this perception of an exquisite beauty amidst the harsh reality of the natural world.

3   Thomas's 'The Untamed' from *The Bread of Truth* (1963) can be read as a discourse on this duality in which the poet employs the metaphor of two gardens, the one natural, the other cultivated, to illustrate this favouring of the elemental over the tamed.

4   Beginning with his earliest published work, Thomas has been more or less consistently preoccupied with these harsher conditions of nature, even at times suggesting their singularly dehumanising force as in, most famously, 'A Peasant'. See also the less well-known 'The Country' in *Young and Old* (1972) as an equally powerful acknowledgement of nature's potentially corrupting force. I would add, however, that, stylistically, Thomas does develop in these depictions from an early and intense lyricism often reminiscent of Coleridge and Yeats, an almost sensual linguistic luxuriating, into the more spare and sharply edged style with which he is typically associated, the early lyricism becoming gradually smoothed out and winnowed down into a minimalist delight in the qualities of bareness, bleakness, and endurance.

5   Thomas's use of 'concede' here seems to imply an acceptance under duress, and gestures toward a wider tension in the poetry as a whole between allowance and disallowance of divinity, between dual forces of willed faith and instinctive doubt. In Chapter 6 I will examine Thomas's 'Echoes' from the collection *H'm* (1972) in which he uses the word to denote not presence but absence.

6   I am thinking also of poems such as 'Llananno', like 'The Bright Field', also from the 1975 collection *Laboratories of the Spirit*. Of course no poem can be purely mystical since Aquinas's 'abstraction from the senses' entails a necessary failure of language. Where nature mysticism employs natural imagery, the experience of

pure mysticism, by its very definition, resists expression. Language, being necessarily grounded in sense-experience, must fail to adequately communicate a
purely mystical experience that entirely transcends such grounding. While
descriptions of pure mysticism must 'fall back' upon metaphor and simile, they
are, in the end, incommunicable experiences. See, for example, Henry Vaughan's
'The World'.

7   Thomas makes a similar admission in his *A Year in Lleyn* (1990). See
    Autobiographies, page 169.

8   Despite this denial Thomas does appear in some of the early poems, such as 'The
    Airy Tomb' from *The Stones of the Field* (1946), to flirt with a kind of pantheism
    reminiscent of Wordsworth's 'A slumber did my spirit steal' and even William
    Cullen Bryant's 'Thanatopsis'. See also Thomas's poem beginning '"And what
    is life?"' from *The Echoes Return Slow* (1988). Similarly, Anthony Conran, in his
    article 'R. S. Thomas as a Mystical Poet', points to lines in 'The Minister' (1953)
    as depicting 'the pagan apprehension of deity in natural forces' (1979: 12).

9   Indeed, the *OED* defines 'sacred' as 'made holy by association with a god or other
    object of worship'.

10 For more on this 'bi-culturality' see Jason Walford Davies's '"Thick Ambush of
    Shadows": Allusions to Welsh Literature in the Work of R. S. Thomas', and M.
    Wynn Thomas's 'Hidden Attachments: Aspects of the Relationship between the
    Two Literatures of Modern Wales', both in *Welsh Writing in English*, 1 (1995).

11 I am borrowing the phrase the 'interrogation of silence' from George Mackay
    Brown's 'The Poet'. Like Thomas's, much of Brown's work depicts a harsh world
    of nature that none the less retains a sustaining sacramental power.

12 I will occasionally be drawing attention in these notes to certain parallels in
    Thomas's work with American art and literature. For example, this description
    by Thomas seems striking in its likeness to the American Transcendentalist Ralph
    Waldo Emerson's famous description of the 'transparent eyeball' in chapter 1 of
    Nature.

13 Thomas's experience is not unlike some of those chronicled by William James in
    his *The Varieties of Religious Experience*. For example, James cites Frank Bullen's
    autobiography in which the latter describes his 'conversion' during an accident
    at sea as 'a whole age of delight' (1961: 232).

14 Thomas underscores this metaphorical usage in *A Year in Lleyn* (1990) where he
    writes: 'it is lovely sometimes to spend an hour or two out on the rocks of Braich
    y Pwll, watching the birds go by and comparing the waiting for a migrant bird
    with the waiting for a vision of God' (144).

15 The nineteenth century American painter Winslow Homer's famous 'The Fox
    Hunt' is an equally powerful and remarkably similar image. While Homer's fox
    is not actually bleeding, it is wounded in the flesh by cold and starvation, drag-
    ging its 'wounded belly / Over the snow' as it is preyed upon by hungry ravens.
    In the most remarkable similarity, Homer depicts, at the edge of the vicious
    scene, the red of wild-rose hips above the deep snow, strangely similar to
    Thomas's 'crimson seeds / Of blood ... bold as roses'. Also interesting, in a state-
    ment which is equally applicable to R. S. Thomas, the art critic Philip C. Beam
    comments that 'Homer's recognition of the savagery always latent in nature runs
    like a continuous thread through his late work' (1975: 40).

16 The fish is, of course, a traditional symbol of Christ, the Greek *icthus*, a word which literally means 'fish' but whose letters were often interpreted as an acronym for the appellation 'Jesus Christ, Son of God and Saviour' (*Iesus Christus, Theou Uious Soter*).

17 The poem is comparable in this regard to the American artist Andrew Wyeth's tempera paintings of sea-working men on the rugged coast of Maine in the extreme north-eastern United States: idealised perhaps, in the sense of being held up for admiration, but not sentimentalised, and most importantly, like nature itself, real and enduring. Like Thomas, Wyeth, sometimes referred to as a 'magical realist', returns again and again to familiar and enduring landscapes, and to the subject of human figures, often solitary human figures, within those landscapes, even as part of those landscapes.

4 'Lenses to bear': the scientific world

> The scientist
> brings his lenses to bear and unity
> is fragmented. It is the hand saying
>
> it is not of the body, leaving it
> to the poet, playing upon his timeless
> instrument, to call all things back
> into irradiated orbit about the one word.
>
> R. S. Thomas, 'First Person'

Introduction

In his 1985 J. R. Jones Memorial Lecture entitled '*Undod*' or 'Unity' R. S. Thomas describes a historical marriage between religion and science and its gradual disintegration. According to Thomas a philosophical 'unity of being' was first achieved in the West under the influence of the great monotheistic religions of Judaism, Islam, and Christianity. Such unity was ultimately undermined by religious reactions by the medieval Christian Church to an emerging scientific vision. Rather than an integration and co-operation developing between thinkers in the two realms, there ensued a continuing divergence, competition, and mutual distrust. Thomas writes:

> Some see the Church to blame for trying to stifle scientific research in the Middle Ages. By defending a position which was indefensible, and thus having to give in later on, the Church shook the faith of believers in its teachings. This led, over the centuries, to the freedom and independence accorded the scientist, until, eventually, scientific truth came to be the *only* truth for most of the West's population; and this led, in turn, to people's desertion of the churches. (1988: 30–1)

Thomas goes on to cite reductionism, via Descartes and Darwin, as equally responsible for the continuing fragmentation of this earlier world-view. Descartes he argues, separated matter from spirit and in doing so laid the foundations for a wholly secular investigation of the universe as a kind of inanimate machine:

By creating two parts, matter and spirit, completely separate from each other, Descartes made it possible for the scientist to treat matter as something wholly lifeless, containing innumerable parts, as if it were a vast machine, running on its own. This led in time to a total reductionism, to belief that the whole world was nothing but a machine. (31)

Similarly, Darwin's theory of evolution later exacerbated this reductionism by its assertion of the primacy of man as animal:

Not only was life no more than a collection of hard, material particles; but man was no more than an animal in essence; true, he was a talented animal, with the ability to think and reason, but an animal all the same, born in the same way, possessing the same organs, and dying just like other animals. (31)

In his book *Further Along the Road Less Travelled*, the widely influential American psychiatrist Dr M. Scott Peck, like Thomas, describes a similar historical unity between religion and science, as well as a similar dissolution of that unity. He suggests that philosophers such as Plato, Aristotle, and Thomas Aquinas were actually scientists, deeply concerned with what today we would call the scientific method, with the logic of premises and viable evidence, but whose realms of inquiry included the divine. According to Peck, this integration of religion and science remained intact until the end of the seventeenth century when, because of growing conflicts between the Church and scientists, not least the indictment of Galileo by the Inquisition in 1633 for his continued adherence to Copernican theory, there developed an 'unwritten social contract' of mutual non-interference in which religion and science agreed to proceed afterward within separate domains. By the eighteenth century 'supernatural knowledge' was said to be the proper concern of religion, and 'natural knowledge' that of science. Peck argues that such an agreement, by substantially easing tensions between the Church and scientists, constituted a significant move towards peace, effectively ushering out the Inquisition, helping to abolish slavery and to establish democracy, and 'giving birth to a technological revolution beyond anybody's wildest expectations, even to the point of paving the way for the development of a planetary culture' (1993: 179). Peck's conclusion, however, is that for our own time such divisions no longer prove beneficial; that in the twentieth century they became so rigidly accentuated as to be compartmentalising and, ultimately, destructive.

What is important here is not merely that Thomas and Peck, lead-
ers in their respective fields and countries, appear to agree on the existence of an historical unity between religion and science and the forces
which ultimately destroyed that unity but, rather, that both men find the
loss of such unity to be of singular importance to their own age; that both
seem to be lamenting the gradual disappearance of a more primitive view
in which matter and spirit were one. Even more, both authors seem to
imply the possibility that fundamental to humankind is a desire for such
unity, the fulfilment of which desire they see as necessary not only to
human happiness but possibly even to human survival.

The question remains why Thomas and Peck see such separation as
having become destructive. A look at R. S. Thomas's work suggests that
an inability to imagine relationships between subject matter, not only
between religion and science, may prove detrimental in at least three
ways. The first of these is by making artificial and simple a reality that is
complex. Compartmentalisation of thought is, for Thomas, a distortion
of our experience of an interrelated reality. If strict categories are tempt-
ing because less subtle and therefore less painful to handle, they may also
constitute an inferior reflection of actual experience. Second, the simplification of a complex reality may, in the end, deny the possibility of paradoxical modes of thought, restraining thought within an either/or
framework and effectively barring it from the more imaginative and often
higher intellectual realms which typically operate on a model of
both/and. For example, as Peck points out, it was Bernhard Riemann,
the nineteenth-century German mathematician, who challenged the
theory that two parallel lines never meet, and by so doing laid the foundations for the geometry named after him, as well as for much of
Einstein's later work (1993: 73–4). Finally, compartmentalisation may,
ultimately, invalidate the struggle towards unity and wholeness, intellectual, spiritual, even physical, which Thomas seems to suggest is basic to
human existence and the search for meaning. What we can see in the
poetry is an ongoing preoccupation with the dangers of such compartmentalisation and a steady pressure towards a reintegration of thought
corresponding exactly to these points. The poetry depicts a reality that
is complex, interrelated and paradoxical, and it derives its most forceful
impetus from a basic struggle towards unity. In particular Thomas's deep
concern with science is characterised by a lament over its separation from
other areas of thought, from poetry, theology, morals, and by an ongoing struggle to reintegrate these areas, to think, in poetry, of 'supernatural knowledge' in a scientific way, and of 'natural knowledge' in a
supernatural way.[1] What seems to prove ultimately destructive in

Thomas's view is not the *desire* for understanding which science poses but the pursuit of that desire divorced from any attention to an innate spiritual searching after wholeness. A. M. Allchin suggests just this in his book *Praise Above All: Discovering the Welsh Tradition*:

> No one could pretend that the growth of such [scientific] knowledge has been or is unimportant in the last two centuries. But it is the onesided development of such knowledge at the expense of all other forms of knowing which is one of the principal factors in the crises of meaning and meaninglessness which besets us today. No society can devote its energy and attention exclusively to the question 'how', to the almost total neglect of the question 'why', without suffering mortal consequences. (1991: 74)

It is an overemphasis on the redemption of human beings materially which Thomas sees as potentially catastrophic. In this he is himself a philosopher in the ancient sense of which Peck writes, but presiding over a modern world, over the break-up of older unities of thought, and over what he sees as the increasingly deadly fallout of those divisions. Of course Thomas's position is not simple. For example, he suggests in the poem 'Pre-Cambrian' from *Frequencies* (1978) that scientific inquiry itself may be dangerous, that

> Plato, Aristotle,
> all those who furrowed the calmness
> of their foreheads are responsible
> for the bomb. (23)

And yet, as we shall see in Chapter 7, Thomas seems to suggest as well that philosophical or scientific inquiry is one of the paths to spiritual awareness, to renewed awe and spiritual regeneration. He writes, for example, in 'One Life' from *Mass for Hard Times* (1992) that

> Growing up
> is to leave the fireside
> with its tales,
> the burying of the head
> between God's knees.
> It is to perceive
> that knowledge of him comes
> from the genes' breaking
> of an involved code,
> from the mind's parallel
> at-homeness with missile and scalpel. (56)

Here is just one example of the highly paradoxical nature of Thomas's thought, his rejection and affirmation of science, his acknowledgement of subtlety, complexity, interrelatedness. To recognise this wideness and this relentless drive towards integration in Thomas's work is to acknowledge the size and the difficulty of the poetic task he has set himself, his standing in the stream of scientific and popular progress, perhaps not to turn it back but rather to divert it a little toward integrity and away from what he sees as a dangerous compartmentalisation.

The accusation that Thomas *is* merely one who would 'turn the clock back' has, at times, been popular. In his article 'Confronting the Minotaur: Politics and Poetry in 20th Century Wales' David Smith suggests that R. S. Thomas, among others, is guilty of a 'wilful re-grasping of a lost tradition …, an ahistorical primitivism …, a wistful Utopianism that invariably looks and sounds like a holistic past that never existed except in the timeless ante-room of the history mansion' (1979: 9–10, 13). It may be true in reading of Thomas's

> long absorption with the plough,
> With the tame and the wild creatures
> And man united with the earth (*Song* 1955: 115)

that there sometimes comes the temptation to view the poet merely as a country vicar venting his *hiraeth* for the alleged simplicity of a pre-industrialised Wales. In fact, Thomas admits in his autobiography, *No-one*, that

> The tendency was always in him to look back and to see the past as superior … Heavy industry had not [yet] reached south Wales to plunder and deface it, making the nation top-heavy … R. S. always saw the industrial revolution as Wales's main disaster. (98)

Yet, despite that 'long absorption' and the nostalgia for an earlier age, it must be acknowledged that, if not always affectionately, Thomas is, at the same time, unflinchingly realistic and even forward-looking in his depictions of contemporary life. One thinks, for example, of the poet's declaration in 'Looking at Sheep' from *The Bread of Truth* (1963) :

> But images
> Like this are for sheer fancy
> To play with. Seeing how Wales fares
> Now, I will attend rather
> To things as they are. (48)

Similarly, Thomas admits in the poem 'Petition' from *H'm* (1972):

> One thing I have asked
> Of the disposer of the issues
> Of life: that truth should defer
> To beauty. It was not granted. (2)

In the first instance Thomas echoes somewhat Wallace Stevens's preoccupations with the relation between the imagined and the real in his
'Man with the Blue Guitar'.[2] The second seems to be a deliberate
reworking of Keats's '"Beauty is truth, truth beauty"'. But in both
instances the effect is to deflate a romantic idealism in which truth is consistently aesthetically pleasing, in favour of a more strenuous 'seeing' of
'things as they are'. Although Thomas is both nostalgic and romantic in
his tapping of history and his vision of an ideal, not to see that tendency
in Thomas as working in conjunction with a strenuous realism and constant forward probing effectively denies much of the richness and complexity of his work.

A look at the place of science in that work confirms this dedication
to 'things as they are'. Few would disagree that an engagement with
modern science, with its vocabulary, sources, and wider implications
became increasingly central to the poet's work in later years, even while
critical comment on that centrality, and even urgency, has remained
sparse. As early as 1968, in the poem 'The Place' from *Not that He
Brought Flowers,* Thomas refers to himself as 'a man vowed / To science'
(45). In the poem 'Prayer', which closes *Later Poems* (1983), he
acknowledges a lifelong dedication to science:

> Baudelaire's grave
> not too far
> from the tree of science.
> Mine, too,
> since I sought and failed
> to steal from it. (214)

Indeed, speaking privately in Manafon as recently as 1998 Thomas
remarked on his continuing 'obsession' with science and technology. This
chapter examines the source and nature of Thomas's position on science,
his path to that position, and, throughout both of these, the rich poetic
manifestations of that position. I will also examine Thomas's prose-
writing as, in some ways, the clearest articulation of that position on science. By turning to these 'prose sources' one can understand more easily
the sometimes hidden lines of continuity which thread these often radically forward-looking poems.[1]

Preoccupations and intentions

Ned Thomas's 1992 article for *Planet* entitled 'R. S. Thomas: The Question about Technology' provides a rare and useful point of departure into the subject of science in Thomas's poetry. For example, he makes clear in the article that the poet has long been fascinated by the *language* of science:

> From quite early on in his poetry we find words and phrases with a scientific and technical ring to them: 'frost's cruel chemistry', 'time's geometry', 'the embryo music dead in his throat' [and] by the later volumes, terms such as *virus, molecule, cell, gene, frequency, equation* are part of the way he apprehends reality. (1992: 59–60)

He also suggests a certain 'complexity and tension' in the poet's attitude towards science by turning to the poem 'Homo Sapiens 1941' and interpreting the aeroplane at the centre of the poem as 'unambiguously destructive' and depicted in 'words which suggest a mechanical and ruthless purpose', while also indicating that simultaneously in the poem 'there are phrases that invite our admiration, our pride in human achievement even: "hosts of ice … weigh down his delicate wings" and "daring the starlight above the stiff sea of cloud"'(55). Perhaps Ned Thomas's most important insight in the article, however, concerns the separation he implies between R. S. Thomas's acceptance and use of the *language* of science on the one hand and his apparent hostility to the *ideas* which underlie and give rise to that language on the other. He cites the poet's engagement with a scientific vocabulary and, as a somewhat separate issue, considers the 'complexity and tension' he sees in the poet's attitude towards the ideas of science which give rise to that vocabulary. Part of what this chapter suggests is that although Ned Thomas, more than any other critic, has perceptively sown the seeds of a long-neglected inquiry into the importance of science for R. S. Thomas, it remains for those insights to be pursued, both 'backward' to their more explicit source in the prose, and 'forward' to their fuller manifestations in the poems. For example, although he unearths a scientific register in the work of R. S. Thomas and indicates a slight expansion in that register, he neglects to explore the important overall development in that register and the driving force behind it. Similarly, while suggesting a 'complexity and tension' in Thomas's relation to science, he fails to get to grips with the source(s) of that complexity, to reconcile that tension, or to indicate whether these issue from a vague confusion or ambivalence on the part of the poet, or whether they could be the result of a more careful and ongoing investigative process. Perhaps most importantly, Ned Thomas fails to 'deconstruct' the term *science* into its constituent parts or to differentiate it from its natural offspring, 'technology', all of which becomes vital if one is to understand the significant role which science came to play in Thomas's work.

While clearly it is the *ideas* of science which must give rise to its *language*, it is none the less language, diction, actual words which, for R. S. Thomas as a poet, seem to form the starting point in his own preoccupation. What we find in his earliest work is a fairly basic scientific register used infrequently, with a primarily artistic relish, and with little apparent concern for any deeper, associated dilemmas. As we have already seen, Ned Thomas cites 'Lament for Prytherch' from *Song at the Year's Turning* (1955) to indicate Thomas's early use of a scientific diction: 'time's geometry / Upon your face by which we tell / Your sum of years' and, 'Your heart that is dry as a dead leaf / Undone by frost's cruel chemistry' (99). These references to geometry and chemistry, while striking artistically, harbour no deeper judgements on the subjects themselves. This proves true of most of Thomas's early use of a scientific vocabulary. Words such as 'embryonic' (*Stones*, 22), 'gestation' (*Stones*, 23), 'retina' (*Acre*, 33), 'analytic' (*Song*, 97), 'membraned' (*Song*, 111), 'equations' (*Song*, 115), 'lenses' (*Supper*, 27), 'scalpel' (*Supper*, 40), 'litmus' (*Supper*, 42), 'obstetrics' (*Tares*, 10), 'virus' (*Tares*, 11), 'neurosis' (*Tares*, 19), 'nodes' (*Tares*, 36), 'satellites' (*Tares*, 43), 'test-tube' (*Bread*, 7), 'molecules' (*Pieta*, 15), 'voltage' (*Flowers*, 28), 'placenta' (*Flowers*, 33), are almost all used primarily as aesthetic devices, as aids to imagery rather than as indicators of any moral or political position on science itself. However, what begins gradually to emerge, beginning with Thomas's 1972 volume *H'm*, is not only a significant expansion of that register to include a more sophisticated and complex *range* of words but also a simultaneous proliferation in the frequency with which these scientific words are used. This expansion and proliferation are indicative of a deepening philosophical undertow in the poet's work; that from the 1970s onward Thomas's use of the scientific register is characterised by an *escalating irony* as he moves from a younger poet's preoccupation with the mere language of science as a mode of artistic expression to a moral philosopher's anxious concern with the sources and wider implications of those words. For example, Thomas writes in 'No Answer', from the 1972 collection *H'm*:

> Knowledge is power;
> The old oracle
> Has not changed. The nucleus
> In the atom awaits
> Our bidding. (7)

Not only do 'nucleus' and 'atom' expand Thomas's scientific register, raising it to a higher level of sophistication, but clearly the vocabulary is loaded with a new political weight. What began for Thomas with the word emerges here as a deeper awareness of, and struggle with, ideas *behind* the word. Those philosophical struggles with science, and his taking up of a position in relation to it, gradually add to his use of scientific language a distinctive irony, arming the later poems with a moral and political aggression unseen in the earlier work. Without forcing the poems into an artificial framework, it seems one can see a kind of dialectical progress over the course of Thomas's long preoccupation with science in which the 'thesis' of the word as 'art-object' is gradually challenged by the 'antithesis' of the word as 'moral signifier' and, finally, transformed in a 'synthesis' of the former two toward an understanding and use of the word as, simultaneously, art-object *and* moral signifier. Of course the aesthetic use of the word is never abandoned by Thomas in this 'progression'. We might as appropriately speak of a transfiguration of the word as art-object towards a greater potency and militancy of purpose. For example, in the poem 'Christmas Eve' from *No Truce with the Furies* (1995) Thomas writes:

> Erect capital's arch;
> decorate it with the gilt edge
> of the moon. Pave the way to it
> with cheques and with credit –
>
> it is still not high enough
> for the child to pass under
> who comes to us this midnight
> invisible as radiation. (13)

A similarly honed political edge can be felt in the opening lines from 'Afallon' in the same collection:

> It is Adam's other
> kingdom, what he might have
> inherited had he
> refused the apple, the nuclear
> fruit with the malignant core. (25)

In both of these examples we can see a dual use of the scientific register both as a contribution to the poem's aesthetic life and to its stringent irony and underlying political purpose. Such 'activist intentions' in Thomas's poetry are less surprising in light of remarks made in his 1963 W. D. Thomas Memorial Lecture titled 'Words and the Poet' where he makes clear the fact that a political purpose often underlies his work as a poet:

> There is always lurking in the back of my poetry a kind of moralistic or propagandist intention. It is as though, having found that I had a slight gift for putting words together to make poems, I used that gift as the best way I knew for getting a particular message across. (1964: 83)

Of equal importance in this regard is Thomas's poem 'After Jericho' from *Frequencies* (1978) in which he writes:

> There is an aggression of fact
> to be resisted successfully
> only in verse, that fights language
> with its own tools. (43)

This is precisely the origin of the irony so characteristic of Thomas's later poems concerning science, a fighting of language with its own tools, the juxtaposition or admixture of a scientific register with a more traditional diction as a means of waging battle against what the poet sees as the destructive excesses of a science cordoned off from wider perspectives.

The last section of this chapter takes up Thomas's early position, as he argues it in the prosework, on the theoretical use of scientific language in poetry, turning to the poems themselves to illustrate his practice of that theory. Chapter 5 defines the term 'science', as used by Thomas, by dividing it into realms of 'pure' and 'applied'. It is in this chapter that I will detail the development in Thomas's position on applied science or 'the machine', illustrating how an early balance of ease and trepidation towards applied science gradually gives way to the emergence of a deepening concern and an 'escalating irony' in the later work. Chapter 5 also takes up the two primary sources of Thomas's accumulating critique of applied science and examines the three poetic techniques according to which he achieves this 'escalating irony'. The final section of Chapter 5 looks briefly at a few of the poems in which Thomas envisions the possibility of a Wordsworthian unity between technology and poetry before taking up his position on pure science, in particular modern physics, as he contextualises it in Old Testament theology. Looking primarily at his 1988 article for *Planet* entitled '*Undod*' or 'Unity' one discovers a surprising argument in support of pure science as an effective opening to philosophy, as uniquely integrative, and as not only facilitating the highest modes of paradoxical thought but as, for Thomas, a force and method of spiritual regeneration.

The question of language

A curious confusion emerges in the closing to R. S. Thomas's 1963 W.
D. Thomas Memorial Lecture, 'Words and the Poet'. First, describing
his own poetic ideal he writes:

> At times there comes the desire to write with great precision and
> clarity, words so simple and moving that they bring tears to the
> eyes, or, if you like, as Wordsworth said, are 'too deep for tears' …
> This is where the one syllable, the four letter words come into their
> own. They can have particular force. One remembers lines such as
> that by Wilfred Owen in 'Futility': 'Was it for this the clay grew
> tall?' Plain simple English words, yet so often they are the best. It
> is a case of 'central peace subsisting at the heart of endless agita-
> tion'. Art is not simple, and yet about so much of the best, whether
> in painting, poetry or music, there is a kind of miraculous simplic-
> ity. Some of Shakespeare's greatest effects are produced with every-
> day words. There is Lear's 'Take it away; it smells of mortality'; or
> Cleopatra's 'Do you not see my baby at my breast, that sucks the
> nurse asleep?' … I think that as long as there is poetry, it will keep
> reverting to that native plainness and simplicity … It is as though,
> for poetry, general words will do, with occasional glimpses or
> insights for added effect, as in Rosetti's [sic] 'The woodspurge has
> a cup of three'. (1964: 83–4)

This striking declaration and illustration of striving for simplicity in
poetry, for 'plain simple English words', is itself not problematic until we
see it set against remarks made in the paragraph which directly follows
it. There Thomas discusses what he sees as a widening urban experience
and the emergence of a 'new vocabulary' required to accommodate and
express that experience:

> Once an eye for nature and a flair for describing it were the natural
> appurtenances of a poet. Even if the audience were townspeople,
> the fields were never far away, the towns being small. Most of that
> has changed and is going to change still more. The common envi-
> ronment of the majority is an urban-industrial one. The potential
> audience of a poet is one of town dwellers, who are mostly out of
> touch, if not out of sympathy with nature. Their contact with it is
> modified by the machine. This is tending to deprive country-rooted
> words of their relevance. The new modes of experience, the new
> subjects, the new vocabulary are creating the impression that the
> old words are outmoded. Rossetti's word-spurge [sic] has given
> way to 'the belt feed lever and the belt holding pawl' of Richard

Eberhart. And this is a problem which all poets must face … One
of the great questions facing the poet is: Can significant poetry be
made with these new words and terms? (84–5)[4]

In this second quotation Thomas appears suddenly to be questioning the
viability of his own theory as just set out in the previous paragraph, prod-
ding poets and poetry not toward simplicity but, with Eberhart, toward
experimentation with a 'new vocabulary' and accommodation of an
emerging 'urban-speak'. Not only does he predict a loss of relevance for
simple country words such as Rossetti's 'woodspurge', he appears to be
simultaneously warning the extinction of those poets who do not keep
pace sufficiently with their increasingly urban-industrial readerships.
More riddling still, Thomas goes on to conclude the lecture by revert-
ing to his original position, numbering *himself* amongst those poets destined for extinction, unwilling to abandon the old, 'outmoded' forms for
the new, thereby effectively reversing his earlier support of the necessity
of experimentation with a new vocabulary. In answer to his own question 'Can significant poetry be made with these new words and terms?'
he writes:

> In theory the answer is frequently an affirmative one. People say:
> 'I don't see why not'. They quote words such as chromosomes
> as being actually attractive. My own position is usually to allow
> this as a legitimate theory, but to ask in practice, 'Where are the
> poems?' (85)

As a final complication to all of this apparent shifting of allegiances we
can say, in hindsight, that Thomas was himself destined to write such
poems, against what appear to be his own scruples, if not derision. And
yet in the lecture he seems adamant in his final (if theoretical) rejection
of such experimentation:

> Perhaps it is my ignorance of other languages that makes me say
> this. Maybe they are issuing from the presses in Germany or
> Czecho- Slovakia. Maybe it is too soon, and there has not yet been
> time to assimilate or absorb the enormous amount of fresh knowl-
> edge and its vocabulary. But I remember Coleridge's saying to the
> effect that the opposite of poetry is not prose but science. We have
> yet to prove that we can have both. I remember also Wordsworth's
> 'human heart by which we live'. The poet's function and privilege
> surely is to speak to our condition in the name of our common
> humanity in words which do not grow old because the heart does
> not grow old. (85)

Thomas rejects in this final quotation his earlier implication that a poet
is in large measure driven by the dictates of his audience and the language
of predominating experience. Here he depicts not the separating power
of exterior experience but an interior unity between poet and reader
which adheres in spite of those increasingly divergent experiences. He
also seems to reaffirm that, for the expression and communication of that
'common humanity', the old vocabulary is best; that the old words 'do
not grow old because the heart does not grow old'. His final conclusion
appears to be that a simpler poetic diction not only is not 'outmoded'
but is particularly and uniquely *relevant* as a language which binds interiorly a people increasingly divided on a more physical and experiential
level.

    Two poems published in the 1980s, however, are singularly affir-
mative of experimentation with the vocabulary of science. In the little-
known 'Vocabulary' from *Destinations* (1985) Thomas seems to suggest
not only the inevitability of these new words but the necessity for an
entirely new genre of poetry under the revolutionary influence of science. In the poem's first stanza vocabulary is imaged as a restless bird,
singing in its cage of time. By stanza two the bird becomes a kind of
phoenix, prone to death and rebirth:

>   You are dust; then a bird
>   with new feathers, but always
>   beating at the mind's bars. (11)

And in a final conflation of the image at the close of the second stanza
the poet is depicted as a 'new Noah' sending the bird to search for 'safe
ground'. The allegorical implications achieved by this development of
images are both complex and powerful. The old vocabulary seems to
have come to the end of its natural life's cycle. The new vocabulary, risen
from the ashes of the old, is sent out into a world destroyed, according
to the myth, by the flood-waters of God's wrath, in response to the corruption of humankind. But, strangely, the post-diluvian world to which
the bird vocabulary is sent to search for 'new life' is a modern world of
steel; the sprig it plucks is not a 'green' poem, as of old, but a 'new poem',
metallic and gleaming, product of a scientific world:

>   A new Noah, I despatch
>
>   you to alight awhile
>   on steel branches; then call
>   you home, looking for the metallic
>   gleam of a new poem in your bill.

It would seem, according to 'Vocabulary', that, while the poet retains a place in this new world, while he has been preserved from the flood, as it were, he has also been radically altered by the experience, forced into an acceptance not only of a modern technological world but of a new vocabulary and, indeed, of a new poetry which, rather than being actively set down by the poet, is necessarily *received* from the wider world over which the poet has little control. This same idea is set out again by Thomas in his 1988 collection *The Echoes Return Slow*, albeit in a new, though no less forceful, image:

> 'Not done yet,' mutters
> the old man, fitting a bent
> poem to his broken bow. (75)

The old poet here is pathetic, 'not done', and yet naively unaware of his broken tool and the deformed poem which will never fly. It is, in a sense, the poet himself who is broken here, less old in his age than in his adherence to an outmoded style. The narrator's surprising reaction to the image is to declare:

> So I refine
> my weapons: beams, gases;
>
> composer of the first
> radio-active verses.

The question remains, what to make of all this apparent confusion concerning the language of poetry. What *is* R. S. Thomas's position on the use of a scientific vocabulary? In his own words 'can significant poetry be made with these new words and phrases?'. And what is one to make of the apparently shifting ground found in his remarks on the subject in 'Words and the Poet' and in the poems we have looked at above?

One answer to the curious confusion concerning language which we find in Thomas's 'Words and the Poet', and one that the majority of Thomas's poems support, is that so far as it can be said that Thomas, in 'Words and the Poet', is setting out a philosophy of language, that philosophy is grounded in the precision and power of a simple diction, while at the same time remaining fluid enough to accommodate the possibility of experimentation with a newer, urban-industrial or scientific diction, despite the clash of such experimentation with the poet's more fundamental impulses. We might view Thomas both as the old man in the poem from *The Echoes Return Slow*, and as the nuclear warrior from 'Vocabulary'. Not only does he seem to hold to both positions in theory, but turning to the poems one finds a 'miraculous simplicity' born of

'plain simple English words', standing alongside a more radical experimentation with the 'new vocabulary' of modern science. As I have
already mentioned, such experimentation becomes widespread only in
the later poems, where it is often characterised by an 'escalating irony'
which I will look at more closely in Chapter 5. None the less, it is possible to see these dual forces of simplicity and experimentation working
more or less in tandem across Thomas's oeuvre. A brief chronological
sampling from the poems helps to illustrate this. For example, Thomas's
second volume, *An Acre of Land* (1952), is stylistically devoted to the
lyrical but precise use of predominantly Anglo-Saxon and monosyllabic
words. Repeatedly we come across lines as pure and powerful as these
from 'The Hill Farmer Speaks':

> I am the farmer, stripped of love
> And thought and grace by the land's hardness;
> But what I am saying over the fields'
> Desolate acres, rough with dew,
> Is Listen, listen, I am a man like you. (17)

And yet even as early as this one might suggest just a glimmer of the
poet's later preoccupation with a 'newer' language and ironic tone in the
final lines of 'The Welsh Hill Country' in which we are told that the man
still farming at Ty'n-Fawnog is 'Contributing grimly to the accepted pattern, / The embryo music dead in his throat' (7). Contrasts between a
dedication to simplicity of utterance and a forward-looking poetic experimentation become more clearly accentuated by the volume *Pietà*
(1966). The poem 'Gifts', for example, communicates the sense of a linguistic reduction down to essentials:

> From my father my strong heart,
> My weak stomach.
> From my mother the fear. (17)

Of course by 'linguistic reduction' I do not mean to suggest simplicity
either of technique or of effect or meaning. The precision of these
clipped lines, their spare diction, their omission of main verbs and con-
junctions, may, for a moment, obscure the fact that the actual object(s)
of the poet's 'fear', and the more exact implications of 'strong heart' and
'weak stomach' remain open to a wide range of interpretation. Beneath
the 'simplicity' of these lines one discovers a heightened resonance, and
the possibility of multiple or complex inference. Juxtaposed to such linguistic paring down, however, we find in the same volume more technically complex phrases such as 'viruses invade the blood', 'the geometry

of their dark wings', and 'the molecules and the blood's virus', vocabulary and evocations clearly moving the poetry in a different direction.
Thomas's collection *H'm* (1972), which I have suggested signals a turning by the poet towards a deeper engagement with scientific language
and issues, often retains the lyricism so characteristic of his early work.
In the poem 'Pouf', for example, he writes:

> It was March.
> A wind
> Blew. Sudden flowers
> Opened in the sea's
> Garden. (13)

But in a poem like 'Earth', also from *H'm*, one finds not only a more
complex vocabulary but a corresponding convolution of thought and
manipulation of imagery, all of which contribute towards a sense of the
poem less as the reflection of wisdom recollected, and more as a strenuous and unfinished activity, a reaction involving various degrees of flux,
strain, and distress:

> We are misled
> By perspective; the microscope
> Is our sin, we tower enormous
> Above it the stronger it
> Grows. (28)

Moving to the 1980s, Thomas's volume *Experimenting with an Amen*
(1986) exhibits perhaps the most extreme combinations of traditional
diction and experimentation with a more technical vocabulary. One finds
there lines such as these from 'Nativity':

> The moon is born
> and a child is born,
> lying among white clothes
> as the moon among clouds. (46)

And yet standing in dramatic contrast are these lines from 'Reply' in the
same volume:

> Do the molecules
> bow down? Before what cradle
> do the travellers from afar,
> strontium and plutonium, hold out
> their thin gifts? (65)

What is perhaps most important in the comparison here is that both poems concern the birth of Christ, and yet the presentation of each, the diction employed, the tone achieved, even the stanzaic formatting, are clearly at odds, emanating from different sources as it were, the former rooted in an extreme simplicity which lends it a bardic or visionary quality, the latter rooted in a more radical experimentation and political protest. We can see this same duality in Thomas's final collection, *No Truce with the Furies* (1995). Note the almost elemental austerity of the following lines from 'At the End' in which the simplicity of language, of utterance, not only echoes the room's physically spartan interior but, by implication, creates a sense of the narrator's own spiritual interior as similarly unencumbered:

> Few possessions: a chair,
> a table, a bed
> to say my prayers by,
> and, gathered from the shore,
> the bone-like, crossed sticks
> proving that nature
> acknowledges the Crucifixion. (42)

And yet in contrast to the stillness which emanates from 'At the End', we come, only a few pages later, to these lines from 'Negative' which are fraught with the terms and tensions generated by modern science:

> A child came
> and what I thought in his hand
> was the key to the kingdom
> turned into a retort
> and test-tube, and his caliper eyes
> were being stretched for measuring
> the widening gap between love and money. (50)

What becomes clear here is that Thomas's use of language derives from two divergent sources: from an impulse towards simplicity and even, at times, austerity of diction, as well as from an impulse towards experimentation with the new language of science. Part of what I will turn to now in Chapter 5 is the way in which that emerging linguistic experimentation is intimately linked with the intensification of Thomas's philosophical concerns over the moral value of applied science.

Notes

1   The titles of two of Thomas's collections themselves attest to this effort towards the reintegration of religion and science: *Laboratories of the Spirit* was published in 1975, and *Experimenting with an Amen* was published in 1986.
2   I am thinking in particular here of the first section of Stevens's poem in which he writes:

> They said, 'You have a blue guitar,
> You do not play things as they are.'
>
> The man replied, 'Things as they are
> Are changed upon the blue guitar.' (165)

Parallels between Stevens and Thomas are less surprising in light of M. Wynn Thomas's report, in his 'Introduction' to *The Page's Drift: R. S. Thomas at Eighty*, that 'scarcely a day has passed in thirty years without his [Thomas's] reading a poem by Wallace Stevens' (1993: 12).

3   This focus on the prose work as 'source' no doubt runs counter to the Formalist orthodoxy which would insist on the integrity/autonomy of individual poems. It is not so much that Thomas's poems concerning science cannot stand alone, but rather that they register the effects of an argument by the poet whose roots are more visible in prose.
4   This excerpt from Thomas's 1963 'Words and the Poet' has its source in the poet's short 'Preface' to *The Batsford Book of Country Verse* which he edited two years earlier in 1961. Besides illustrating a long-term preoccupation with the relation of poetry to an increasingly scientific or industrial environment, the earlier version, written as an introduction for young readers, is remarkable for its candid eloquence.

5 Science and nature

Introduction: pure and applied science

Having dealt with the issue of the language of science, one must return to the dilemma pointed up earlier by Ned Thomas's reading of 'Homo Sapiens 1941': how does one begin to reconcile R. S. Thomas's apparently simultaneous condemnation and admiration for the objects and ideas which underlie that language? As I have already suggested, Thomas seems to move gradually from a preoccupation with the language of science for the purposes of art into a moral philosopher's more anxious musings over the nature of science itself. In this chapter I will trace those musings, and examine their various manifestations in the poems.

The first step in this task is to define the word 'science'. Though Ned Thomas's article is entitled 'The Question about Technology', he continually employs the combination 'science and technology', while offering little differentiation between the two. However, in order to follow the poet's thought in this area one must delineate on the one hand 'pure science', as an abstract activity of reasoned thought, an abstract empirical investigation and the understanding brought to light by such and, on the other hand, 'applied science' or technology, what R. S. Thomas refers to as 'the machine', as the practical transformation and application of that pure science into a physically working reality. In this way pure science can be thought of primarily as a process of interior reasoning, while applied science can be considered technological development, the physical manifestations of the conclusions of pure science. Thomas himself makes a similar clarification when he writes, in his autobiography, *No-one*, (1985) that

> perhaps it wasn't pure science that was to blame, but applied science, the kind that was used under financial pressure to exploit and exhaust the earth's resources in order to satisfy the needs that science herself had created. (108)

In the light of this statement the temptation is to see a strict dichotomy. It might be argued, though erroneously I think, that R. S. Thomas's 'position' is one that validates pure science while demonising its application in technology. It is true that Thomas is rarely sparing in his judgement of what the machine has produced:

> Wales today is a land of pylons and wires, a land of television masts and police poles, a land of new roads full of visitors rushing to the sea, where the planted forests and the caravan parks are fast swallowing the remaining open ground. (99)

And yet Thomas's reference to 'the kind' of applied science indicates a more complex position, a recognition of applied science as both creative and destructive in its potential. Indeed, we read, a bit earlier in the autobiography, of another example of applied science not as destroying but as saving:

> Porth Neigwl was an exceedingly dangerous bay for the old sailing ships, and though he was so much inclined to praise the past at the expense of the present, seeing the waves rolling in so fiercely R. S. would give thanks that the machine had arrived, to save ships from being at the mercy of such seas. (91–2)

Clearly Thomas's position is more fluid than absolute. What is beginning to emerge here is the possibility of the judgement of applied science not in any absolute sense, but according to its particular intentions and effects. But while this idea clearly forms a part of Thomas's position, it is by no means indicative of his whole view. As a poet Thomas constantly probes toward and examines the sources of ideas. To grasp the considerable force and subtly of his position on science we must follow him both 'backward', into the causes, and 'forward', into the implications of science, apart from the mere 'weighing up' of effects. Not surprisingly, this probing toward foundations leads, in the end, to the poet's probing the very nature of human existence and the relation of humanity to the divine. It is in this way that the so-called 'science poems' are, equally, 'religious poems', wrestling, as virtually all of Thomas's work does, with perennial questions of existence and meaning.

Merely haunted: the birth of the machine

Thomas's use of a fairly wide range of scientific words in the early work prior to *H'm* in 1972 is clearly evidence of a developing scientific awareness and interest. We have already seen how his early deployment of those words is primarily aesthetic, as opposed to ironic or political. The treatment of science as an idea is primarily occasional in the early work. When it does occur it is mostly restricted to treatment of some aspect of applied science, or technology, what Thomas refers to as 'the machine'. These early treatments of science as a political force, which I shall examine now, are often accomplished with somewhat of a flourish, with a lightness of touch and even a relish which disappears in the later, more serious and caustic work. Although the seeds of that later seriousness concerning science are certainly present in the collections prior to *H'm*, as we shall see, they are somewhat diluted, their effects balanced, by the poet's confidence in older ways which, it would seem, have yet to be deeply threatened.

'Cynddylan on a Tractor' from *An Acre of Land* (1952) is the first of Thomas's poems to be concerned with 'the machine'. What strikes one immediately is the poem's light-hearted tone, its sense of engaging play. Cynddylan on his tractor is far from threatening because the narrator himself appears primarily bemused by the sight, even from the opening line in which he takes the reader in as an equal and friend: 'Ah, you should see Cynddylan on a tractor' (16). There is a benign condescension in this opening line that invites us to share not alarm but pleasure at the sight of the 'new man now, part of the machine, / His nerves of metal and his blood oil'. The poem forms a single image, a snapshot of the quixotic Cynddylan

> Riding to work now as a great man should,
> ... the knight at arms breaking the fields'
> Mirror of silence.

The final couplet, both by image and by rhyme, seals up this comic effect:

> And all the birds are singing, bills wide in vain,
> As Cynddylan passes proudly up the lane.

However, while the narrator may appear bemused at this sight, the poem's mock-heroic tone can be viewed also as somewhat of a façade, as masking a darker agitation at work under the poem's surface. There is a certain poignancy and even plangency for example in the poem's second line: 'Gone the old look that yoked him to the soil'. The ethos of this line is one not only of emancipation but also of loss and the beginnings of grief, though the good-natured mocking of lines 1 and 3 effectively deflate these deeper sentiments. More prominently, it would appear that Cynddylan's tractor has delivered him from slavery to the soil, has freed him, raised him even to the status of a master:

> The clutch curses, but the gears obey
> His least bidding, and lo, he's away
> Out of the farmyard, scattering hens.

Not only is Cynddylan seemingly the master of the machine, the master of the farmyard, the breaker of the field's mirror of silence scattering the foxes, the squirrels and the jays, we are also told that

> The sun comes over the tall trees
> Kindling all the hedges, but not for him
> Who runs his engine on a different fuel.

The accumulating sense here can be seen as one of *false* freedom, of violent displacement, of rending of an older and humbler way of life in which the farmer once co-operated as part, rather than master, of nature. Cynddylan can, after reflection, be viewed as tragic and even pathetic, as a man deceived, inflated by momentary pride to press onwards in ignorance toward his own inevitable doom at the hands of the machine. Though he has 'lost the old look that yoked him to the soil', trading his humility for what seems to him mastery and liberation via the machine, Cynddylan can be seen ultimately to have taken on a more dire and destroying burden.

It is possible of course that a tragic rather than a comic reading is encouraged not so much by the poem itself as by familiarity with the dark quality of Thomas's later poems on the machine. I would suggest that a middle view comes closest to the truth here, that Thomas intends *both* senses, and that the poem is ultimately tragi-comic: a dark foreboding in the narrator is tempered, and even subsumed at this stage, by a quiet confidence in the endurance of a more ancient tradition. This tension between confidence in an unmechanised agricultural tradition and yet fascination with, and fear of, an impending force that may effectively separate humankind from that tradition is characteristic of Thomas's early treatment of applied science.

While a tentative discomfort with mechanisation may seem to lurk beneath the surface of 'Cynddylan on a Tractor', Thomas's 'The Lonely Furrow' and 'Farm Child', both also from *An Acre of Land*, reaffirm a human confidence in the sure wisdom of the earth prior to the appearance of the machine. The narrator of 'The Lonely Furrow' 'sat on a tall stool / At learning's gate' but later 'found in the mind's pride / No peace, no rest' (36). Traditional 'education' is portrayed here as lacking in the power to satisfy a deeper human longing which only 'field and plough' can quench.[1] Despite the loneliness of his chosen profession, the farmer's satisfaction is palpable in the poem, a return to first things:

> Then who was it taught me back to go
> To cattle and barrow,

> Field and plough;
> To keep to the one furrow,
> As I do now?

If not the school or the schoolmaster, who, indeed, was it that taught this return to simpler things of the earth? Why does the farmer not remember? It is possible to locate that giver of more ancient wisdoms in the exquisite closing to 'A Line from St David's', from the 1963 collection *The Bread of Truth*:

> Somewhere a man sharpens a scythe;
> A child watches him from the brink
> Of his own speech, and this is of more
> Importance than all the visitors keeping
> A spry saint asleep in his tomb. (7)

The learning here is an almost mystical passing on of instinct in a silent and unconscious ceremony of deeply religious significance. Paradoxically, the 'saint' is pictured here as both 'spry' and 'asleep in his tomb', implying an active spiritual force emasculated by the superficial observance of the 'visitors'. The image of the lulled saint underscores the largely unobserved yet potent spiritual force transpiring between the man and the child in the lines that directly precede it. The power of the image of the boy watching the man sharpen the scythe is the very same power which keeps science and mechanisation effectively at bay in these early poems, which allows us to laugh with as yet not too deep an irony at the sight of Cynddylan on his tractor. Of course, like Frost's 'The Road Not Taken', 'The Lonely Furrow' can be read as the narrator's acceptance of his work as a poet, his keeping 'to the one furrow', over the lure perhaps of academic scholarship or 'the mind's pride'. But whether the return the narrator makes is to the lonely furrow of poetry or to farming, the image remains of nature's unique ability to satisfy.

'Farm Child' reiterates this superiority of nature's wisdom by imaging in ten lines a village boy's life and physical appearance as bred free of the constraints of formal schooling and civilisation. We are told that

> his head is stuffed

> With all the nests he knows, his pockets with flowers,
> Snail-shells and bits of glass, the fruit of hours
> Spent in the fields by thorn and thistle tuft. (37)

The boy's learning is achieved not through the study of books but through the very tactile experience of nature. And in contrast, if not contradiction, to many of the Prytherch poems which depict the farmer as being slowly primitivised in a *de*volutionary progress by the dehumanising forces of nature, the farm child seems uniquely integrated and protected by those forces, elevated to a rare beauty and even sophistication. Of his physical description, so reminiscent of Patrick Tuohy's painting *A Mayo Peasant Boy*, Thomas writes:

> Look at his eyes, see the harebell hiding there;
> Mark how the sun has freckled his smooth face
> Like a finch's egg under that bush of hair
> That dares the wind, and in the mixen now
> Notice his pose; from such unconscious grace
> Earth breeds and beckons to the stubborn plough.

In the final phrase Thomas accepts the fact of 'the stubborn plough', the life of agricultural toil, that waits for the boy, and yet the whole ethos of the poem points to a breeding in the boy of 'unconscious grace' by the force of all things natural. He is, as it were, haloed by that unconscious grace, existing somehow 'before the fall' according to the beauty not only of his natural learning but also of his ignorance.

Still, Thomas does view such innocence as under threat in these early collections. His confidence in the safety of an older way of life is often countered by an awareness of the new threat of nuclear destruction posed by the technological developments of science. For example, in the 1958 collection *Poetry for Supper* Thomas writes of 'the new physics' terrible threat / To the world's axle' (37). And, in a more ironic imagining of a similar sentiment, which we shall look at more closely later, he writes, in the poem 'The Garden', from *The Bread of Truth* (1963):

> Out of the soil the buds come,
> The silent detonations
> Of power wielded without sin. (20)

Perhaps most pertinent here is Thomas's warning to Iago Prytherch in the poem 'Too Late' from *Tares* (1961):

> Can't you see
> Behind the smile on the times' face
> The cold brain of the machine
> That will destroy you and your race? (25)

Clearly Thomas is deeply aware in these early poems of a certain threat
posed by science, both to the traditional way of life of the farm communities of Wales and to the existence of the world as a whole. But
one feels that generally in these early poems the danger perceived, if
increasingly urgent, is not yet imminent, but is, rather, a brooding
danger, a possibility still to be successfully resisted. Poems such as
'Cynddylan on a Tractor' may be somewhat darkly fringed at times,
but depictions like these of a serious alarm concerning science are few
in these early collections. Instead, we meet characters such as Job Davies
of 'Lore' from *Tares* (1961), 'Mowing where the grass grew, / Bearded
with golden dew' at dawn (35). Job Davies might easily be the
farm child who once watched from the brink of his own speech a
man sharpening a scythe, who returned to the one furrow. His strength
and confidence, even at eighty-five years old, seem boundless as he
holds to the ways of his fathers, boldly defying any power of the
machine:

> Rhythm of the long scythe
> Kept this tall frame lithe.
>
> What to do? Stay green.
> Never mind the machine,
> Whose fuel is human souls.
> Live large, man, and dream small.

Unlike his alter ego Cynddylan, Job Davies is well aware, even in his
defiance, of the dangers of the machine. But his warm flippancy, his
childlike audacity, is heartening, giving one the sense, again, that,
after all, there is little yet to fear. As we shall see, that sense of
confidence in older ways begins gradually to wane in the decade
of the 1970s, giving way, in the end, to the embattled and sometimes
embittered poems on science which we find in Thomas's later collections.

Deepening alarm in *H'm* and after

Beginning with the volume *H'm* in 1972 Thomas's uncertainty regarding applied science can be seen to evolve into outright alarm and contention. Indeed, one need only read the opening poem of *H'm* to sense
a militancy towards the machine which stands in stark contrast to the
more playful treatment of applied science we have just seen in the earlier
work:

> I took your hand,
> Remembering you, and together,
> Confederates of the natural day,
> We went forth to meet the Machine. (1)

The next twenty-five years and fifteen collections of poetry witness the poet's deepening struggle to come to terms not only with the machine but with the whole scientific endeavour, pure as well as applied. Writing from the remote Llŷn peninsula in north-west Wales, Thomas, in *H'm* and after, turns his full attention upon the dilemmas he sees posed by science:

> Although my love of nature and of the heart of the countryside is still as deep, I do not write about them so often any more. Faced with the great developments in technology, the lack of faith in the old traditions, and the omnipresence of the aeroplanes practising above our heads in the Llŷn Peninsula, my poetry has grown (some would say deteriorated) to be more abstract ... Lleyn is not an escape, but a peninsula where I can be inward with all the tension of our age. (*A Year*, 1990: 151)

I want to look briefly at the expansion in Thomas's use of the scientific register beginning in the 1970s as an indicator of this deepening engagement with the 'tension of our age'. I will be primarily concerned here, however, with looking *through* that change in vocabulary and into the more exact nature of Thomas's struggle with the machine and, finally, into his ideas concerning pure science. Of course there *are* a handful of poems in which, with Wordsworth, Thomas envisions a possible unity between applied science and poetry, and I shall examine these in the final section. But besides being few in number, such poems are indeed just that: visionary, brief contemplations of an ideal set within the framework of a much darker polemic.

Thomas's use of a scientific vocabulary in the early poems is, as we have already seen, a basic one, employing words uncommon perhaps to poetry, but common enough in general usage as not to require definition. One need only sample the later work, however, to find that, in addition to the intensified use of that early scientific vocabulary, the poet begins to employ new terms not common to everyday usage. We see a new sophistication in the register as words are introduced which are not only radical to poetry and, for most readers, in need of definition, but which indicate a vastly more specialised knowledge of scientific themes and procedures. For example, in *Laboratories of the Spirit* (1975) Thomas writes of 'the mirror of a refracted / timescale' (4). In *Later Poems*

(1983) we encounter the phrase 'the mind's kiloherz' (190). *Experimenting with an Amen* (1986) opens with the poem 'Formula' which includes Einstein's equation for relativity, and later in the same collection we come to the terms 'strontium' and 'plutonium' (65). Even in *Welsh Airs* (1987), a collection devoted to issues of Welsh culture and politics, we can find the phrase 'the Doppler / effect of the recession of our belief' (54). Add to the list terms such as 'pulsars' (*Frieze*, 1992: 11), 'Thermo-Dynamics' (*Echoes*, 33), 'twin helix' (*Echoes*, 109), 'quasars' (*Counterpoint*, 1990: 49), 'Tricyano-aminopropene' (*Counterpoint*, 55), 'leptons' and 'quarks' (*Mass*, 63), and one begins to sense the extension in Thomas's awareness of, and poetic concern with, the issues of science, the reality of his being 'inward with all the tension of our age'.

What then, for Thomas, is 'wrong' with applied science? We find the poet preoccupied in his prose work *A Year in Llŷn* with the question posed by Yeats whether one would agree to live the same life again, knowing what it holds in store. Thomas writes: 'I have thought many times that I am not like Yeats, willing to live it all again' (119). And a bit later: 'Am I glad to have been born? There's a question! Yeats said that he would be willing to live it all again. Would I? An answer to the contrary seems abhorrent' (124). We find in the poem 'Then' from *No Truce with the Furies* (1995) an explicit 'answer to the contrary' in which it is perhaps not so much the poet's rejection that surprises as it is the stated reason for that rejection:

> The bone's song will be:
> 'Let me sleep. I am not
> Yeats. I cannot face
> over again the coming
> of the machine'. (21)

It is precisely as a witness to the birth and growth of applied science that Thomas feels he cannot submit to relive his life. The lines imply not merely questioning and discomfort concerning the machine, but an agonising by the poet which cannot but arouse our curiosity as to its ultimate source, especially given that applied science or technology is so often greeted as a progressive convenience.

Division: the first threat

A close examination of the later poems which deal with the machine indicates two major sources for the angst voiced in 'Then'. The first of these is that applied science, in this case everything from electricity to the internal combustion engine, and perhaps most importantly the instruments of the mechanisation of farming which, historically, these made possible, is, in some degree, destructive, in Thomas's view, of a more ancient relationship between humankind and the earth.[2] As we have seen in Chapter 3, that relationship is, for Thomas, essentially spiritual and even sacred. Applied science, for Thomas, is 'man's unnatural quarrel / With the chaste earth', destructive of humankind's integration with the actual physical substance of nature and also therefore of a certain psycho-spiritual health which he sees that integration as uniquely affording (*Acre*, 1952:24). In this Thomas is not merely a 'green' poet but, rather, part of an ongoing Welsh poetic tradition from Taliesin in the sixth century to Dafydd ap Gwilym in the fourteenth century, to such writers as Gwenallt and Waldo Williams in the twentieth century, in which the physical world in time is accepted and depicted as one side of an eternal whole.

Thomas's second and most widely apparent source of angst over the emergence of applied science is an extension of the first. He suggests that humankind's apprehension of its spiritual identity and source is most possible, most probable, within the context of the natural world as ongoing revelation. According to this position, humanity comes close to *requiring* nature for a true experience of self, as well as for a true experience of deity. The breaking of intimacy between humanity and nature which technology represents for the poet thus becomes both self-alienating and God-alienating, precluding a sense of integration and purpose whose absence is the primary characteristic of modernist anxiety. With few exceptions Thomas denies in the later poems the possibility of compatibility between the individual soul's search for its identity and source and the developments of applied science, to the extent that the two are often depicted in a relation of inverse proportion. For Thomas, an expanding technology increasingly results, as we shall see, not only in contraction of the soul but in flight of the divine.

To contextualise Thomas's position as I have outlined it here, many of these 'objections' to applied science are echoed by his Welsh contemporary, the poet David James Jones (1899–1968), most often referred to by his bardic name of Gwenallt. Thomas writes in *No-one* of his friendship with Gwenallt, whom Jason Walford Davies, in the 'notes' to his translation of *No-one*, refers to as 'one of the most striking Welsh-language poets of the twentieth century' (182). In his poem '*Y Ddaear*' or 'The Earth', Gwenallt's opening lament is strikingly similar to Thomas's own, especially as we find it in his early work:

> How intimate was the earth in days gone by,
> As intimate as a neighbour, and fluent in the Welsh dialects;
> We kept her in good shape, and we brought forth her colours,
> The colours of wheat, barley and oats;
> We put a wave in her hair with the ploughshare,
> And combed its sheen with the clanking harrows. (200–1)

These opening lines of gentle nostalgia give way, in the second half of the poem, to a more biting indictment of applied science as the breaker of such intimacy. As the poem shifts to the present tense one encounters a corresponding shift in vocabulary to more technical words and phrases such as 'laboratory', 'factory', 'cogged', 'an alien chemistry', 'a machine's syntax'.

> The earth has been converted into a vast laboratory,
> The cowshed into a factory where cogged cattle chew the cud …
>
> An alien chemistry is making the soil barren.
>
> The earth no longer speaks man's homely language:
> Her speech has a machine's syntax; the grammar of x,y,z:
> The neighbour has become a distant monster;
> A monster whose hydrogenous jaws
> Are about to swallow the husbandry and civilization of man.
>
> > Pylons where once were angels
> > And the concrete damming the brook.

We can see in these final lines an alienation which Gwenallt depicts as the result of the machine's increasing predominance. The sentiments and language of 'The Earth' are remarkably similar to Thomas's own: the loss of a vital intimacy with the earth and a resulting barrenness, physical as well as spiritual; a linguistic and spiritual fragmentation achieved; applied science as a monster swallowing 'the husbandry and civilization of man', the displacement of spirituality (angels) by applied science (pylons), a 'damming' by technology which is indicative both of a stoppage and, more importantly, of a 'damning' or casting out by condemnation of more traditional life-sources in nature (the brook). While Thomas's position concerning applied science is, ultimately, as we shall see, more accommodating than Gwenallt's as we find it in 'The Earth', both poets, contemporaries in separate languages, show a deepening concern for its escalating ramifications.

'Welsh Summer' from *Laboratories of the Spirit* (1975) is a good example of what I have described as Thomas's first objection, the effect on humanity of technology's destruction of the earth. One notices immediately an imagery similar to that just seen in Gwenallt's 'The Earth':

> It is the machine wins;
> the land suffers the formication
> of its presence. Places that
> would have preferred peace
> have had their bowels opened; our
> children paddle thoughtlessly there in the mess. (6)

It is not simply that the land, imaged here as a body, suffers under the machine. Equally powerful is the word 'thoughtlessly', representing as it does both a lack of awareness and an actual absence of thought. We can see here an insidious quality to the machine whereby, under the guise of 'improvement', it recoils, collapsing a vital intimacy between humankind and nature. If we juxtapose this depiction of collapse from 'Welsh Summer' with lines from 'Fugue for Ann Griffiths', in *Welsh Airs* (1987), we can get a clearer view of what Thomas seems to be implying. In the latter poem he describes

> A nineteenth century
>   calm;
> that is, a countryside
>   not fenced in
> by cables and pylons,
> but open to thought to blow in
>   from as near as may be
> to the truth. (50)

In these lines the proximity of truth and the freedom of thought correspond directly to the unmechanised nineteenth-century countryside. The scene might easily be read as a metaphor for the mind in nature, with the implication of a psycho-spiritual 'calm' deriving from the very absence of the machine.

One recognises a lament similar to that of 'Welsh Summer' in the poem 'Gone?' from *Frequencies* (1978). The poem opens with a description of the countryside's destruction by the machine and, with it, the destruction of an older way of life:

> Will they say on some future
> occasion, looking over the flogged acres
> of ploughland: This was Prytherch country?

> Nothing to show for it now: hedges
> uprooted, walls gone, a mobile people
> hurrying to and fro on their fast
> tractors; a forest of aerials
> as though an invading fleet invisibly
> had come to anchor among these
> financed hills. They copy the image
> of themselves projected on their smooth
> screens to the accompaniment of inane
> music. (34)

In the poem's closing lines anger over the land's degradation gives way to a deepening grief over the disappearance of the man once linked to that land, who

> accepted it, as a man
> will who has needs in him that only
> bare ground, black thorns and the sky's
>   emptiness can fulfil.

The title 'Gone?', by the end of the poem, has come to signify not only the land as it once was, nor even only the race of men who worked that land, but equally the two as one and their lost *relation*, the tragedy of dis-integration according to which those constant 'needs' are now to be constantly frustrated.

This is not to say that Thomas is altogether uncompromising towards the machine or that he perceives any least encroachment by applied science as somehow absolute in its effect. In his poem 'Good' which closes the collection *Laboratories of the Spirit* (1975) we find the machine as part of an idyllic scene. The old farmer in the poem, feeling 'A chill in the flesh' that 'tells him that death is not far off / now', surveys his life and the valley below:

> He sees the stream shine,
> the church stand, hears the litter of
> children's voices …
>
> His garden has herbs growing.
> The kestrel goes by with fresh prey
> in its claws. The wind scatters the scent
> of wild beans. The tractor operates
> on the earth's body. His grandson is there
> ploughing; his young wife fetches him
> cakes and a dark smile. It is well. (65)

The grandfather shows little concern here for the presence of the machine that possibly made its entrance during his lifetime. It is, rather, part of a satisfying whole. This apparent tolerance, standing in some contrast to Gwenallt's 'The Earth', is not merely a grudging compromise to an inevitable reality, but rather an affirmation of contextualisation, of balance and priority. There is not the least sign of the machine as destructive in this brief sketch, but neither does it eclipse the predominant integration of the scene. The stream, the church, the voices, the garden herbs, the kestrel, the scent of wild beans, the sexual energy between the young farmer and his wife and, indeed, between all of these connected elements, their nearly erotic interplay, creates a fabric into which the machine is absorbed without danger, into which the machine takes its place as subservient, disarmed as it were, or harnessed within a larger, more powerful dimension.[3] This is a key point in Thomas's position on applied science. What he calls 'the machine' becomes not applied science *per se* but a system of values according to which the *en masse* production, possession, and use of technology outweigh every other consideration. It is this rampant *de*contextualisation of applied science which Thomas views as harmful, its increasingly unbridled independence by which it becomes a kind of Frankenstein's monster, a changeling, achieving not only a life and a will of its own but its virtual indispensability as well. Thomas's most explicit depiction of this independence and indispensability occurs in the poem 'The Other' from *Later Poems* (1983) in which the machine speaks in the first person:

> Come out, they shouted;
> with a screech of steel
> I jumped into the world
> smiling my cogged smile,
> breaking with iron hand
> the hands they extended.
>
> They rose in revolt;
> I cropped them like tall
> grass; munched on the cud
> of nations. (180)

In closing the poem Thomas goes on to depict both the machine's crippling of the poet and the poet's increasing dependence upon, and even addiction to, the machine:

> I took him apart
> verse by verse, turning

on him my x-ray
eyes to expose the emptiness
of his interiors. In houses
with no hearth he huddles
against me now, mortgaging
his dwindling techniques
for the amenities I offer.

In contrast to the poem 'Good', the machine here is not mastered and
contextualised but mastering and decontextualised, conquering its
human creator.

Fierce divine

Having examined Thomas's first objection to applied science as effectively separating humankind from its more ancient and proper place as
a part of nature, I will turn now to his second objection, the obscur-
ing and even displacing by applied science of the poet's experience of
divinity. Before turning to this second major objection, and as a kind
of bridge to it, I will look briefly at one further implication for Thomas
of the machine's destruction of what he sees as a more ancient relationship between humankind and the earth. Despite his reputation as
a poet of absence, Thomas sometimes portrays as attributes of deity
both a radical presence and a consuming desire, most often depicted
in the poems as a wildness and a fierceness made manifest in and
through the experience and the images of nature.[4] For Thomas, the
machine, in the degree to which it separates humanity from nature,
simultaneously separates it from the experience of these divine attributes, both from a divine presence which the poet depicts as constantly
overflowing human containment and control and resisting human
domestication, as well as from a consuming desire or fierceness, not
the wrath of an Old Testament God, but rather a divine love for humanity perceived to be so intense as to be portrayed most often as a kind
of insatiable longing or hunger after humankind. In the poem 'The
Indians and the Elephant' for example, from *No Truce with the Furies*
(1995), Thomas depicts both this ubiquity of divine presence as well
as this divine aggression toward unity. Like the blind Indians in the
poem who explore the elephant by touch, crying out that it is like a
tree or like a rope, so Thomas claims humankind's explorations of the
divine are similarly blind, its descriptions similarly piecemeal and inadequate. He writes:

> I, though I am
> not blind, feel my way
> about God, exploring him
> in darkness. Sometimes he is
> a wind, carrying me off;
> sometimes a fire devouring
> me. Rarely, too rarely
> he is as the scent
> at the heart of a great flower
> I lean over and fall
> into. (48)

The imagery here suddenly shifts from the tangible and finite elephant of the opening lines to the more abstruse imagery of spiritual experience. Corresponding to that shift, the whole tone of the poem modulates from the comic to the mystical. Deity becomes, in these lines, a wind, a fire, a scent, shrouded in darkness. What is important here as well is the sheer unpredictability of the divine, and the consequent vulnerability of the explorer: the narrator is at risk in the experience of deity, is carried off by that wind, devoured by that fire, he falls into the heart of the great flower. There is a marked absence of ontological certainty in the narrator's ongoing explorations that can be countered only by trust in the necessary and complete surrender he is forced to make in his terrifying experience of a deity which is without boundary and beyond control. Nor does Thomas stop merely at the description of such divine ubiquity and human dependence. The final lines of the poem depict a sudden, rapid movement forward and downward, as it were, out of an amorphous mystical experience and into a series of precise images:

> But always he surrounds
> me, mostly as a cloud
> lowering, but one through which
> suddenly light will strike,
> burnishing the cross
> waiting on me with spread wings
> like the fiercest of raptors.[5]

Just as the poem appears to peak in an image of encompassment by the lowering cloud, Thomas draws out of it, in quick succession, three sharply focused snapshots: the sudden, striking light, the burnished cross, the fiercest of raptors. Viewed in slow motion, as it were, we can visualise the emergence of these images, the light descending from the lowering cloud, which in turn illuminates the cross in its flash, revealing not the suffering Christ but the hunting bird of prey. Despite this motion in time, the effect is one of simultaneity in which the strike of light is itself the strike of the 'waiting' raptor. In this startling final image we find not the beckoning of a meek deity but his, her or its attacking descent as a bird of prey, propelled by a desire to 'kill' and consume the poet, in order to be made one with him. My point here is that the emotional or mystical experience of divine presence and desire which these images represent is precluded, for Thomas, by a bur-geoning scientific revolution which is not only destructive of the nat-ural context and imagery of that experience but which, most importantly, suffocates that experience by an exclusive and uncompro-mising adherence to the rational, analytic mind alone. Thomas reiter-ates this point just a few pages after 'The Indians and the Elephant' in the poem 'Raptor'. Although both poems lament an anthropomorphic shrinking of God, 'Raptor' depicts that shrinking as a product, specif-ically, of the scientific mind:

> You have made God small,
> setting him astride
> a pipette or a retort
> studying the bubbles,
> absorbed in an experiment
> that will come to nothing. (52)

It is the replacement of a mystical experience of the divine with an attempt at its scientific measurement which Thomas descries as belit-tling here, and he proceeds after the indictment of these opening lines to a powerful description of deity as an enormous, hunting owl, fright-eningly defiant of any human domestication or analysis. Deity becomes something

> abroad in the shadows,
> brushing me sometimes
> with his wing so the blood
> in my veins freezes, able
>
> to find his way from one
> soul to another because
> he can see in the dark.
> I have heard him crooning
> to himself, so that almost
> I could believe in angels,

> those feathered overtones
> in love's rafters, I have heard
> him scream, too, fastening
> his talons in his great
> adversary, or in some lesser
> denizen, maybe, like you or me.

Here applied science effectively blunts man's spiritual awareness by creating the illusion of having domesticated the presence and escaped the desire which Thomas finds reaching through the experience and images of nature. It is precisely this blunting which he depicts, for example, in the poem 'Calling' from *Experimenting with an Amen* (1986) in which the telephone becomes an artificial barrier to God, a kind of shield from divine presence and desire, replacing what is uncontrollable and therefore frightening (deity) with what is seemingly controllable or tame (technology). In the poem's final lines the narrator yearns for a breakdown or, in this case, a break*through* in that artificial distancing of deity by the machine:

> So many times I have raised
> the receiver, listening to
> that smooth sound that is technology's
> purring; and the temptation
>
> has come to experiment
> with the code which would put
> me through to the divine
>
> snarl at the perimeter of such tameness. (31)[6]

'Technology's purring' represents here a 'tameness' which precludes an experience of the divine. This is reiterated again in 'Preference' from the 1992 *Mass for Hard Times* where Thomas writes of children 'revelling among tame / toys' and of scientists whose 'god / is the old nameless god / of calculus and inertia' (32). In closing the poem, however, and in juxtaposition to these images of a domesticated God, he writes again of an experience of the divine that is neither tame nor certain:

> I have wakened in the night,
> my hair rising at the passing
> of presences that were not human;
>
> switched on the light on articles
> and upholstery, and switched it as soon
> off in preference for the dark places
> to the certainty of our domestication.

The lamp here, like the telephone in 'Calling', creates a sense of certainty which may dispel 'the dark', but which, in so doing, also denies an experience of the other, non-human 'presences' which inhabit that darkness. Indeed, much of Thomas's work can be read as an intuitive, creative probing of 'darkness' as a spiritual realm which defies rational understanding. The final lines of 'Preference' encapsulate this nicely as a 'preference for the dark places / to the certainty of our domestication'. The poem 'History' from *Experimenting with an Amen* (1986) also employs this imagery of a preferred darkness disturbed by the machine:

> As the sun went down
> the lights came on in a million
> laboratories, as the scientists attempted
> to turn the heart's darkness into intellectual day. (44)

One senses here not only the poet's preference for the 'heart's darkness' but an affirmation of the *necessity* of that darkness, the danger of an unending 'intellectual day' from which all shadow and darkness have been eradicated. In all of these examples Thomas seems to depict applied science not as opening up a 'new frontier' but, surprisingly, as a manifestation of *timidity*, as a *retreat* into rationality from the 'darker', less predictable, but more powerful, realms of spirit.

Displacement: the second threat

This brings us to Thomas's second major objection to applied science: Its displacement of the divine. In the later poems Thomas depicts not only a fundamental incompatibility between these spheres of reason and spirit but, more explicitly, a displacement by applied science of religion. Evidence of a general incompatibility abounds. In the poem 'Soliloquy' for example, from *H'm* (1972), God states:

> Within the churches
> You built me you genuflected
> To the machine. (30)

Similarly, in 'Those Times' from *The Way of It* (1977), the poet writes that the

> Scientists worked away
> with their needles, a shroud for the spirit. (7)

Likewise, in 'Asking', from *Experimenting with an Amen* (1986), Thomas asks:

> Did I see religion,
> its hand in the machine's,
> trying to smile as the grip
> tightened? (51)

There is a sinister humour to these strangely 'cartoon' images or 'snap-shots' of incompatibility between applied science and religion. Such incompatibility gives way ultimately, however, to more disturbing images of actual displacement. Thomas writes, for example, in the 1992 collection *Mass for Hard Times*:

> 'Come,' life said
> leading me on a journey
> as long as that
> of the wise men to the cradle,
>
> where, in place of the child
> it had brought forth,
> there lay grinning the lubricated
> changeling of the machine. (60)[7]

Here, expectations raised in the poem's first stanza are exploded, in the second, by the Christ-child's actual displacement by the machine. Thomas's description of that machine as a grinning, lubricated changeling, as a likeness that is both evil and laughing, produces a powerfully lurid effect. The exact nature of this displacement seems to involve an inability of the exclusively rational mind to tolerate the prescriptions of Christian love which Thomas claims can be identified by 'the unreasonableness of its music' (*Mass*, 67). For example, in 'St Julian and the Leper' from the 1968 *Not that He Brought Flowers*, the poet writes of St Julian

> contaminating
> Himself with a kiss,
> With the love that
> Our science has disinfected. (12)

And in 'The Casualty' from *Laboratories of the Spirit* (1975), he claims:

> I went on with that
> metallic warfare in which
> the one casualty is love. (21)

In a more ironic depiction of that 'unreasonableness' of love the poet writes in 'Sonata in X' from *Mass for Hard Times* (1992):

> 'I love you.'
> 'How much?'
> '$1^{32} \times \sqrt{-1}$.'
> 'Wait a minute, let me
> compute my thanks.
>   There.
> Meet me tonight
> at SH 126 243
> so we may
> consummate our statistics.' (84)

Of course the square root of minus one is technically a non-representable sum. The fact that the equation which the poet sets out in answer to the question 'how much?' is nonsensical only accentuates the poem's commentary on the inability of science to define or quantify love. As Thomas develops these ideas of incompatibility and displacement we begin to see not only religion being precluded or forced out by the machine but increasingly the active flight of the divine from the investigations and probings of science. It seems that the threat Thomas perceives in applied science is not rationality, but rationality removed from a wider perspective. As we have already seen in the poem 'Good', it is not the presence of the machine but its predominance, its elevation above any contextualising relationships which the poet finds abusive. That unnatural elevation becomes, for the poet, the equivalent of pride, a repetition of the sin of Adam according to which humanity experiences again its alienating of the divine. In 'Winged God' from *No Truce with the Furies* (1995) Thomas underscores that alienation, referring to humanity as

> that alienating shadow
> with the Bible under the one
> arm and under the other
> the bomb. (51)

In these lines Thomas seems to suggest a hypocritical collusion between 'bible' and 'bomb', depicting, through the use of irony, what he sees as an incompatibility of opposites in keeping with his position as a pacifist and his long involvement in the Campaign for Nuclear Disarmament or CND (See *No-one*, 44, 96–8 and *A Year in Lleyn* 156–7). Deity in the poem is winged specifically for retreat from this man of science, armed with bible and bomb, of whom Thomas asks:

> how
> can he return home
> when his gaze forages

beyond the stars? Pity him,
then, this winged god, rupturer
of gravity's control
accelerating on in the afterglow
of a receding laughter?

'Home' here is clearly interior, spiritual home, a condition, not a place, precluded by the contrastingly outward probings of science. Interestingly, the final sentence in the poem is not declarative but interrogative, like the first. Ought one, Thomas asks, pity the man of science, the 'winged god', for his knowledge and capability which here become the very instruments of his alienation of the divine? We can juxtapose the laughing God who recedes in 'Winged God' to an earlier portrait of the divine as suffering its own peculiar self-alienation because of the machine. In 'God's Story' from *Laboratories of the Spirit* (1975) the victim is not helpless humanity at the hands of an all-powerful God but, rather, a vulnerable God at the hands of the machine:

> God,
> looking into a dry chalice,
> felt the cold touch of the machine
> on his hand, leading him
>
> to a steel altar. 'Where are you?'
> he called, seeking himself among
> the dumb cogs and tireless camshafts. (7)

And yet 'God's Story' is merely an exaggerated inversion of the idea central to 'Winged God'. Both poems present Thomas's account of a profound spiritual desolation, what I have called alienation, whose source resides in the exclusivity and dispersive potential of rational thought. Divine retreat from the intrusions of modern science becomes a recurring motif in these later poems. In 'Bleak Liturgies' for example, from *Mass for Hard Times* (1992), the poet writes,

> We have captured position
> after position, and his white flag
>
> is a star receding from us
> at light's speed. (63)

Thomas, in these poems, often depicts a God which may approach humankind's stillness, its intuitive vigilance and waiting, which may even allow its blind explorations, as in 'The Reason' from *Mass for Hard Times*, but which repeatedly flees from this more active and strictly rational pursuit via science which seeks less to recognise or to know, and more to discover, name, and master the divine, which seeks, like Adam and Eve in the Genesis myth, to *become* the divine. In *The Echoes Return Slow* (1988) Thomas prays to be made free from this temptation to define deity strictly in rational terms:

> Anonymous presence
> grant that, when I come
> questioning, it is not with the dictionary
> in one hand, the microscope in the other. (115)

In these lines, again, Thomas is deriding not science as itself but the method of science as an approach to deity. It is precisely the *exclusivity* of an analytic, scientific perspective which, increasingly, Thomas comes to view as harmful, and which accounts in much of his later work for what I have termed an 'escalating irony'. In these later poems we see Thomas reacting against science as an instrument of measurement and division rather than as a method of wonder and unification.

'An aggression of fact': three techniques of irony

I will close this chapter by examining Thomas's use of irony in these later poems on applied science. In Chapter 4 I suggested that the poet's purely aesthetic usages of a scientific diction in his early work give rise in the later poems to an 'escalating irony'. I am suggesting by this the poet's assignation of a doubleness to words and phrases which effectively undermines their literal sense or face value. We can find in these ironic poems a submerged vehemence created by the bending back of words upon themselves, an anger more caustic because it resists outright expression in favour of a heightened tension between literal use and underlying intention. In these poems Thomas makes language recoil back on itself to display a highly charged political aggression. In the poem 'After Jericho' from *Frequencies* (1978) Thomas writes consciously of this civil war of words:

> There is an aggression of fact
> to be resisted successfully
> only in verse, that fights language
> with its own tools. (43)

What I am interested in here is the idea of fighting language with its own tools. Such an expression is itself an appropriate definition for Thomas's particular use of irony. His fight against 'an aggression of fact', can be interpreted as the 'fact' of applied science, his method being to absorb the language of that fact and turn it to his own purpose by driving it against itself. He concludes the poem:

> Smile, poet,
>
> among the ruins of a vocabulary
> you blew your trumpet against.
> It was a conscript army; your words,
> every one of them, are volunteers.

The opposing vocabulary is, in this case, the scientific register which Thomas employs, pictured here as a conscript army compelled by force to a particular purpose. The irony Thomas creates in these poems occurs in his turning that weaker conscript army back upon itself.

Thomas employs three main techniques to create such irony. By far the most prominent of these is a method of 'simple sarcasm' in which the words set down by the poet imply the opposite of their literal sense. He also employs a method I will call 'mixing' in which images of science and religion are closely incorporated so as to highlight a moral disparity between them. Finally, what might be called 'image reversal' is a more sophisticated method of mixing in which the development of a given image, scientific or religious, is achieved in the terms of its opposite, creating, by inversion, a politicised statement.

'No Answer' from *H'm* is an example of simple sarcasm in which Thomas writes:

> Life is too short for
> Religion; it takes time
> To prepare a sacrifice
> For the God. Give yourself
> To science that reveals
> All, asking no pay
> For it. (7)

The often subtle insincerity upon which such irony relies is typically brought into sharper focus in these poems by lines in which either the poet seems to become suddenly candid, thus underscoring his intentions by relief, or those intentions are made unmistakable by a

sudden inflation of sarcasm. In the case of 'No Answer' the candid literal force of the closing lines sharpens our sense of the sarcasm present in the earlier lines, revealing at the source of anger a wellspring
of grief:

> Over the creeds
> And masterpieces our wheels go.

Second, we find examples of what I have called 'mixing' in the poems
'The Hearth' and 'Postscript', also from *H'm*. In 'The Hearth' Thomas
depicts scientists and statesmen as magi in the story of Christ's birth. The
intention here, however, is to illustrate, through the anachronistic
mixing of these images, the vast disparity the author finds between the
original magi and their modern counterparts, as well as the threat which
the latter pose to the infant saviour, symbol of vulnerable love: Thomas
calls them

> travellers
> To a new Bethlehem, statesmen
> And scientists with their hands full
> Of the gifts that destroy. (18)

The irony here is not resident so much in the literal 'message' of the
lines as in the yoking of disparate images of scientists and statesmen as
gift-bearers to the infant Christ. Such yoking creates a kind of violent
subterranean force in the poem which explodes outwards. Thus, while
the poem's 'message' seems clear, namely that these 'new' Magi, here
both politicians and scientists, have not come seeking spiritual enlight-
enment or proffering religious homage but as antagonists, the poem's
broader 'meanings' are predominantly emotional. For example, what
exactly is this 'new Bethlehem' for Thomas, why are the travellers going
there, and what are 'the gifts that destroy', a phrase reminiscent of
Homer's Greeks bearing similar gifts at Troy? One is left to speculate
on possible 'answers' to these questions, and yet my point here is that
the anachronistic blending of images in these lines is powerfully suggestive, even prophetic of impending doom, deep mistrust, overwhelming fear, and increasing anger, all emerging from what Thomas
sees as a deepening chasm between these realms of reason and spirit.
In a sense, the poem's considerable emotional resonance is achieved
precisely through an allowance for literal ambiguity. Similarly, in
'Postscript' Thomas writes:

> As life improved, their poems
> Grew sadder and sadder. Was there oil
> For the machine? It was
> The vinegar in the poet's cup. (22)

Here not only do we encounter the simple irony of the word 'improved' in line one, but a mixing in which oil for the machine becomes vinegar in the poet's cup, an image which immediately recalls the vinegar offered to Christ at the crucifixion. Thus we come to see, again by inference, the poet as saviour. The oil for the machine, as the vinegar offered the poet (Christ) further heightens the bitter doubleness of 'improved', since the improvement here is at once a taunting of the divine and a crucifixion of the artist.

In the later collections such as *Counterpoint* (1990) and *Mass for Hard Times* (1992) Thomas's use of this technique of mixing becomes widespread, as well as blistering in its political effects. In *Counterpoint* for example, Thomas writes

> On a bone
> altar, with radiation
> for candle, we make sacrifice
> to the god of quasars
> and pulsars, wiping
> our robotic hands clean
> on a disposable conscience. (49)

And a bit later in the same collection:

> Tricyano-aminopropene–
> it is our new form
> of prayer, with biological
> changes as an Amen. (55)

In both of these poems we encounter a radical mixing in which the highly technical language of applied science, words such as 'radiation', 'quasars', 'pulsars', and 'Tricyano-aminopropene', are yoked to traditional religious images evoked by words such as 'altar', 'sacrifice', and 'prayer'. The combination of these words and images in an essentially ironic rendering creates a dramatic cross-current in these poems in which the two spheres or realms, that of applied science and that of traditional religion, continually undermine each other, but in which they are none the less tightly bound in a kind of excruciating tension which illuminates what, for Thomas, is their ultimate disparity. 'Bleak

Liturgies', a longer poem central to the collection *Mass for Hard Times*, becomes a full-blown polemic on this disparity between applied science and religion and, as such, sustains an ironic mixing to sharpen its significant edge:

> What Lent is the machine
> subjected to? It neither fasts
> nor prays. And the one cross
> of its Good Fridays is the change
>
> over of its gears. Its Easter
> is every day when, from the darkness
> of man's mind, it comes forth
> in a new form, but untouchable as ever. (62)

According to Thomas here, although the machine does not partake of the suffering and death remembered in the Christian observance of Lent, it does enjoy, perversely, a kind of daily Easter or resurrection. I would suggest that just as the 'changeling of the machine' displaced the Christ-child in the poem from *Mass for Hard Times* (1992) examined earlier, so here the resurrected Christ is displaced by the machine, not a divinity since it issues 'from the darkness / of man's mind', but a force none the less transformed, independent, spiritualised, and 'untouchable as ever'. My point here, again, is simply that this mixing by Thomas of the language and images of applied science with those of traditional religion, creates a subverting tension in these poems which is held up without being resolved, and that such continually subverting tension is the source of the dark emotional force in these works which make them so startling and effective.

Third, Thomas's most sophisticated use of irony is achieved by his employment of the technique I have termed 'image reversal'. Perhaps the best example of this occurs in 'The Garden' from *The Bread of Truth* (1963), cited earlier in this section. While the nine short lines of the first stanza are successful in their depiction of an ordinary garden as a place of refuge and rest, it is the final five lines of the poem that suddenly and radically expand that sense:

> It is the old kingdom of man.
> Answering to their names,
> Out of the soil the buds come,
> The silent detonations
> Of power wielded without sin. (20)

The garden in these lines is Eden, 'the old kingdom of man', the place of innocence and delight. It is clearly Thomas's depiction of the buds as 'silent detonations' however, which is most striking and which constitutes the image reversal. Here the innocence, which is the central feature of the poem, is implied not in positive terms but by a conjuring of its opposite, its absence. The whole dramatic impact of the poem is rooted in Thomas's choice of the technical 'detonations' over the more obvious 'explosions'. Tempers, automobiles, thunder, and eggs all may explode. It is a word exhausted by common usage and multiple associations. Only bombs however detonate. It is a word still pristine by its very restriction to a single and literal association. Because of that restriction the poet's use of it to describe the buds is a 'first use' in the sense that its association has been created rather than received.[8] More importantly perhaps, Thomas goes on in the final line of the poem to elongate this reversal. The buds become 'silent detonations / Of power wielded without sin', that single closing line itself becomes a kind of detonation, exploding the poem's meditative predictability into a frenzy of complex implications. One becomes suddenly aware, for example, of the *new* kingdom of man on the other side of the fall, as well as of those less silent detonations of power wielded *with* sin. The Edenic innocence residing at the heart of the poem is suddenly thrown into dramatic relief, made radically poignant and fragile by contextualisation within its opposite, its absence, within the fall from Eden with its further implications of sin, guilt, and war. The poem suddenly bristles with political nerve, poised between humankind's flight to innocence and its partaking of evil. The irony of the poem, its crafted doubleness, resides precisely in this implication that innocence is, at least in part, the absence of its opposite.

Thomas employs this technique of image reversal again and again. For example, the poet asks in 'Nuclear' from *The Way of It* (1977):

> What word so explosive
> as that one Palestinian
> word with the endlessness of its fallout? (19)

In the poem 'Ritual' from *Experimenting with an Amen* (1986) he writes of scientists as having become priests,

> working away in their bookless
> laboratories, ministrants
> in that ritual beyond words
> which is the Last Sacrament of the species. (28)

In 'Waiting' from *Welsh Airs* (1987) he writes:

> The Book rusts
> in the empty pulpits above empty
> pews, but the Word ticks inside
> remorselessly as the bomb that is timed soon to go off. (48)

And in the poem 'Doves' from *Frieze* (1992) he states that

> doves, too,
>
> are explosive. In the porches
> of the peace conference, memories
> of their earlier fall-out insist
> militantly on their being kept in a cage. (10)

The reversals Thomas achieves in these examples are essentially dramatic: The 'word' becomes, like the bomb, 'explosive', it 'ticks inside / remorselessly', its detonation creates 'fall-out'. The scientists become priests, 'ministrants' of 'the Last Sacrament of the species'. And, in the last example, the doves of peace must be restrained by the would-be peacemakers for fear, again, of their explosive potential. Not only are these examples of a technique by Thomas but in all of them one senses an expanded propagandist intention behind the art-object. Thomas suggests a latent but surprisingly aggressive power in 'the word', 'the Book', the 'doves', which he raises up in tension and, more importantly here, in opposition to what he sees as the *de-unifying* force of applied science.

What we have seen is that from the 1970s R. S. Thomas's poetry becomes increasingly and, at times, radically preoccupied both with the language of science and with the sources and implications that underlie that language. Perhaps more than any other contemporary poet in English, Thomas has sought to utilise an expanding scientific register, giving to his poetry a daring linguistic transfusion. Likewise, he has sought, in poetry, to come to terms morally with a burgeoning and complex technological revolution unparalleled in human history, and by so doing has achieved in this poetry on science a highly contemporary political edge. As we have also seen, however, Thomas's positions concerning the language of science and its wider ramifications are far from simple. It remains in the final section of this chapter to examine the poems in which the poet envisions, with Wordsworth, a possible unity between science and poetry. I will also, in this final section, attempt to uncover the grounding and context for Thomas's position on science in his reading of Genesis. Finally, I will look at the poet's position, in both the prose and the poetry, concerning the possibility of the healing of a historical dichotomy between science and religion, discussed in section one of the chapter, through an affirmation of the investigations of pure science, in particular of modern physics.

Inheriting Wordsworth's dream

In order to understand more fully Thomas's dilemma concerning science and nature it is helpful to examine the first explicit treatment of that dilemma by Wordsworth. In his 1802 'Preface' to *Lyrical Ballads* Wordsworth writes of an imagined relationship between poetry and science:

> If the labours of Men of science should ever create any material revolution, direct or indirect, in our condition, and in the impressions which we habitually receive, the Poet will sleep then no more than at present; he will be ready to follow the steps of the Man of science, not only in those general indirect effects, but he will be at his side, carrying sensation into the midst of the objects of the science itself. The remotest discoveries of the Chemist, the Botanist, or Mineralogist, will be as proper objects of the Poet's art as any upon which it can be employed, if the time should ever come when these things shall be familiar to us, and the relations under which they are contemplated by the followers of these respective sciences shall be manifestly and palpably material to us as enjoying and suffering beings. If the time should ever come when what is now called Science, thus familiarised to men, shall be ready to put on, as it were, a form of flesh and blood, the Poet will lend his divine spirit to aid the transfiguration, and will welcome the Being thus produced, as a dear and genuine inmate of the household of man. (1974: 141)

Two hundred years later, most would agree that the 'labours of men of Science' have clearly created a 'material revolution' in the condition of society well beyond what Wordsworth could have supposed possible. The discoveries of science *have been* made 'manifestly and palpably material to us as enjoying and suffering beings'. Of greater importance here though is that Wordsworth's prediction that the poet will 'follow in the steps of the Man of Science … carrying sensation into the midst of the objects of Science itself' proves, in the case of

R. S. Thomas, to be oddly both true and not true. For example, as we have seen, according to his use of a scientific register and the changes occurring in that register and its use, Thomas has, in some sense, followed 'in the steps of the Man of Science', actively, even eagerly, absorbing the new vocabulary and the new knowledge which science has produced and integrating both of these into poetry. One is forced to add, however, that although Thomas has made the discoveries of science the 'proper objects of the Poet's art', it is perhaps not in the sense that Wordsworth, in his 'Preface', intended. Thomas's carrying of sensation into the midst of science, like his integration of the objects of that science into art, is not, primarily, a sign of compatibility between poetry and science but more an act of rebellion in which the poet alternately defends poetry from science and attacks science as not only imminently dangerous but as poetry's mortal enemy, with whom coexistence is rarely an option. But while Thomas seems, in the poetry, to be consistently at war with science, or at least with its practical applications, there *are* instances, glimpsed earlier in 'Vocabulary', when he, like Wordsworth, envisions the possibility of an integration between science and poetry. He hints at such a possibility in the poem 'Emerging' which opens the collection *Laboratories of the Spirit* (1975). In the poem's final lines the narrator imagines, and seems to embrace, 'the tall city / of glass that is the laboratory of the spirit' as a future destination in which, albeit experimentally, science and poetry can commingle (1). In the poem 'Suddenly' from *Later Poems* (1983) he writes of an experience of divine presence in which not only nature but science too has become the mouthpiece of God:

> I listen to the things
> round me: weeds, stones, instruments,
> the machine itself, all
> speaking to me in the vernacular
> of the purposes of One who is. (201)

In these lines deity speaks to the poet not only through nature, as 'weeds' and 'stones', but, in a startling progression, also through 'instruments' and 'the machine itself'. Also important, these 'objects' all speak to the poet 'in the vernacular' a word that seems here to indicate not a spoken 'language' but, rather, a lack of formality and artifice, an authenticating *intimacy* of intuited communication. Finally, these 'things' do not speak of divinity itself but 'of the purposes of One who is', thus becoming, for Thomas, not chance manifestations of a ruling chaos but integral parts of an ongoing creation, an ordered universe. Both 'Emerging' and 'Suddenly' appear to run strangely counter to the current of Thomas's apparent condemnation of applied science as we have seen it thus far. Just two years later we find in the collection *Destinations* (1985) not only the poem 'Vocabulary', treated earlier as a possible affirmation of the validity of a new scientific diction in poetry, but the title poem 'Destinations' whose closing lines bear a striking similarity to Wordsworth's sentiments in the 'Preface'.

'Destinations' is a prophetic poem in which travellers, who have been 'waylaid by darkness', might easily be viewed as representations of humankind as a whole, reminiscent of the couple in 'Once', from *H'm*, who 'went forth to meet the machine' (1). Unfrightened by the experience of darkness, the travellers in 'Destinations' push forward hopefully 'to the light', toward the future and the salvation of an imagined wholeness (17). In the poem's final lines Thomas describes that future salvation as a brightness 'which is science / transfiguring itself in love's mirror', clearly an echo of Wordsworth's view that science must first be transfigured by poetry in order to put on 'flesh and blood' and be welcomed as a 'dear and genuine inmate of the household of man'. In both of these poems, as well as in others such as 'Numbers' from *Frieze* (1992), Thomas seems to be suggesting a possibility which his predominating *experience* of science painfully precludes, as if affirming, momentarily, Wordsworth's dream against the more bitter contention which he has come to accept as real. In these poems Thomas, for an instant, partakes of Wordsworth's bold, nineteenth-century, Romantic optimism, and the longing for that ideal which one senses in these few poems further accentuates in Thomas's work on science an underlying plangency over that which may be hoped for, may be dreamed of, but which, ultimately, is not.

In one of Thomas's last poems, 'How?', from his *Six Poems* (1997), a special, limited edition by Celandine Press, it is exactly this sense of plangency which emerges, largely stripped of its customary mask of irony, more vulnerable and, hence, disarming:

> How shall we sing the Lord's song
> in the land of the electron,
> of the micro-chip? Are these also
> ingredients of a divinity
> we have been educated to misunderstand?
> Our dependence on him is anticipated
> by our expertise …

In a universe
that is expanding our theologies
have contracted. We reduce
the God-man to the human, the human
to the machine, watching it demolish
forests faster than we can grow even
one tree of faith for our Saviour
to come down from.

As a romantic, Thomas has inherited from Wordsworth the dream of an intimate reciprocity between poetry and 'the objects of science'. But two decades after Wordsworth's 'Preface' Thomas depicts an experience not only of division but of contention between these fields whereby the expansions of technology threaten destruction of the spiritual experiences which, for both poets, form the wellspring of poetic inspiration and expression. The poem 'How?' depicts a science which mutes poetry's ability to sing, an expertise which precludes any dependence upon deity, and an expansion in knowledge which contracts theology and leads, ultimately, to self-destruction. But why, for Thomas, is Wordsworth's dream an unrealisable one? Why are the divisions between science, poetry, and religion so acute. In the final pages of his autobiography, *No-one* (1986), one discovers a 'theology of division' underpinning the poet's position on science:

> It appeared to R. S. many times that it would have been far better had man not tasted the fruits of the tree of the knowledge of good and evil. How often he has shown how unsuited he is to use that knowledge for the glory of God and the benefit of his fellow human beings. And yet it is equally difficult to imagine the earth without the mind of man probing and searching and challenging itself to make the best use of his discoveries and devices. (107)

For Thomas, the duality of good and evil which inhabits the objects of science is merely reflective of the same forces competing within the human psyche. In this quotation from *No-one* Thomas views science not with scorn but as a natural function of the mind. It is not science but the split mind which Thomas sees as dangerous. In the quotation he traces that split mind to its origins in the temptation and fall of humanity as depicted in Genesis. This passing reference to the story of 'the fall' is, none the less, central to Thomas's understanding of the world. By examining the Genesis text more closely we can begin to see that Thomas's struggle with science is one in which he must come to terms, both intellectually and emotionally, with a division between humanity and the divine, with a disfiguring guilt inherent in that division, and with the frightening weight of the responsibility of free will.

In Genesis 1.28–9 we are told of Adam and Eve that

> God blessed them, and God said unto them, 'Be fruitful and mul-
> tiply, and replenish the earth, and subdue it and have dominion
> over the fish of the sea, and over the fowl of the air, and over every
> living thing that moveth upon the earth.' (*Reader's Bible*)

While 'the fall' of man and woman in chapter 3 of Genesis negates nei-ther human superiority in the order of creation nor this earlier com-mand to subdue and administer dominion over it, the context within which that command must be carried out has been none the less rad-ically altered by the 'act of disobedience'. In an effort to become divine themselves, Adam and Eve achieve a fundamental and pervasive alien-ation from their creator. The author of Genesis describes them as driven from the garden to toil and to die, separated from the tree of life by a flaming sword. This physical imagery of separation seems meant, at least in part, to underscore a more interior transformation in the very nature of human reality. The act of rebellion rends the eternal world, spawning a separate and separated world in time in which virtually every aspect of human life becomes subject to division. Because of that divi-sion the very powers with which humanity were originally endowed, the power of reason and of free will, become, after the fall, double-edged as it were. Subjection of the earth and the administration of dominion over it no longer occur within the stable context of assured unity, but instead within a rather more dark and dangerous context of separation, ignorance, and temptation. The pursuit of knowledge is, for Thomas, an endeavour fraught with guilt, temptation, and the danger of self-annihilation. Barbara Prys-Williams highlights this sense of guilt and temptation tied to the pursuit of knowledge when she sug-gests in her 1996 article on Thomas's *The Echoes Return Slow* as auto-biography that

> Thomas feels scientists are impiously tampering with dangerous
> knowledge beyond man's right to know ..., that the blandishments
> of science have diverted human beings from God's intended pur-
> pose for them, repeating, in a sense, Adam's first sin, perhaps with
> equally disastrous results. (114–15)

In 'This One', from *H'm* (1972), we find not a condemnation of the sci-entist but, by inversion, a vindication of the farmer as one heroically resisting the 'temptation' and 'fall' which Thomas suggests may be endemic to scientific pursuit. He describes how

> patiently this poor farmer
> Purged himself in his strong sweat,
> Ploughing under the tall boughs
> Of the tree of the knowledge of
> Good and evil, watching its fruit
> Ripen, abstaining from it. (3)

By its depiction of the unmechanised labour of the farmer as a form of abstinence from original sin and therefore as 'Edenic' or pure, the poem further highlights the importance, for Thomas, of a humanity 'fallen' through science. Poems such as 'The Gap' (*Laboratories of the Spirit*), 'Publicity Inc.' (*Later Poems*), 'Adam Tempted' (*Mass for Hard Times*), and 'Afallon' (*No Truce with the Furies*) all continue this thread according to which Thomas sees the machine as in some way closely linked to the fall in Genesis. Understanding the importance of that theological grounding for Thomas goes a long way toward helping to explain an apparent duality in the poet's position which might otherwise be considered paradoxical, ambivalent, or even obscure. For example, it is within the context of that grounding that Thomas can assert, in *No-one*, that God 'has revealed Himself through the mysterious processes of the creation, as He did, perhaps, to Einstein and Schrödinger', and only a few pages later to bewail that 'the mind of man has discovered a power that is endangering his own future ..., that is certain to lead to a war that will destroy all the work of the centuries in addition to mankind itself' (106, 108). This is the source too of that 'complexity and tension' pointed up by Ned Thomas in his reading of 'Homo Sapiens 1941'. The aeroplane at the centre of that poem is both 'unambiguously destructive' and at the same time awe-inspiring because the potentials competing in science are, for Thomas, the forces of dark and light competing within the human psyche itself, what he calls in 'Economy' from *Frieze* (1992),

> the split
>
> mind that is half in love
> with the instruments of division. (13)

Thomas's 1992 collection *No Truce with the Furies* further intensifies the imagery of this division. In 'Incubation' the poet writes:

> We are fascinated
> by evil; almost you could say
> it is the plumage we acquire
> by natural selection. There is a contradiction
> here. (55)

And in 'Hallowe'en' Thomas warns the loose spirits hungry to return to stay where they are:

> 'This is no world for escaped beings
> to make their way back into.
> The well that you took your pails
> to is polluted. At the centre
> of the mind's labyrinth the machine howls
> for the sacrifice of the affections'. (63)

Here the machine is not an alien changeling introduced magically, as it were, from sources without but, rather, seems wholly interior and even fundamental to the human psyche, existing 'At the centre / of the mind's labyrinth'. Again we can see that Thomas's quarrel with science is, at its source, a quarrel with the human mind, its division originating in an alienation from unity brought about through free will, and whose legacy is a battle against the temptation to evil.

Towards healing: the case for pure science

Having highlighted the story of the fall as the proper context of Thomas's position on applied science, I want to emphasise again that the poet's thought and work are not *only* a lament over division, not characterised *only* by these sometimes dire depictions of guilt and dread. If Thomas's work concerning the machine is primarily concerned with divisions reflected by, and characteristic of, applied science, much of the poet's work concerning pure science portrays a powerful drive towards the *healing* of such division. Rather surprisingly, Thomas often prophesies a future synthesis according to pure science in which the need for unity and the need for understanding, the spiritual and the material, art and science, are recognised equally and pursued in tandem. In the poem 'Mediations' for example, from *Laboratories of the Spirit* (1975), Thomas recognises the possibility of spiritual experience specifically through the investigations of pure science:

> And to one God says: Come
> to me by numbers and
> figures; see my beauty

in the angles between
stars, in the equations
of my kingdom. Bring
your lenses to the worship
of my dimensions: far
out and far in, there
is always more of me
in proportion. (17)

This, of course, is precisely the opposite of Thomas's sentiments in 'First Person' in which he states emphatically that 'The scientist / brings his lenses to bear and unity / is fragmented' (*Mass*, 1992: 18). Here pure science kindles spiritual or religious wonder, not reducing the dimensions of the divine but rather, exploring their vast reach. Similarly, the scientists in the poem 'They' from *The Way of It* (1977) are called by the narrator 'The new explorers', and are depicted as discovering the divine through a science which, here, becomes an alternative to prayer:

Have I been too long on my knees

worrying over the obscurity
of a message? These have their way, too,
other than prayer of breaking that abstruse code. (28)

It seems, in both of these poems, that Thomas has made his peace with the 'otherness' of the scientific endeavour, realising not only that 'These have their way, too' but that 'their way' may, in fact, be a viable supplement to the poet's own. Indeed, in 'Roger Bacon', from *Frequencies* (1978), Thomas imagines the scientist's religious faith to be the result of an experience of God specifically in and through science:

Yet
he dreamed on in curves
and equations
with the smell of salt petre
in his nostrils, and saw the hole
in God's side that is the wound
of knowledge and
thrust his hand in it and believed. (40)

We see a unity here between the dream and the fact, between the experience of God and the experience of science. While scientific knowledge here forms the wound of Christ, that is, while it plays a part in

the crucifixion of the divine, it also becomes, paradoxically, the opening (both literally and symbolically) to religious faith, a probing of
wounded flesh which is the catalyst here of belief.[9] It seems that simultaneous to Thomas's angst over the displacing force of applied science
in these later poems, we can see emerging the affirmation of a restored
unity and spiritual regeneration made available through modern
physics. Thomas writes, for example, in 'Nuance', from *No Truce with
the Furies* (1995),

> there were
> the few who waited on him
> in the small hours, undaunted
> by the absence of an echo
> to their Amens. Physics' suggestion
> is they were not wrong. Reality
> is composed of waves and particles
> coming at us as the Janus-faced
> chooses. We must not despair.
> The invisible is yet susceptible
> of being inferred. To pray, perhaps, is
> to have a part in an infinitesimal deflection. (32)

Shocking here is the suggestion by Thomas that the knowledge afforded
by the discoveries of modern physics facilitates humankind's understanding of the nature of God and of prayer.[10] Scientific knowledge here
anticipates and corroborates intuitive knowledge. Thomas's most dis-
cursive remarks on this idea of science contributing to the reawakening
of spiritual hope can be found in his essay '*Undod*' or 'Unity' (1988) in
which he points to Fritjof Capra's *The Tao of Physics* as a book 'which is
full of hope of regaining the old faith of the West in unity of being
through the most recent discoveries and theories in the world of physics'
(33). It is worth quoting at some length Thomas's remarks concerning
this hoped-for synthesis:

> Gradually in the course of this century the realization has grown
> that matter is not half as solid as the materialists would like to
> believe, and indeed that it is so immaterial that it is more akin to
> spirit than to conventional matter ... By shifting the emphasis away
> from matter as something solid to something closer to a field of
> force, contemporary physicists have come to realize just how mys-
> terious the universe is, and that we need qualities such as imagina-
> tion and intuition and a mystical attitude if we are to begin to
> discover its secrets.

What is striking here is not only Thomas's assertion that the methods typically employed by the artist – imagination and intuition – have become appropriate to the scientific endeavour, but more his insistence that the scientific endeavour become the catalyst of a religious faith. Science, in this way, becomes radically expanded to embrace both the desire for unity and the desire for understanding. Indeed, the two desires become one. Thomas claims:

> Contemporary physics' version of the nature of being is far more similar to that of a poet or a saint. The physicist believes in a living web, which connects everything in the entire universe. All living things are related to each other, and no part of the universe can be harmed or abused without awakening echoes throughout the whole web. (33).

In this light R. S. Thomas's poetry is clearly not to be viewed simply as an indictment of science. Nor, as it turns out, is his treatment of science in the poems contradictory or even enigmatic. The 'escalating irony' employed in his use of the scientific register is one method of battle not against science as an endeavour, but against the unbridled indulgence in scientific thought for the sake of a technological development that pursues humankind's material salvation to the exclusion of a fundamental need for a unifying spiritual vision and accompanying sense of wonder. As we have seen, such indulgence and development Thomas views not only as alienating but as effectively self-destructive. What Thomas envisions through Physics, however, is a dynamic alternative in which the objects of religion, the objects of science, and the objects of art are one, an existence which simultaneously believes and hopes (religious), seeks and understands (science) and sees and praises (poetry). Thomas writes of this conflation of seeking, understanding, and praying within the context of modern physics in his *A Year in Lleyn* (1990) as well:

> The new knowledge, physics especially, has reduced matter to a state of thin vapour like a current that connects two electrical charges. The physicists came to see how amazing the universe is in which we live, and the tricks that time and space can play. Behind the atoms were found smaller particles, and behind those, others still smaller. If man were to succeed in travelling faster than the speed of light, he would disappear, and the universe with him, into a huge black hole. Therefore the sense of holy dread returned. As the Book of Job puts it, 'Then a spirit passed before my face; the hair of my flesh stood up'. Therefore when I stand at night and look towards the stars, and think of the galaxies that stretch one after the

other to oblivion, while remembering that it is all within finite space that is still expanding, I am not a dreamer belonging to the old primitive lineage of Lleyn, but someone who, partaking of contemporary knowledge, can still wonder at the Being that keeps it all in balance. (145)

It is this same vision of a unity regained through science, in this case both pure and applied, which Thomas underscores in the final pages of his autobiography, *No-one*, where he writes that he has

> lived long enough to know that the discoveries and the theories of the scientists have given birth to a universe that even the imagination of man fails to comprehend. Space is huge. For years the astronomers have revealed the distance between us and the nearest star. And beyond that, there is star after star, galaxy after galaxy; and having come to the borders of our own galaxy, there is only another galaxy, and so on almost to eternity ... Aren't we back with the people who wrote the Bible, who would confess that such knowledge was too wonderful for them? (105)

What we find here is a significant *deconstruction* by Thomas of notions concerning both religion and science in which the two areas become less opposites standing in diametrical opposition to one another, and more co-ordinates, sharing similar aims of seeking, understanding, and praising in a movement towards the realisation and articulation of meaning.

What we discover then in Thomas's work concerning science is never a single or simple 'position' but a multidimensional, considerably complex, and ongoing engagement with science in which paradox often emerges as a force not of contradiction but of tension, as one manifestation of a 'unity of being' which the poet would *uncover* and *recover* through art. Among other things, I have highlighted in these chapters on science the significant development in Thomas's poetic use of a scientific register and the deeper philosophical concerns which have driven that development from casual to experimental and ironic. I have highlighted as well Thomas's conditional 'acceptance' of applied science and, with Wordsworth, his sometimes surprising vision of its possible contextualisation within what he views as an older way of life grounded in nature. I have argued that Thomas's concern and poetic use of 'the machine' is not merely for mechanisation or even a mechanisation which breaches contextualisation, but for a force originating within the human psyche itself, the product of a basic alienation from divinity which he traces to the mythic 'fall' of humankind. Finally, I have set out to illuminate Thomas's preoccupation with pure science, and in particular with modern physics, not only as a potentially unifying force, but as an essentially imaginative, intuitive, and therefore artistic approach to the world.

It remains to take up in Part III Thomas's search for deity as it reaches with growing intensity across his poetic oeuvre. As we shall see in Chapters 6 and 7, the search for deity is, for Thomas, a natural extension both of the exploration of identity and of the confrontation with environment that we have focused on in the first two parts of the book. Chapter 6 will examine Thomas's search for deity as it is chronicled most intensely in the 'mythic' poems of *H'm* (1972). Chapter 7 will focus on Thomas's existential contexts, on the experience of spiritual absence known as the *via negativa*, and, finally, on the emergence, beginning strongly in the collection *Destinations* (1985), of experiences of renewed spiritual presence in the *via affirmativa* mode.

Notes

1 One might profitably contrast this separation between traditional education and natural learning to George Mackay Brown's 'Countryman' in which the two types are quietly assimilated, the schoolboy's experience giving way naturally to the farmer's turning of 'Black pages on the hill' (1996: 142).

2 Writing in *The Echoes Return Slow* (1988) of the mechanisation introduced to farm communities in Wales following the Second World War, Thomas claims that, amongst farmers, 'The only casualties [have] been the old wisdom, the old skills of the land' (34).

3 Evidence of Thomas's view of a naturally erotic relation of humanity to nature abounds in the poet's early and highly lyrical work, perhaps the most explicit example of which is his lament for the loss of that eroticism in the poem 'Song' from *The Stones of the Field* (1946).

4 Again, Norman MacCaig, while avoiding Thomas's more formally 'religious' context, none the less echoes him in this idea, writing in 'Reversal' from *The World's Room* (1974) of a domestication of nature as diminishing the 'music' of wildness. In the poem MacCaig describes a blue hare's skeleton, found preserved in a peat bog, as a wild, and, paradoxically, living substance. For him, as for Thomas, this kind of experience of wildness in nature combats a growing alienation, imaged as an actual physical atrophy, and makes possible the re-emergence of a substantive 'true self'.

5 I have already examined, in Chapter 3, certain parallels between the use and depiction of nature in the work of Ted Hughes and R. S. Thomas. It seems important to note here, though, that Hughes's use of the crow, in his 1970 collection *Crow*, remains in keeping with a traditional trope that views the bird as suggestive of evil. In contrast, Thomas's explicit use of the raptor as a representative of the Christian God of love appears unprecedented as well as strangely

paradoxical, since the term 'raptor', ornithologically an order of birds of prey, is also synonymous with 'rapist', 'abductor', 'plunderer', and 'robber' (*OED*).

6 This same image is employed in the poem 'Numbers' from *Frieze* (1992).

7 This image is prefigured in the 1990 collection *Counterpoint* in the poem beginning 'Come close. Let me whisper.'

8 Norman MacCaig writes of his own compulsion to create fresh associations in the poem 'Still Going', from *The World's Room* (1974), in which he depicts the land using images of the sea. MacCaig refers to such associations as 'incorrigible metaphors' and suggests that the creation of such 'new' perspectives issues from a kind of poetic double vision, from a tension between the 'feverish' and the 'icy' eye.

9 The image of the wound in God's side into which the scientist thrusts his hand is, of course, an allusion to the story of 'doubting Thomas', one of the twelve apostles of Jesus who refused to believe in the rumoured resurrection until he had probed the wounds of Christ. See John 20.24–30.

10 It should be noted that Thomas's 'The Combat', from *Laboratories of the Spirit* (1975), and 'Gradual', from *Later Poems* (1983), both depict physics as falling short of any complete realisation of the divine. However, despite their portrayals of the limitations of physics in a spiritual realm, these poems can be seen as further evidence of Thomas's affirmation of pure science, not as a replacement for, or even as providing a definition of, divinity, but as one possible inroad to spiritual experience and religious faith.

Part III
Expanding deity

6 Theologies and beyond

Introduction

This chapter begins with an examination of the philosophical grounding for R. S. Thomas's 'religious poetry' as found in his 1966 article 'A Frame for Poetry' and in his 1963 'Introduction' to *The Penguin Book of Religious Verse*. It then examines Thomas's 'mythic' poems by focusing on the 1972 collection *H'm*. Chapter 7 examines Thomas's '*via negativa*' and '*via affirmativa*' poems by concentrating on the collections *Frequencies* (1978) and *Destinations* (1985), in which these 'types' are most pervasive. This examination of individual collections allows one a view into the most concentrated treatment and development of such themes by Thomas, as well as a deeper grasp of the character of the individual volumes, each of them significant milestones in the oeuvre as a whole. My chief purpose in these final chapters is to highlight and explore what might be called Thomas's 'reconfiguring' of theology, that is, his insistence on the central validity and importance of individual spiritual experience, both as absence and as presence. That insistence radically expands the category 'religious poetry' towards what Thomas calls, in his 'Introduction' to *The Penguin Book of Religious Verse* (1963), the 'imaginative representation' of an 'experience of ultimate reality' (64). His religious poetry can be seen not merely as 'devotional' but as primarily *exploratory* of wider dimensions of the notion of deity, and, in particular, the relation of deity to human experiences of suffering, doubt, and despair. Such 'reconfiguring' constitutes one of Thomas's major achievements. Through such reconfiguring he, more than any other recent, poet, reinvigorates the genre of English-language religious poetry, reshaping it to reflect a contemporary spiritual experience, a reshaping which, as M. Wynn Thomas has recently attested, qualifies Thomas as 'an aristocrat of the language and one of the modern world's greatest religious poets' (Jones and Evans, 1999: 13).

The sudden proliferation of R. S. Thomas's 'religious poems' beginning in the 1970s follows closely on his move from Eglwysfach, near the mid-Wales coast, to Aberdaron, on the Llŷn peninsula, in 1967. With the move to Aberdaron in the remote north-west there appears in Thomas's poetry a waning of earlier preoccupations with Welsh rural life and the struggle for national identity in favour of an intensification of the personal search for deity. In his autobiography *No-one* (1986) Thomas writes of himself that 'having reached Aberdaron ... he turned to the question of the soul, the nature and existence of God'. (76). And later in the autobiography:

> He wrote political, patriotic poetry in English, and then fell quiet. He portrayed the life of the small farmer as an act of protest against the ignorance and apathy of the rich and the well-off. But through those poems ran a religious vein that became more visible during his last years. After all, there is nothing more important than the relationship between Man and God. (104)

Beginning in earnest with the volume *H'm* in 1972 it is the vicissitudes of that 'relationship between Man and God' which Thomas's work primarily reflects.[1] Two significant characteristics emerge with this turning in the 1970s towards a distinctly 'theological' poetry. First, in their drive and method the poems become notably metaphysical, reflecting an intense *intellectual* drive towards spiritual understanding which is propelled by an equally intense *emotional* urgency. One finds in these poems an intense compression forged under what seems a barely restrained emotional charge. The poetry becomes 'wrought' in the sense of being 'highly worked', seeking the mind's understanding by force of 'the heart's need'.[2] One is reminded of Eliot's claim in his lecture 'The Varieties of Metaphysical Poetry' that the major characteristic of such poetry is its 'fusing sense with thought' (1993: 58). While Eliot sees Dante and Donne as the masters of such poetry, he goes on in the lectures to write of the French poet Jules Laforgue as sharing a similar disposition and drive:

> He had an innate craving for order: that is, that every feeling should have its intellectual equivalent, its philosophical justification, and that every idea should have its emotional equivalent, its sentimental justification. (1993: 212)

The drive behind, and manifestations within, Thomas's religious poetry beginning with *H'm* are strikingly similar to what Eliot elucidates here: an uncompromising search for natural links between thought and feeling, for an intellectual conception which can adequately answer emotional experience, and, in turn, the contextualisation of those experiences within a viable frame of speculative thought.[3] One encounters in these poems an often painful yoking of the disparate elements of these 'two worlds' as, repeatedly, Thomas presses towards a reckoning between religion and life.[4]

The second significant element which emerges from, and becomes characteristic of, these religious poems is a potent spiritual thirst. While despair is often and rightly discussed as a key element in Thomas's religious poetry, it needs to be added that the quality of that despair is one of intense spiritual yearning or thirst. Eliot helps in this as well. Commenting on Tennyson's *In Memoriam* in his *Essays Ancient and Modern*, he writes that

> It is not religious because of the quality of its faith, but because of the quality of its doubt. Its faith is a poor thing, but its doubt is a very intense experience. *In Memoriam* is a poem of despair, but of despair of a religious kind. And to qualify its despair with the adjective 'religious' is to elevate it above most of its derivatives. (1936: 177)

Although clearly Thomas's faith is not 'a poor thing' but, rather, a living thing, that is, stronger or weaker, waxing and waning, but never static, Eliot's main point in these lines never the less seems entirely relevant. Thomas is a religious poet, and even a despairing poet, in precisely this sense, according to the nature of his insatiable thirst for, and drive toward, a spiritual source. Using Eliot's qualification of despair as 'religious' it seems that Thomas's despair, like Tennyson's, is elevated 'above most of its derivatives', that it can be seen not as the collapse of final resignation but, rather, a strenuous suspension, an ongoing tension between searching and waiting, as, for example, in 'Tidal' from the collection *Mass for Hard Times* (1992):

> The waves run up the shore
> and fall back. I run
> up the approaches of God
> and fall back …
>
> Let despair be known
> as my ebb-tide; but let prayer
> have its springs, too, brimming,
> disarming him; discovering somewhere
> among his fissures deposits of mercy
> where trust may take root and grow. (43)

Finally, although I will not be pursuing further any specific parallels between Thomas and Eliot in this chapter, I do want to suggest that

Thomas's religious poetry is part of the modernist discourse associated
with Eliot, a discourse in which the urgency and honesty of the spiritual
quest effectively overturns the tradition and register of 'devotional' verse
in favour of increasingly more radical approaches to, and wider possibilities concerning, the human search for ultimate meaning. By 'devotional'
I mean here primarily that poetry which utilises dogmatic or 'institutionalised' forms, in language, content, or a combination of the two, to
make implicit assumptions of a shared faith between writer and reader.
In particular I am referring to the use of an immediately recognisable
religious register often closely identified with traditional prayers, ser-
mons, and hymns, which indicates an apprehension of deity as *benign* and
present. While I am not arguing against the possible sincerity or merit of
such poetry, I am suggesting that Eliot and Thomas are innovative in
depicting, in a new register, the reality and urgency of their individual
spiritual experiences.

Beginning with *H'm* (1972), Thomas's 'religious poems' can be
viewed as emerging into three branches which I define in these chapters
as 'mythic', '*via negativa*', and '*via affirmativa*'. The poems I have
labelled 'mythic' are characterised primarily by an exploration of, and
often confrontation with, an anthropomorphised creator-God which is
typically distant, impersonal, predominantly fierce, and, often, ferocious.
Most often these mythic poems reiterate, in a radically non-traditional
way, a creation narrative as a means of examining the nature of a
monotheistic God and the ultimate meaning of its relation to humanity.
In this way the poems are distinctly 'mythopoeic' or myth-making, theological speculations, allegorical openings into the possibility of underlying truths about the nature of deity. The mythic poems are to be found
primarily in the collections *H'm* (1972) and *Laboratories of the Spirit*
(1975). By contrast, the poems I have signified as '*via negativa*' are concerned with the poet's search for a personal deity less anthropomorphised
and exterior than ubiquitous and interior. The *via negativa* poems are
most often characterised by a sense of absence as, paradoxically, the ear-
mark of a divine presence, as well as by an often impending spiritual
despair, and by asceticism, silence, and waiting as, increasingly, the only
available means of spiritual approach. These poems are mainly to be
found in the collections *Laboratories of the Spirit* (1975), *Frequencies*
(1978), and *Experimenting with an Amen* (1986). Finally, in keeping
with the idea of these 'types' as 'branches', one finds, simultaneous to
and, as it were, punctuating these mythic and *via negativa* poems,
expressions by Thomas of instances of spiritual presence and affirmation.
In these poems one senses Thomas's gradual emergence from an ascetic

posture of empty waiting and the experience of deity as absence, towards a regained experience of divine presence, towards a resurgence of spiritual hope and the relaxation of a characteristically bitter contention with divinity, towards acceptance, serenity, and even joy. In so far as there is any 'progression' from one 'type' to another it is, loosely and not strictly, a slow evolution by Thomas out of the *via negativa* stance towards an emphasis on the experience of spiritual presence, towards expressions which can be labelled '*via affirmativa*'. This gradual emergence finds its strongest expression in the 1985 collection *Destinations*, though it occurs intermittently prior to this, and its manifestations continue into Thomas's final work.

Philosophical grounding

In exploring the philosophical grounding for Thomas's religious poems it is important to emphasise its intellectual breadth. It is according to that breadth that Thomas is able to discard the more 'devotional' models of 'religious verse' while at the same time retaining and re-emphasising, in a new way, what he considers to be the primacy of a 'religious frame' for poetry. His expanded definitions for such terms as 'religious frame' and 'religious truth' enable him to *transform* and *reinvigorate* so-called 'religious verse', updating it to accommodate the keen probing, the honest doubt, and, often, the alarming despair characteristic of the search for deity in a postmodern age. I am suggesting that by neither insisting on traditional models of poetic piety nor jettisoning altogether the possibility of religious 'answers' to the searching questions posed by twentieth-century sensibility concerning the existence of deity and its relation to humanity, Thomas's grounding allows him effectively to *transfuse* the genre of religious verse by widening its relevance to the whole experience of life.

In his 1966 article for the *Times Literary Supplement* entitled 'A Frame for Poetry' Thomas argues that 'it is within the scope of poetry to express or convey religious truth, and to do so in a more intense and memorable way than any other form is able to' (90). Although one can infer from the phrase 'within the scope' that, for Thomas, all poetry need not be 'religious', he makes clear his opinion that poetry is somehow uniquely suited to the expression of 'religious truth'. He goes on in the article to suggest a compatibility, what he calls a 'symbiosis', between the two professions of priest and poet, and even suggests the possibility that the conscious abandonment of such a 'religious frame' may propitiate a kind of literary decline:

So far as we can tell, there are no works of poetry being produced in English today that are of comparable stature with those
of Chaucer, Spenser, Shakespeare or Milton. Whether these writers themselves were avowedly Christian or not, they wrote within
a Christian framework. Is there a relation between the decline of
Christianity ... and the decline in works of high poetry? Many
like to associate poetic decline or inferiority with a consciously
adopted Christianity, Wordsworth being the *locus classicus*. But
why blame Christianity for our failure to produce high poetry, if
Christianity is no longer a major force in our culture? (92)

Thomas raises three important questions by his suggestion in these lines
that religion forms the proper frame or context within which poetry can
do its best work. First, what, for Thomas, constitutes the 'religious
framework' of poetry? Second, what is the nature of the 'religious truth'
which he feels poetry is so aptly suited to express? And third, what is the
nature of the relation Thomas seems to envisage between religion and
poetry? Because Thomas was a priest in the Anglican Church in Wales
for forty-one years (1937–78) and a poet engaged deeply with philosophical questions concerning the existence of deity and the nature of its
relation to humanity, his answers to these questions become central to
an understanding of his life and work.

It is in his 'Introduction' to *The Penguin Book of Religious Verse*
(1963) that one begins to find answers to these questions and, as such,
the 'Introduction' becomes indispensable to an understanding of the
philosophy which underlies Thomas's religious poems. In the
'Introduction' Thomas defines religious poetry as the 'imaginative representation' of 'an experience of ultimate reality' (64). He warns of
this definition as 'sticking somewhat loosely to orthodoxy', and one
can immediately see that 'imaginative representation' and 'ultimate reality' allow for tremendous leeway, both on the side of poetry and on
the side of 'religious truth'. In particular, use of the term 'ultimate
reality' broadens the category not only beyond the doctrinal confines
of the Christian Church but beyond institutionalised religion as a
whole. The phrase is clearly subjective in its application, allowing for
a wide-ranging *multiplicity* in the understanding and experience
of divinity.[5] Thomas's subject divisions in the anthology into 'God',
'Self', 'Nothing', 'It', 'All', are examples of this wide view of what constitutes 'ultimate reality'. In particular the category 'Nothing' significantly widens the traditional parameters of 'religious poetry' by making
room for expressions of spiritual absence and despair. Thomas writes
that:

> Neither the Middle Ages' obsession with death, nor the ability of contemporary poets such as John Crowe Ransom to describe despair so movingly, are necessarily indicative of their satanic allegiance. Poems such as the 'terrible' sonnets of Gerard Manley Hopkins are but a human repetition of the cry from the Cross: '*Eloi, Eloi, lama sabachtani!*' The ability to be in hell is a spiritual prerogative, and proclaims the true nature of such a being. (66)

Thus, while he readily admits in the 'Introduction' to attempting 'to broaden the meaning of the term "religious" to accommodate twentieth-century sensibility', and while he owns that such an attempt may 'arouse the indignation of the religious, more especially the Christian, reader', Thomas defends these efforts at expansion with the assertion that 'it is not necessarily the poems couched in conventionally religious language that convey the truest religious experience' (65). His claim is that 'wherever and whenever man broods upon himself and his destiny, he does it as a spiritual and self-conscious being' (66). According to this statement most, if not all, of Thomas's poems, overtly religious or not, would fall within the parameters of a new 'religious poetry', an indication, again, of the wide breadth of his view.[6] Such observations by Thomas in the 'Introduction' are not merely prefatory to his choices for the anthology, but are important indicators of the broad mind-set out of which his own religious poems can be better understood. To borrow an expression from Douglas Dunn's appraisal of Hugh MacDiarmid, Thomas's religious poetry is 'not an art of simple rediscovery so much as one of transfiguration in the crucible of modern sensibility' (1992: xix).

According to these definitions one can begin to see more clearly Thomas's answers to the three questions raised above. In answer to the first question it becomes apparent in the 'Introduction' that, for Thomas, a 'religious frame' is composed not of a body of dogma but, rather, of belief in an 'ultimate reality' which is primarily experiential and therefore subjective. Likewise, concerning the nature of 'religious truth' posed in the second question, it is, Thomas suggests, the individual experience of that 'ultimate reality', again, a 'religious truth' clearly unconfined by traditional religious dogma. In answering the third question concerning the nature of the relation between religion and poetry Thomas's answer is implicit in the foregoing responses: the relation between religion and poetry is, for Thomas, clearly organic. The individual's subjective experience of ultimate reality itself becomes the natural stuff of poetry. Indeed, according to his own definitions, to cast off the 'religious frame' for poetry is, for Thomas, to abandon poetry itself since what Thomas calls 'the frame' is at once religious frame, religious truth, *and* poetic substance. In the 'Introduction' he further suggests, with Coleridge, that the imaginative expression of the experience of ultimate reality in poetry not only imitates but very nearly *partakes of* the action of deity itself. He writes:

> The nearest we approach to God he [Coleridge] seems to say, is as creative beings. The poet by echoing the primary imagination, recreates. Through his work he forces those who read him to do the same, thus bringing them nearer the primary imagination themselves, and so, in a way, nearer the actual being of God as displayed in action. (64)

According to this, the act of writing, the imaginative expression of the experience of ultimate reality, as well as the act of reading, the reflexive imagining of that experience, become a transformation, a meta morphosis of writer and reader into the process, and therefore the very being, of deity. Together with his definition of religious poetry as the 'imaginative representation' of 'ultimate reality', this suggestion of the poet as 'echoing the primary imagination', as uniquely *recreating*, points to a philosophical grounding in Thomas which is significantly wider than is often supposed. And it is this intellectual 'breadth' that is one of the most important characteristics and contributions of Thomas's religious poems: the expansive and inclusive nature of his intellectual position regarding the personal experience of ultimate reality as the essential raw material of poetry.

Mythic: the shock of *H'm*

The shock of the collection *H'm* (1972) begins with its opening poem, 'Once', which features all of Thomas's mythic elements. First, the poem is distinctly mythopoeic or myth-making, reworking a creation narrative which, while not perhaps 'true' in its literal sense, is none the less meant to probe 'truths' concerning the human condition which transcend the confines of physical time and space. Second, the poem's mode is clearly prophetic-apocalyptic, that is, authoritative in tone (prophetic) and visionary in aspect (apocalyptic). Third, the poem features an anthropomorphised creator-God, omnipotent and 'other', the object of fear. Finally, underlying the poem's text one discovers an implicit imaging and questioning of that creator-God, and even of creation itself, concerning human meaning and purpose. When viewed in conjunction with the second point above, this final characteristic bears an irony worth noting. While 'Once' is singularly authoritative in tone, it is also singularly speculative in its underlying drive. While the poem's rhetoric is deliberately fashioned to assert 'truth' in clipped, bold declaratives, beneath this mask of infallibility the poem is an expression primarily of possibility. Thus 'Once' is effectively split in its 'personality'. Driven at its source by a questioning angst, its manifestation, its overriding poetic voice and gesture, remain cool and self-assured, strangely *un*questionable in the authenticity of its authority. It is important to recognise this discrepancy since it indicates these mythic poems to be, fundamentally, theological probings and even deconstructions by Thomas of monotheism and its relationship to the actual, physical, and human world, what J. P. Ward, in his book *The Poetry of R. S. Thomas*, refers to as 'the mythic figuring and refiguring of God' (1987:84).[7] With *H'm* Thomas presses forward in an intensely focused way towards the discovery of a religious understanding which can match experience. Indeed, D. Z. Phillips, in his book *R. S. Thomas: Poet of the Hidden God*, views *H'm* as finally relinquishing the poet's search for a 'theodicy' which can answer the charge of human suffering and as embracing, rather, a deity whose very identity is somehow intimately bound up in that suffering. In highlighting this embrace, Phillips not only underscores the radical nature of Thomas's religious stance but also suggests that Thomas's answer to the philosophical 'problem of evil' is a view of deity characterised not by the divided imperatives of omnipotence *or* love, but by an omnipotence which *is* love, which is 'self-emptying' and which therefore encompasses both the good and evil, a sordid combination which the poet finds endemic to human existence. Such a view of divinity, according to Phillips, allows Thomas a faith response in keeping with his own experience:

> The poet turns his back on the kind of religious impulses which seek to explain away the torment and suffering in the world. The poet insists that such facts must be embraced rather than ignored ... The poet shows us a religious faith which actually depends on embracing the mixed character of human life in a way which does not deny its character. (1986: 77)

My main point here is that the mythic poems are not merely an intellectual exercise for Thomas but are attempts to render religion in terms of actual human experience without denying or over-simplifying, in language or content, either one. This section focuses closely on the mythic poems as, specifically, examples by Thomas of theological expansions towards what might be called a 'spiritual realism', a reworking of more

dogmatic structures in favour of a poetic grappling with spiritual struggle, and even paradox, which is nearer, both in its language and its substance, to individual spiritual experience than to stricter theoretical
constructions of the objective nature of God.

'Once', the opening poem of *H'm*, begins with God's creation of
Adam, the first man, significantly a poet, who narrates his own beginnings:

> God looked at space and I appeared,
> Rubbing my eyes at what I saw.
> The earth smoked, no birds sang;
> There were no footprints on the beaches
> Of the hot sea, no creatures in it.
> God spoke. I hid myself in the side
> of the mountain. (1)

The creation of man in these lines occurs not as the biblical formation
by God from clay, but as a conjuring from space, a nearly comic sleight
of hand. There are, however, two other aspects to focus on in these lines.
The first is the man's reaction to the sight of the created world around
him, the second his reaction to the sound of God's voice. The man rubs
his eyes at the sight of the created world, presumably in some wonder,
and yet we can infer from the description of the world in lines 3–5 that
it is a wonder at least partially tinged with fear:

> The earth smoked, no birds sang;
> There were no footprints on the beaches
> Of the hot sea, no creatures in it.

The creation here may be pristine, but it is also primeval and desolate, as
yet untamed by occupation or age, and hence, if only by implication,
dangerous. We also find in these opening lines that, despite the apparently 'unfallen' state of the man, the voice of God precipitates in him fear,
flight, and hiding: 'God spoke', we are told, and 'I hid myself in the side
/ of the mountain'. While Thomas leaves the reader to guess precisely
what that divine utterance might have been, what is most important here
is that the sound of that voice, the *first* sound of that voice, the first communication between creator and created, elicits not trust or comfort in
the man but fear and an instinctual flight towards self-preservation from
what is perceived to be a singularly threatening deity. This sense of the
created world as lonely and dangerous, and of deity as mighty and fear-
some, is amplified in the poem's second and final stanza. Thomas writes:

> In the brown bark
> Of the trees I saw the many faces
> Of life, forms hungry for birth,
> Mouthing at me. I held my way
> To the light, inspecting my shadow
> Boldly.

The sense in these lines is of life as a journey, an important motif for Thomas, but, more specifically, an uncertain journey in which the poet is forced to hold his 'way / To the light', a journey plagued by shadow and pain, and the mouthing 'faces of life', 'hungry for birth'. These ideas of a distant God, of life as a journey through the 'dark' of longing, of the necessity of a courageous probing of one's shadow-self, of the stamina required for holding one's way to 'the light', are characteristics central to Thomas's understanding of human existence, and it is in these mythopoeic renderings that one can see them most plainly and power-fully united.

In the final lines of 'Once' the poet introduces Eve as 'rising towards me out of the depths / Of myself'. This evocation of the creation of woman is striking and important. By substituting the biblical formation of Eve from the sleeping Adam's rib with this awareness by the man of her organic growth out of his own vital substance, Thomas intensifies an intimacy between the two which compensates for their apparent alien-ation from the creator, as well as their apparent loneliness within the nat-ural world they are to inhabit. More than companion and counterpart, the two are, Thomas suggests, one and the same.[8] In the poem's final lines Thomas further consolidates that intimacy and its compensatory force in the hostile world that awaits them:

> I took your hand,
> Remembering you, and together,
> Confederates of the natural day,
> We went forth to meet the Machine.

In these final lines one finds not only a powerful affirmation of human intimacy, but the necessity of that intimacy within the natural context of war. The two key words in these final lines are 'Confederates' and 'Machine', indicating as they do that the man and woman enjoy not only a mystical union of sorts but a military objective as allies against 'the Machine'. While Thomas refrains from defining 'the Machine' here, his use of the word as a proper noun indicates it to be a force of evil which stands pitted against the couple. And while this image is capable of being contextualised within a Christian framework, these final lines seem to hint more than a little towards a kind of Zoroastrianism in which the forces of light and dark are seen to march forth into battle for possession of the world. Thomas seems to be suggesting in 'Once' not only the inexplicable reality of evil but the nature of existence as a warring struggle against that reality, in which divinity has relinquished its omnipotent hold and in which ultimate outcomes have yet to be determined.

What we discover, then, in 'Once' is a poem which pursues insight into both the nature of deity and into the nature of human existence by re-posing, re-inventing, and re-interpreting traditional 'actions' of a monotheistic creator-God. These philosophical or imaginative reworkings form the core of virtually all of Thomas's mythic poems. What is striking in this regard is that while Thomas's probings in the mythic poems remains constant, his conclusions often range. While one may infer a certain philosophical 'picture' or 'position' from a poem such as 'Once', that conclusion is very likely to stand more or less at variance with depictions in alternative mythic poems. Largely because of such speculative variance on Thomas's part, the mythic poems, as a whole, are both complex and dynamic, as opposed to simple and static replications of a given formula.

Of the thirty-seven poems which make up the collection *H'm*, fully eleven can be labelled 'mythic' according to the characteristics I have already discussed above. Having examined 'Once', I will now turn to five of these poems in order to underscore, despite the similarity of their means, their alternating emphases and conclusions and, in doing so, to encourage a view of Thomas's mythic poems not as static or repetitive but as creating, by their cumulative effect, a kind of philosophical montage of intensified spiritual pursuit. Indeed, a sequential comparison of these five poems indicates a pattern with regard to Thomas's depiction of deity which, beginning with divine indifference, goes on to alternate between divine violence and divine compassion, finally ending in a curious synthesis of all of these characteristics. This alternating pattern encompasses, in total, the following six poems: 'Echoes' (4), 'Making' (17), 'Island' (20), 'Repeat' (26), 'Soliloquy' (30), 'The Coming' (35). I will examine four of these poems in addition to 'Once', as an introduction, and 'Other', as an example of the synthesis Thomas finally achieves between these two alternating poles of divine violence and compassion.

Although in 'Once' Thomas images deity as secondary to the ruminations of the man, in 'Echoes', just a few pages later that deity becomes both central and active. The first nine lines of the poem revolve around three central elements. First, the separation between divinity and its creation; second, the imperious and consuming anger of that divinity;

and third, the pain experienced by the creation as the result of these.
Thomas begins the poem:

> What is this? said God. The obstinacy
> Of its refusal to answer
> Enraged him. He struck it
> Those great blows it resounds
> With still. It glowered at
> Him, but remained dumb,
> Turning on its slow axis
> Of pain, reflecting the year
> In its seasons. (4)

These lines indicate a creator-God alienated from its own creation and
'enraged' by such unaccountable separation to the point of violence.
However, concerning the sources of such alienation and violence there
is a certain ambiguity. For example, God's question 'What is this?' indicates a concealed referent. Similarly, we find a strange 'obstinacy' in the
earth, an unexplained 'refusal to answer'. Even after the 'great blows'
dealt it by God the creation remains unaccountably 'dumb'. What *is* clear
in these lines, and what appears most important to Thomas in the poem
thus far, is that this suffering of the creation, whatever its ultimate source,
is a defining characteristic, the 'slow axis / Of pain' on which it is
doomed to turn. In the poem's second half God's 'answer' to the 'dumb'
earth, a dumbness which underscores God's essential loneliness and the
need, in so far as one can posit divine need at all, for intimacy or relat-
edness with a seemingly independent creation, is to create animals and,
ultimately, human beings:

> God looked at it
> Again, reminded of
> An intention. They shall answer
> For you, he said. And at once
> There were trees with birds
> Singing, and through the trees
> Animals wandered, drinking
> Their own scent, conceding
> An absence. Where are you?
> He called, and riding the echo
> The shapes came, slender
> As trees, but with white hands,
> Curious to build.

It seems at first in these lines that God's overriding need for communication, for dialogue with the creation, may be indicative of a divine compassion defeating the earlier impulse to punish. But despite the ability of the new creatures to communicate, to 'answer', they do so by 'conceding an absence'. In so far as these creatures possess a 'knowledge' of their origin, it is as absence only. The gap, the uncomfortable silence between creator and created remains. God is forced to utter the cry 'Where are you?', and humanity hears that call not directly, but only faintly, as 'echoes' they must 'ride'. The implication of distance is explicit. In the final lines of the poem the communication which finally does occur across that distance between the humans and God comes in the form of blood, of sacrifice:

> On the altars
> They made him the red blood
> told what he wished to hear.

What is shocking in these final lines is the blatant absence of any divine compassion. One finds here that Thomas's God has shifted from pining for intimacy to demanding satisfaction, homage, sacrifice. What one finds in 'Echoes' is not a silent or indifferent god but a divinity whose wounding, rather than giving way to a more deeply loving regard, requires blood.

Having highlighted the divine indifference of 'Once' and the divine violence of 'Echoes', one finds in the poem 'Making' the emergence, finally, of divine compassion. Before examining this development however, it is important to stress a basic continuity established by Thomas in these three poems and, indeed, in the mythic poems as a whole. In addition to their opening with similar images of an anthropomorphised creator-God at work, 'Once', 'Echoes', and 'Making' are all characterised by an ethos of overwhelming loneliness and alienation.

In 'Once' not only does man hide himself 'in the side / of the mountain' upon hearing God speak, he is similarly alienated from the rest of nature, which, in its own turn, is removed from the divine. Thomas writes that

> In the brown bark
> Of the trees I saw the many faces
> Of life, forms hungry for birth,
> Mouthing at me. (1)

The loneliness and alienation that are common and central to these poems are reflected in these anonymous 'faces', 'forms' without voice which are desperate for a 'birth' denied them. The faces are isolated and haunting, just as the narrator of the poem is himself isolated and haunted by them.

In 'Echoes' one finds a similar fault-line or separation by which God becomes enraged at the creation for its dumbness, its 'refusal to answer', and punishes it accordingly. This divine propensity for violence is further echoed in God's sinister spreading of bacteria in 'Making' (4). Nature, in 'Echoes', remains unconnected from its source in the divine, 'conceding / An absence'. And finally, God in the poem is forced to call out to the humans, 'Where are you?', who hear only the echoes of that cry over the distances between.

In 'Making' nature is depicted, again, as 'faces' which 'stared in / From the wild', an image which clearly creates an inside/outside dichotomy and the sense of a barrier, as of glass, not to be transgressed. The existence of nature is not indicative of its deeper presence in relation to divinity, forcing God to admit:

> Yet still an absence
> Disturbed me. (17)

'Once', 'Echoes', and 'Making' are poems in which God, nature, and humanity exist in fragmentation, alienation, and essential loneliness, rather than in a more organic connection. Such alienation forms the overriding ethos, the most basic premise, the common ground and frame out of which the poems emerge. It is precisely this frame which ties the mythic poems into a single developing body. While, as we shall now see, Thomas's depiction of deity in 'Making' stands in stark contrast to his depictions in 'Once' and 'Echoes', that contrast emerges from within this common ground. Viewed in this way the individual mythic poems can be seen not as contradictions, but subtle modulations or counterpoints, not primarily as individual works, although they are clearly capable of standing alone, but as a succession of movements in a musical suite.

The final lines of 'Making', while emerging from this common ground, none the less indicate a substantial development in Thomas's depiction of the nature of divinity. God, as the narrator, relates:

> I slept and dreamed
> Of a likeness, fashioning it,
> When I woke, to a slow
> Music; in love with it
> For itself, giving it freedom
> To love me; risking the disappointment. (17)

Here, finally, is the God of love so painfully absent from 'Once' and 'Echoes'. These lines reveal not only the selflessness of the love-force underlying the act of creation but the empowerment of that creation via free will, and the acceptance, by God, of a necessary vulnerability as the result of such empowerment. What we have in 'Making' is thus the complement to 'Echoes' rather than the contradiction. Thomas is not, in these poems, restricting divinity to wrath or love but, rather, driving forward speculations, drawing out strands in a philosophical reckoning with the whole idea of monotheistic divinity. Far from any narrow assertion of a single truth, Thomas is widening the approach in these mythic poems to an understanding not so much of what divinity is, but of what divinity could be, holding up, at the same time, the possibility, and perhaps even the necessity, of paradox as the defining characteristic of such an answer.

Finally, as yet another aspect of this 'comprehensive effect' it should be noted that although in 'Once' Thomas narrates in the first-person omniscient *as the man*, and while in 'Echoes' he narrates in the third-person omniscient *as the narrator*, in 'Making' he, for the first time, assumes the first-person omniscient *as God*. These shifting perspectives in the mythic poems are an effective means of directing reader focus. In 'Once' the reader is primarily drawn down, into what Thomas views as the predicament of human existence; in 'Echoes' the reader is forced out, to the wider perspectives of relationship between God, creation, and humanity, and in 'Making' the reader is taken in, to speculation on the more precise and fundamental nature of deity. Again, these shifting perspectives, when seen together, serve to broaden rather than to restrict the theological context of Thomas's probing.

If 'Making' introduces into the mythic poems the possibility of love as the predominant characteristic of a creator-God, 'The Island', just a few pages later, reverts in its emphasis to a deity of wrath and thereby highlights the alternating pattern of these mythic poems in *H'm* between depictions of divine violence and compassion:

> And God said, I will build a church here
> And cause this people to worship me,
> And afflict them with poverty and sickness
> In return for centuries of hard work
> And patience. (20)

Whereas in 'Making' human free will is the chief manifestation of divine love, in these lines the retraction of that free will seems to be the effect of divine displeasure: 'I will build a church here / And cause this people to worship me'. The disappointment risked by God in 'Making' has been not only realised here but, as in 'Echoes', transposed to anger, the clear inference being that humanity, according to Thomas, has not, of its own free will, chosen the practice of worship. These opening lines indicate not only a divine anger, jealousy, and outrage but the determination by deity to compel such worship through force of superior strength, to grind humanity into dependence by affliction with poverty, sickness, and pain, despite 'centuries of hard work / And patience'. In the remaining four lines of the first stanza the omniscient narrator proceeds to describe this failure of humanity in terms of the physical structure which God, in the poem's opening line, vows to construct:

> And its walls shall be hard as
> Their hearts, and its windows let in the light
> Grudgingly, as their minds do, and the priest's words be drowned
> By the wind's caterwauling.

It is, for Thomas here, a human lack of receptivity to the divine, a lack of acceptance of and dependence on the divine to which God reacts: the hard heart, the grudging mind, the deaf ear. And yet what seems so disturbing in the poem as a whole is, first, that the punishment which God metes out for such 'failings' seems disproportionately severe and, second, that divinity becomes virtually consumed by human emotion, by offended love, essentially by grief, and subsequently seeks to redress that grief through a brutal exacting of revenge:

> All this I will do,
>
> Said God, and watch the bitterness in their eyes
> Grow, and their lips suppurate with
> Their prayers. And their women shall bring forth
> On my altars, and I will choose the best
> Of them to be thrown back into the sea.

In these lines God's wrath appears frighteningly unbounded. Not only that, there seems, perversely, to be a divine enjoyment of the long suffering of humanity. Thomas ends the poem with the declaration:

> And that was only on one island.

While the narrator seems to wink from behind this final line in a kind of tongue-in-cheek acknowledgement of the poem's extremity and severity, it is, none the less, a grim humour which does little to subvert the poem's dark concern. 'The Island' raises and sustains the question whether Thomas in these mythic poems embraces a decidedly malevolent creator, a Puritan God of wrath, bent on the punishment, through suffering, of human sin.

While the answer to this question may appears to be 'yes', it helps to view 'The Island' not as a strict philosophical 'answer' by the poet but as driven by Thomas's longing to understand human suffering. The poem's ultimate preoccupation is with the source of, and reason for, poverty, sickness, pain, and loss. In dealing with this 'problem of pain' Thomas is faced again with the paradox of a New Testament God of compassion and forgiveness and the relation of that God to human suffering. Thomas, rather than embracing a malevolent God, is exploring in 'The Island', as a possible answer, the model of an Old Testament God of the sort found in the Pentateuch and the Psalms, whose passion is characterised not only by love and forgiveness, but by demands, conditions, anger, jealousy, and wrath. The God of 'The Island' is most productively viewed as a single exploration of a single aspect of monotheism, and is significantly restricted by removal from its proper context in the mythic poems as a whole.

As if to drive home this necessity of viewing the individual mythic poems as creating an alternating pattern within the wider context they form together, Thomas provides us in 'The Coming' with a configuration which emerges from this Old Testament grounding to anticipate the Christian incarnation. Central to 'The Coming' is not God's wrath but the helpless state of humanity and the son's pity, upon witnessing that state, as the key to the Christian incarnation, crucifixion, and redemption. In marked contrast to 'Echoes' and 'The Island', it is not the divine *infliction* but the divine *alleviation* of human suffering which is central to 'The Coming'. Thomas writes in the first stanza:

> And God held in his hand
> A small globe. Look, he said.
> The son looked. Far off,
> As through water, he saw
> A scorched land of fierce
> Colour. The light burned
> There; crusted buildings
> Cast their shadows; a bright
> Serpent, a river
> Uncoiled itself, radiant
> With slime. (35)

As in so many of Thomas's mythic poems, one becomes aware at once of the distance, the metaphorical gap, between creator and creation. Though deity in these lines holds the earth 'in his hand', the son sees it 'Far off, / As through water'. Even the title 'The Coming' indicates the separation inherent to the relationship. Most important here, however, is the narrator's description of the earth as barren waste, a stage of divine neglect and human suffering. It is, Thomas tells us, a land scorched, burned by light, littered with crusted buildings, radiant not with beauty but with slime. Indeed, Thomas's description of 'a bright / Serpent, a river' can be seen, by its effective inversion, as an allusion to earth as the habitation of evil. This is, it seems, the earth after 'He struck it / Those great blows it resounds / With still' in 'Echoes', or after the affliction of 'poverty and sickness' dealt it in 'The Island'. In the poem's second stanza Thomas focuses this broad, aerial view down to a more particular place and people:

> On a bare
> Hill a bare tree saddened
> The sky. Many people
> Held out their thin arms
> To it, as though waiting
> For a vanished April
> To return to its crossed
> Boughs.

Though the poem's action is chronologically prior to the Christian incarnation, clearly the yearning in these lines is a collective, platonic 'remembering', a prefiguration or prolepsis of the Christian crucifixion or redemption to come, the 'bare / Hill' being Calvary, the 'bare tree' and 'crossed / Boughs' the as yet untenanted cross. In the same way, the 'vanished April' for which the humans pine can be seen both as an assertion of some remembered Eden, a state of union prior to the human alienation from divinity, and as the Easter resurrection.[9] The whole ethos of the lines is one of sorrow and yearning. Remembering God's decree in 'The Island', 'I will … cause this people to worship me', we find in 'The Coming' a people brought to their knees by suffering, worshipping out of need. One might argue that it is precisely that need which creates the receptivity towards, and acknowledgement of dependence upon, deity which Thomas laments as lost in 'The Island' and which, ultimately, elicits the action of divine love in the poem's closing lines:

> The son watched
> Them. Let me go there, he said.

The act of sacrifice embraced by the son in order to restore a 'vanished April' to suffering humanity is, for Thomas in 'The Coming', the fulfilment of Old Testament narrative as it is re-invented in the mythic poems 'Echoes', 'Making', and 'The Island'. What we can see developing in the mythic poems of *H'm* is a meditation on Judaeo-Christian monotheism and its gradual movement from Old Testament to New Testament paradigms. The context of 'The Coming' is, necessarily, the mythic poems which precede it, on which it hinges, and of which it is, at least partially, the fulfilment. Thomas, at least in part, intends these mythic poems as a theological reconsideration, and even deconstruction, of deity.

'Other', the penultimate poem of *H'm*, provides a synthesis of the disparate images of the divine which have preceded it in the poems 'Echoes', 'Making', 'The Island', and 'The Coming'. I am suggesting not that 'Other' is some kind of deliberate unification or knitting together by Thomas of these paradoxical images of deity, but merely that it reflects divinity as characterised both by jealousy, resentment, and wrath, as well as by sensitivity, grief, and compassion. For example, in 'Other' Thomas writes of God's relationship to creation by stating:

> He loved and
> Hated it with a parent's
> Conceit, admiring his own
> Work, resenting its
> Independence.

This simultaneous pride and resentment towards creation is a combination of ideas found to be strictly isolated in the mythic poems so far, embodying both the ferocity of 'Echoes' and 'The Island' as well as the deeper empathy of 'Making' and 'The Coming'. As in 'Echoes' and 'The Island', God is effectively ignored and excluded by the creation in 'Other' and with a similar result:

> There were trysts
> In the greenwood at which
> He was not welcome. Youths and girls,
> Fondling the pages of
> A strange book, awakened
> His envy. ...

> He began planning
> The destruction of the long peace
> Of the place.

These 'trysts / In the greenwood' between 'Youths and girls / Fondling
the pages of / A strange book', while reminiscent of Hawthorne's
'Young Goodman Brown' or Arthur Miller's *The Crucible*, in which
young Puritans dabble in evil, are, according to Thomas in 'Other', stray-
ings which arouse a divine envy and lead, ultimately, to God's determination, once again, to inflict suffering. However, in contrast to the
mythic poems examined thus far, once that destruction is under way,
God, in compassion, relents:

> He began planning
> The destruction of the long peace
> Of the place. The machine appeared
> In the distance, singing to itself
> Of money. Its song was the web
> They were caught in, men and women
> Together. The villages were as flies
> To be sucked empty.
> God secreted
> A tear. Enough, enough,
> He commanded.

It is not clear in these lines whether the appearance of 'the machine' is
the direct result of God's planned destruction or whether that appearance occurs independently of a divine plan. The question arises in 'Other'
whether the machine originates as a kind of divine punishment or
whether it is an evil somehow exterior to and independent of that divinity. Whatever the answer to this, God's command that its destruction
should cease comes in the poem not authoritatively but as a cry of empathy, a pleading in tears, not as the completion of justice but as an intimate compassion for humanity, much the same as we have seen in
'Making' and 'The Coming'.

In the grim final line of 'Other' the narrator declares that

> the machine
> Looked at him and went on singing.

In this final mythic poem from *H'm* deity is ultimately defeated. More
important, however, is Thomas's suggestion that human suffering continues simultaneous to and independent of divine love and compassion,

that while divinity suffers with humanity, it is none the less somehow incapable of defeating that suffering and, finally, that while prone to envy, wrath, and punishment, divinity is, at least in 'Other', predominantly loving, suffering its alienation from humanity in the same way that humanity suffers its alienation from the divine. I am not suggesting that 'Other' brings the mythic poems of *H'm* to a neat philosophical close. On the contrary, it indicates the ongoing complexity, the subtle shifting and probing of Thomas's mythic poems, their sustaining of a paradoxical tension and the need to view them not so much as independent entities but primarily as a body of poems in *relationship*, whose wider speculations and implications arise not from isolation but from 'abrasion', from the friction of a wider contextualisation.

Notes

1 The volume proves to be a turning point not only in terms of subject matter. With *H'm* Thomas moves away from his early use of traditional rhyme and metre towards the free-verse and syntactical experimentation of his later work, as well as from his long-term publisher, Rupert Hart-Davis, to the London-based Macmillan.

2 The phrase 'the heart's need' is Thomas's own, occurring for the first time in 'The Lonely Farmer' (*An Acre of Land*, 1952) and again in 'Taliesin 1952' (*Song at the Year's Turning*, 155).

3 John Ackerman, in his valuable study *Welsh Dylan: Dylan Thomas's Life, Writing and His Wales* (1998), echoes Eliot's definition, perceptively highlighting a similar quality in the work of Dylan Thomas.

4 Eliot makes quite clear his estimation of the power of such poetry when he writes that 'Humanity reaches its higher civilisation levels not chiefly by improvement of thought or by increase and variety of sensation, but by the extent of co-operation between acute sensation and acute thought' (220–1).

5 It is likely that Thomas inherited the phrase from Bishop John Robinson, who uses it in his influential book *Honest to God* (1963): 'God is, by definition, ultimate reality. And one cannot argue whether ultimate reality exists. One can only ask what ultimate reality is like' (29).

6 Dylan Thomas's declaration concerning his own work that 'These poems, with all their crudities, doubts, and confusions, are written for the love of Man and in praise of God, and I'd be a damn' fool if they weren't', seems underpinned by an understanding of 'religious poetry' arguably similar to that of R. S. Thomas's here (1993. 'Author's Note'). Again, much, if not all, of Dylan Thomas's work might fall within these broadly defined margins, and indeed, R. S. Thomas includes him in the Penguin collection.

7 Robert Langbaum, in his *The Poetry of Experience*, suggests that the dramatic monologue offered Victorians the 'objectification' or distance between poet and narrator they sought following what they often viewed to be a Romantic indulgence in the subjective first-person stance. Thomas's mythic poems can be seen

to function in much the same way, as creating a distance or even persona from which to explore 'objectively' philosophically complex and often paradoxical points of view, while at the same time allowing the poet to 'dramatize an emotional apprehension in advance of or in conflict with his intellectual convictions' (1957: 104). Taking Langbaum further, Carol Christ suggests that such objectifiying devices or masks function for the poet not only as 'defensive armor' but as a means of access to an 'ultimate self' (1984: 36).

8 In contrast to this image of the sexes united in origin and purpose, one might compare Thomas's 'Female', in *H'm*, and 'The Woman', from *Frequencies*, both variations on the creation of woman in which the female is depicted not, primarily, as in union with the male but as pitted against him in a struggle for power, as 'other', serpent-like and seductive.

9 Similarly to the idea I am suggesting here, Henry Vaughan's 'The Retreate' takes as its subject an intuited awareness of pre-existence, a 'remembered Eden'.

7 Absence and presence

Introduction: existential contexts

In the final pages of his autobiography, *No-one* (1985), Thomas comments that

> Our image of God must be transformed, as Bishop Robinson has said. The Church has up to this day produced a great number of thinkers of the quality of Paul and Augustine and Thomas Aquinas and Pascal. But somehow the alternative element in Christianity, the popular, somewhat sentimental element, has displaced the other, with unfortunate consequences to say the least. (107)

The reference to Bishop Robinson in these lines is to his influential best-seller *Honest to God* (1963). The 'transformation' which Robinson argues for, and which Thomas in the quotation endorses, is essentially from a 'deistic' to a 'theistic' understanding and imaging of divinity, that is, from an 'impersonal' to a 'personal' God. Of the deistic conception Robinson writes:

> Here God is the supreme Being, the grand Architect, who exists somewhere out beyond the world – like a rich aunt in Australia – who started it all going, periodically intervenes in its running, and generally gives evidence of his benevolent interest in it. (30)

Robinson juxtaposes this deistic conception of a remote God to an alternatively theistic divinity, a being not impersonal but intimate, a God of *relationship*:

> The difference between the two ways of thought can perhaps best be expressed by asking what is meant by speaking of a *personal* God. Theism … understands by this a supreme Person, a self-existent subject of infinite goodness and power, who enters into a relationship with us comparable with that of one human personality with another. (48)

This shift from an understanding of divinity as impersonal to an understanding of it as personal comprises half of Robinson's argument in

Honest to God. In conjunction with it he also calls for a topographical or directional shift in popular theological imagery from a God 'up there' or 'out there' to a ubiquitous divinity which pervades the created world and, as such, is also distinctly interior. Thus the shift is from an impersonal divinity 'out there' to a divinity realised in relationship, 'in here'. In this second 'phase' of topographical or directional transformation Robinson leans heavily on ideas set out by the existentialist theologian Paul Tillich in his *The Shaking of the Foundations* (1949). In particular Robinson employs Tillich's image of divinity as a 'ground of being': 'God, Tillich was saying, is not a projection "out there", an Other beyond the skies, of whose existence we have to convince ourselves, but the Ground of our very being' (1963: 22).

In a more precise articulation of this idea of divinity as an intimate 'ground of being' Robinson goes on to state that

> God is not 'out there'. He is in Bonhoeffer's words 'the "beyond" in the midst of life', a depth of reality reached 'not on the borders of life but at its centre', not by any flight of the alone to the alone, but, in Kierkegaard's fine phrase, by a 'deeper immersion in existence'. (47)

I am emphasising Robinson's argument, and his references to Tillich, Bonhoeffer, and Kierkegaard, not only to contextualise Thomas theologically but, more in particular, to account for a remarkably similar 'transformation' which occurs between Thomas's mythic poems and those I have designated *via negativa*.[1] As we have seen, Thomas's mythic poems reflect primarily a *deistic* understanding, that is, they set forth a distant and, for the most part, impersonal creator-God. In partial contrast to Robinson, Thomas's deistic divinity expresses wrath as well as divine compassion, but my point here is that whatever the nature of these expressions they occur across significant distances, allowing for little, if any, closer integration between creator and created. Alongside Thomas's mythic poems however, one encounters others in which the poet is clearly seeking out the possibility of a *theistic* God, a God not 'out there' and separate but 'in here' and intimate, whose presence is ubiquitous and therefore as much interior as exterior, Tillich's 'ground of being', whose defining characteristic is the desire for relationship. In a 1983 radio interview, *R. S. Thomas at Seventy*, the poet acknowledges Tillich as influential to his thinking: 'I do like Tillich's idea of the Ground of Being, that God is not a being' (178). But there is a subtlety here which needs to be noted. While Robinson argues for the 'ground of being' as a move towards a personal God of relationship, Thomas emphasises the phrase as indicating that God is not a 'being' at all. This is important to an understanding of Thomas's approach in these '*via negativa*' poems. God, for Thomas, does become personal, but primarily in the sense of being non-anthropomorphic. While images of God become, for Thomas, radically interior and intimate, they remain images of a God of which, as he says, 'personality is only one aspect'. Thomas states in the interview:

> we have been brought up on the Bible to believe that God is a Being, whereas the slightly more impersonal approach of Hindu thought, and Buddhistic thought for that matter, does give me a feeling that this is more what I am after. If there is any contact with an eternal reality I don't want to limit that reality to personality. It is a bit like Wordsworth's Fourteenth book of *The Prelude* with his trip up Yr Wyddfa, Snowdon. It seemed to me a type of majestic intellect. (178)

The shift one encounters between the God of the mythic poems and that of the *via negativa* poems is a shift primarily from the deistic paradigm of an anthropomorphised creator-God which is 'out there' to a ground of being, a 'majestic intellect', an eternal reality which is interior but unlimited, which is intimately personal, but which, as a ubiquitous source, simultaneously spills the boundaries of 'personality' or 'being'. J. P. Ward, in his *The Poetry of R. S. Thomas*, sees this shift as culminating in the collection *Frequencies*, which I shall examine shortly, where 'the writing becomes not a description of God, but a search for God' (83).

Finally, Robinson avows that Tillich's words 'seemed to speak of God with a new and indestructible relevance and made the traditional language of a God that came in from outside both remote and artificial' (22). In contrast to Robinson here, it is important to stress that, for Thomas, the 'discovery' of an understanding of deity as interior in the *via negativa* poems does not constitute a rejection of the mythic mode as erroneous, or even a progression forwards from it. The *via negativa* poems are not to be seen in *contrast* to the mythic poems, not as displacing them, but as distinctly *complementary* to them, as an ongoing exploration or expansion of deity as complex and multi-dimensional. Where the mythic poems are primarily intellectual speculations on the nature of an omniscient creator-God, the *via negativa* poems explore that same God as simultaneously 'subterranean' as it were, a ubiquitous, mystical divinity intuited within the more subtle nuances of interior presence and absence. While one *can* detect in Thomas's religious poems a 'progression', primarily in their imaging of divinity, this progression is towards an expanded conception of deity in which each of the 'successive' elements or aspects remains equally important, held in a reciprocal tension. More important than their 'progression', the mythic, *via negativa*, and *via affirmativa* poems can be seen to establish by such reciprocity a single, unified entity in which no 'type' is diminished, much less replaced, by the emergence or apparent counter-action of another. Together the poems comprise an exploration of the complexity and paradox inherent to the poet's growing apprehensions of deity.[2]

I will turn now to an examination of Thomas's yearning for and probing after such a theistic God by looking closely at the poems I have designated *via negativa*. In the final section of the chapter I will turn to look at poems which, in contrast to the predominant sense of absence which characterises the '*via negativa*' poems, indicate a more positive realisation of that theistic God, depicting divinity not as absence and darkness but as renewed presence or light, an actuality no longer to be inferred.

Via negativa: *Frequencies* and absence

Via negativa, meaning literally 'by way of what is not', is an idea associated largely with mystical theology. Thomas himself uses the term as a poem title in *H'm*. Perhaps the earliest and most comprehensive discussion of *via negativa* occurs in 'The Mystic Theology', the work of the sixth-century Syrian mystic Dionysus the Areopagite, although the idea is perhaps best known in the West through the anonymous English classic of medieval mysticism *The Cloud of Unknowing*. Regardless of particular sources, the idea of *via negativa* is common to eastern mystical traditions predating Christianity, as well as to Christian monastic traditions in the West, both as an approach to and as an experience of divinity. As a technique of approach *via negativa* signifies a deliberate mortification not only of the sensual appetites but of the whole desire of the ego for its own realisation and dominance, as well as of the distraction seen to be posed by the physical world. It insists upon an emptying of the self, a silencing of the individual will, and a patient waiting and watching in these privations for God's approach. For example, in 'The Flower' from his 1975 collection *Laboratories of the Spirit*, Thomas writes:

> I asked for riches.
> You gave me the earth, the sea,
> 　　　　　the immensity
> of the broad sky. I looked at them

          and learned I must withdraw
                 to possess them. I gave my eyes
                 and my ears, and dwelt
          in a soundless darkness
                           in the shadow
              of your regard.
                        The soul
              grew in me, filling me
          with its fragrance. (25)

The register of these lines is clearly that of the *via negativa*, an ascetic withdrawal, the giving up of sight and sound, the dwelling in darkness and shadow. And yet Thomas makes it clear in the opening lines of the poem that such withdrawals, in keeping with the *via negativa* as a technique of approach, are embraced solely in pursuit of spiritual 'riches', a kind of mystical union with the divine. It needs to be emphasised, however, that the actual experience of the divine is not always one of such presence but frequently, rather, of absence. This experience of divinity as absence is rooted in a philosophical logic which asserts that since divinity, by its very nature, must necessarily overflow the created world of the senses, its presence therefore, at least in the higher realms of contemplative prayer, must, paradoxically, be expressed in terms of that which is not, as an actuality to be inferred from the experience of absence. Ward, in his chapter entitled 'God Absent and Present', describes this *via negativa* absence as 'itself an entity, as implying of necessity a presence before, after or beside, by which the resulting absence could have pressure, and seem to hint at something not itself, and so not be mere flat emptiness' (1987: 97). Later in the same chapter Ward writes: 'We can never conceive "nothing" without the outline of a shimmering shape which suggests what has been removed' (105). Thomas's poem entitled 'Via Negativa', from the collection *H'm*, is a good example of this, depicting the sensation of painful absence as itself indicative of divine presence. Thomas writes:

              Why no! I never thought other than
              That God is the great absence
              In our lives, the empty silence
              Within, the place where we go
              Seeking, not in hope to
              Arrive or find. He keeps the interstices
              In our knowledge, the darkness
              Between stars. His are the echoes

> We follow, the footprints he has just
> Left. We put our hands in
> His side hoping to find
> It warm. We look at people
> And places as though he had looked
> At them, too; but miss the reflection. (16)

The absence in these lines is clearly haunted, pregnant with a very distinct, albeit intangible, sense of presence. One notices how the *is* of God's existence in line 2 is an 'absence', an 'empty silence', the elusive 'place', the 'darkness / Between stars', 'echoes', 'footprints', missed 'reflections'. The experience of divinity in these lines can be seen to be predicated upon the sense and signs of absence. God here must be inferred from what is not. It should be emphasised too, however, that the *via negativa* experience of divinity's painful absence is often seen to be tied to the idea of purification, both as the winnowing of a sense-orientated framework inadequate to the fuller apprehension of that which radically transcends all sense experience, and as the gradual purgation of an unworthiness wrought by sin, both of which seem to be a part of what St John of the Cross refers to as 'the dark night of the soul'. Equally, such *via negativa* experiences of absence are often considered a kind of protection against a divine brilliance too powerful to be unmediated, the deep shadow thrown by blinding light, what Vaughan refers to in his poem 'The Night' as the 'dazzling darkness' of the divine. Most importantly however, in all of these various aspects the *via negativa* is to be seen as an experience, even as a diatonic or recurring 'stage', common to prolonged spiritual pursuit, an acceptance of darkness and unknowing in a spiritual journey towards the realisation of what Thomas calls 'ultimate reality' or, in Tillich's phrase, 'the ground of being'.

Like the mythic poems, the *via negativa* poems begin to appear with the volume *H'm* in 1972. But if *H'm* represents the most intensive treatment of the mythic poems, it is the 1978 collection *Frequencies* which manifests most widely Thomas's preoccupation with the idea of the *via negativa* as an experience of deity. In turning now to examine these poems in *Frequencies* I want to stress again that the mythic and the *via negativa* poems occur side by side, that they are contemporaneous and, as such, should not be seen so much as definite 'stages' in a strict theological development by Thomas but, rather, as manifestations of the poet's deepening spiritual probe, his grappling with the nature of deity and its relation to human experience. The title, *Frequencies*, itself indicates a widening range to the poet's probe of divinity, pointing to an awareness of spiritual 'vibrations' or 'signals' coming simultaneously from distances without and within. Far from being disposed of, the mythic God is still very much the God of *Frequencies* as, for example, in 'The Gap', 'The Woman', and 'Play'. Still, with *Frequencies* there occurs a subtle shift away from contemplations of the mythic creator-God towards the possibility of a more intimate or interior divinity. For example, in 'Groping', the fifth poem in the collection, Thomas is writing not of cosmic explorations of a vast God-space beyond but of a journey within the self, the exploration of divinity within an interior landscape:

> Moving away is only to the boundaries
> of the self. Better to stay here,
> I said, leaving the horizons
> clear. The best journey to make
> is inward. It is the interior
> that calls. Eliot heard it.
> Wordsworth turned from the great hills
> of the north to the precipice
> of his own mind. (12)

Thomas, in these lines, seems to have put away, at least temporarily, the mythic creator-God as a vehicle for his intellectualised handling of theological suppositions in favour of a more emotional or intuitive approach to God as a personal 'ground of being'. In contrast to the mythic poems, one senses little irony here but, rather, a gentle transitioning away from probes upward and outward to probes downward and inward, to the possibility of deity within 'the boundaries / of the self'.

Thomas reiterates this shift more explicitly in the final poem from *Frequencies*, 'Pilgrimages'. Both titles, 'Groping' and 'Pilgrimages', suggest action and movement, but with the added implication of a released intellectual tenacity, action characterised by an inherent receptivity. The search goes on in these poems, but in a changed direction, and with an emphasis placed not so much on the goal of empirical knowledge as on the possibility of intuited understanding. For example, Thomas writes in the first stanza of 'Pilgrimages':

> He is such a fast
> God, always before us and
> leaving as we arrive. (51)

This is the mythic creator-God, at large in cosmic space, with the narrator in frustrated pursuit. However, as if exhausted by such outward and grasping pursuit, Thomas writes in the poem's final lines:

> Was the pilgrimage
> I made to come to my own
> self, to learn that in times
> like these and for one like me
> God will never be plain and
> out there, but dark rather and
> inexplicable, as though he were in here? (52)

The inference here is not that the mythic probings of a creator-God were fruitless, but that they have led, finally, to the prospect not of a 'plain' God 'out there', but of a 'dark' God, 'inexplicable' and 'in here'. One senses in these lines not merely a metaphorical shift in 'direction' but a fundamental shift in ethos from an irony characteristic of the mythic poems such as 'The Island' to a posture of genuine relaxation, even surrender, a movement from the active to the passive, from a muscular intellectual ordering to a more accepting humility.[3]

As I have already indicated, Thomas's depictions of the *via negativa* are primarily concerned with the experience of absence rather than with the technique of asceticism. Although he does write of the ascetic's approach to deity, most notably in 'The Flower' and 'Sea Watching', both from *Laboratories of the Spirit* (1975), *Frequencies* is a record of the *via negativa* primarily as experience. This is not to say that Thomas's search for a theistic or relational God is frustrated but, rather, that it results in the paradoxical affirmation of absence as the predominant experience of divine presence. While 'Via Negativa' from *H'm* is probably the single most explicit elucidation by Thomas of that experience of divinity as absence, its echoes go on to pervade the poems of *Frequencies*. For example, we have seen already how in 'Via Negativa' the presence of divinity becomes predicated upon signs of its absence. This motif begins to predominate in the poems from *Frequencies*. In the first stanza of 'The Possession' Thomas writes:

> He is a religious man.
> How often I have heard him say,
> looking around him with his worried eyes
> at the emptiness: There must be something. (33)

While these lines reflect an outward probing characteristic of the mythic poems, the protagonist's experience of 'the emptiness' shows the *via negativa* clearly at work. In particular, while the illocutionary force of the statement 'There must be something' is indicative of despair, that is, of a realisation that, indeed, there *is* nothing, it may also be read as the affirmative corollary to the experience of 'the emptiness' which directly precedes it. According to this latter reading, the exclamation 'There must be something' can be taken literally. It is possible and, given the poem 'Via Negativa', very probable that the experience of emptiness in these lines is, in part and paradoxically, a catalyst to the affirmation of '*something*' in the final phrase. Similarly, in the poem 'Abercuawg' Thomas writes:

> An absence is how we become surer
> of what we want. (26)

Thomas's play on the word 'want' in these lines indicates it to signify both 'desire' and 'lack', and by this expansion he seems to be suggesting that the experience of absence is not only the way in which 'we become surer' of what we desire and what we need, but that, in a paradoxical way, it is precisely the absence which makes those objects real. They exist because they are not. Predating the poem, but co-textual with it, is Thomas's 1976 National Eisteddfod address of the same title in which he expands on this idea, linking it to the creative process:

> Here is no cause for disappointment and despair, but rather a way to come to know better, through its absence, the nature of the place which we seek. How else does a poet create a poem other than by searching for the word which is already in his mind but which has not yet reached his tongue? And only through trying word after word does he finally discover the right one. This is certainly not an example of emptiness, but of becoming. (172)

The comparison here between the poet's search for the word and the poem and the individual's search for God is rich with implication. For Thomas, divinity, like the poem, exists in its absence, somewhere between the mind and the tongue. It is precisely in and through such absence that Thomas claims one comes to know better the nature of that divinity. However, and this is my main point here, like the poem, that 'better knowing' does not emerge to a static passivity, but under the constant pressure of absence, a tension between the mind and tongue according to which the individual seeks relentlessly for an opening, for the right word as it were. In this way the realisation of reality, its dynamic 'becoming', is linked inextricably to the most powerful work of imagination. Thomas does not question the fundamental actuality of the divine or of the poem but, rather, the ability of the individual, through imagination, to realise or create the existence of each according to its absence. This is the root of the paradox out of which the *via negativa* emerges, and I shall turn now to the poems 'Shadows', 'Adjustments' and 'The Absence', all from *Frequencies*, in order to examine it more closely.

Thomas writes in 'Shadows':

> I close my eyes.
> The darkness implies your presence,
> the shadow of your steep mind
> on my world. I shiver in it.
> It is not your light that
> can blind us; it is the splendour
> of your darkness. (25)

It is the narrator's rejection of the sensory world in line 1 which creates the darkness in which presence becomes immediately implied so that shadow, an important motif in Thomas's poetry, becomes suddenly blinding by its splendour. This of course is paradoxical – the blinding splendour of shadow – blinding not by obscurity but by splendour or brightness. Shadow is in fact both the product of light and its opposite, that is, blocked light or darkness. In these lines, however, that blocked light retains, paradoxically, the radiance of its source. Meaning here overflows language. Thomas continues:

> And so I listen
> instead and hear the language
> of silence, the sentence
> without an end. (25)

These lines too find their centre in apparent contradiction. Just as in the first quotation light dwells in darkness, here sound exists in silence. It becomes clear that the discourse of the *via negativa* is one in which words are continually denied their usual associations, in which language itself is 'broken open' to accommodate the possibility of its opposite value in paradox, a clear parallel to Derridean *différance*.

The poem 'Adjustments' reiterates this idea, central to the *via negativa*, in its opening lines:

> Never known as anything
> but an absence, I dare not name him
> as God. (29)

Here we find not only a breaking open of language into paradox but an actual mistrust of language by the narrator as an inadequate signifier of meaning. The poem's title, 'Adjustments', is, in part, a reference to this inadequacy of language and the need to relinquish a more traditional or 'logocentric' understanding of the word. Ben Astley, in his 1998 article '"Somewhere Between Faith and Doubt": R. S. Thomas and the Poetry of Theology Deconstructed', sees this 'breaking open' of language as a manifestation in Thomas's work of 'Derridean deconstruction' in which 'the free-play of the sign destroys any attempt to reduce or restrict the associations of the sign' (77). While this seems true, it should be noted that in the discourse of the *via negativa* the word becomes an approximation, often more accurate in its cataloguing of what a thing, in this case deity, is *not*, rather than of what a thing *is*. The 'free-play of the sign' is indeed achieved, but within a negative context. This alarming re-interpretation of the function of language can be viewed not only as a challenge to the 'tyranny' of the word, freeing meaning from the constriction of a rigid signifier, but as a movement by Thomas towards a moral stance of receptive humility. For example, he writes:

> Patiently with invisible structures
> he builds, and as patiently
> we must pray, surrendering the ordering
> of the ingredients to a wisdom that
> is beyond our own. We must change the mood
> to the passive.

These lines assert the need for a changed stance in relation to both language and philosophy, a stance open to meaning as transcendent of the word and of the reason, meaning as overflowing vocabulary and logic, not to be dictated by the wilful administrations of language and rationality but, rather, received, accepted as larger than both. The movement here is towards a mystical or intuitive awareness as superior to a purely rationalistic understanding. Thomas is emphasising in these poems what he calls in 'Via Negativa' 'the interstices / In our knowledge', that is, the 'gaps' in a rational understanding, not necessarily as a hindrance, but as the actual path towards an increased awareness of deity, a 'knowledge' which defies the expressive capabilities of language. The 'interstices' of 'Via Negativa' become the 'invisible structures' of 'Adjustments'.

This emphasis on absence as presence, on the inability of language to encompass meaning fully, and on the failures of rationalistic thought to comprehend the divine are all, finally, the subject of the poem 'The Absence'. Thomas writes:

> It is this great absence
> that is like a presence, that compels
> me to address it without hope
> of a reply. (48)

Here again, we find Thomas's opening statement to be an affirmation of
the *via negativa*. Linked to this affirmation we find a corresponding mistrust of language by the poet. Not only does the experience of divinity
as absence warn Thomas against hoping for a 'reply' to his address, thus
further acclimatising him to the medium of silence, but twice in these
lines Thomas refers to deity as 'it', further evidence that, for him, language must fail in its most fundamental purpose of naming. He goes on
to elongate the description of absence in these lines into the image of an
empty room:

> It is a room I enter
>
> from which someone has just
> gone, the vestibule the arrival
> of one who has not yet come.

Again, in contrast to the mythic poems, absence in these lines is depicted
not as 'out there', in realms of space, but 'in here', as an interior and
domestic absence, like 'a room I enter'. In keeping with that image, the
hoped-for divinity in these lines, while still anthropomorphised, is
imaged as relational, as someone who has just left or who has yet to
arrive, as an intimate self or relation of the self. This interiority of absence,
and intimacy of a longed-for divinity, are further indications of Thomas's
shift in these *via negativa* poems from a predominantly deistic understanding of an exterior creator-God, to a predominantly theistic understanding of an interior 'ground of being'. Thomas goes on in 'The
Absence' to implicate both language and science as incapable of 'invert-
ing' the paradox of the *via negativa*:

> I modernise the anachronism
>
> of my language, but he is no more here
> than before. Genes and molecules
> have no more power to call
> him up ...
>
> My equations fail
> as my words do.

In these lines scientific knowledge fails as a 'corrective' to the paradoxical nature of the *via negativa*, that is, science fails to make absence *as* absence and presence *as* presence. In the face of scientific advancements towards an expanded knowledge of 'genes', 'molecules', and 'equations', the paradox of the *via negativa* persists. What Thomas seems to be suggesting in 'The Absence' is, first, that deity exists; second, that it can be posited and apprehended on the basis of its absence; and, third, that it continually overflows the rational confines of both language and science. Ultimately, these recurring characteristics of the *via negativa* are employed by Thomas effectively to undermine the exclusivity of rational thought as a ruling discourse by affirming the necessity, at least regarding the search for deity, of a mystical approach and an intuited understanding. The final statement of 'The Absence' is explicit in its expression of this:

> What resources have I
> other than the emptiness without him of my whole
> being, a vacuum he may not abhor?

The question is, of course, rhetorical, Thomas's answer being 'none'. Where language and science fail as 'resources' in the narrator's search for divinity, there remains only the experience of emptiness and the inference of an imagined fullness which can be drawn from it. In the poem's final line Thomas plays on the notion that 'nature abhors a vacuum' by holding up the tension, central to the *via negativa* position, between the enduring existence of that vacuum and yet, according to this 'law', the immanent filling of the vacuum by presence. Thus, the *via negativa*, for Thomas, balances between the emptiness of absence and the fullness of expectation. And it is within that carefully balanced tension and its engendered waiting 'on that lean / threshold, neither outside nor in' that, according to the *via negativa* experience, deity is finally located (10). Such waiting in tension is in keeping with the Kierkegaardian existentialism often associated with Thomas. For example, D. Z. Phillips, in his book *R. S. Thomas: Poet of the Hidden God* (1986), argues that the poet, after rejecting, like Hume's Philo, the 'Argument from Design' for God's existence, embraces in the *via negativa* not only an existentialist angst but an existentialist freedom as well:

> We come to God through a *via negativa*, by coming to see that the
> nature of his will is born not of an external system which gives a
> point to everything, but of a radical pointlessness in things. It is

precisely because there is no reason why things should go as they
do in life that there is a possibility of seeing all things as acts of grace
… It is not by seeking explicit answers, but by seeing why such
answers must be hidden, died to, that the possibility of belief in a
God who is present in all things emerges. (82)

Not only is such 'dying' to a need for answers a characteristically existentialist position held by Thomas, it is at just this point of dying, and by
way of such dying, that patience, stillness, and waiting become, for
Thomas, the keys to an interior freedom, to a 'grace' which Phillips calls
'the givenness of things under a religious aspect' (87).

It is important to note that, for Thomas, depictions of absence associated with the *via negativa* frequently give way to, or are countered by,
depictions of affirmation and spiritual presence. J. P. Ward writes that
'The God who eludes when all palpable things, even the senses themselves, are left behind, can suddenly be experienced in what is immediate and natural' (1987: 98).

Remembering Elaine Shepherd's description of the *via negativa* as
'a darkness which may on occasion … flame with love', I will end this
chapter by turning to examine such 'occasions' in Thomas's work, and
by suggesting that they constitute, by their increasing frequency, the
most recent 'phase' in the poet's spiritual journey (1996: 186). At the
same time that Thomas expands the category of 'religious poetry' to
include spiritual doubt and the experience of absence, he also, albeit
more quietly perhaps, makes his returns in the religious poems to a very
traditional and, in many ways, Celtic spirituality of affirmation and presence. Esther De Waal, in her book *Celtic Light: A Tradition Rediscovered*
(1997), underscores what she sees as a major characteristic of that spirituality. Writing of her experience of viewing the Celtic high crosses at
Monasterboice, Ireland, she writes:

I was being confronted here for the first time with a starkly dramatic statement of what I was to find time and again as I came to
understand better the Celtic way of seeing the world: this ability to
hold things together. (7)

Later in the book she adds that

David Jones once said that the favourite phrase for any artist must
be that of psalm 122 where Jerusalem is described as a city 'at
unity in itself', and he added that in Welsh that word translates
as interjoining, the crafting between the whole and the parts.
(135)

Together these two observations articulate an idea which I have already suggested is a central theme for R. S. Thomas: the struggle for whole-ness. While critics often and rightly focus on the characteristic angst of Thomas's poems, on their stark realism and level, unflinching gaze, and while it is true that such angst is produced, in part at least, by the disparity between that realism and an ideal vision, this emphasis on realism risks ignoring the poet's 'ability to hold things together', his 'crafting between the whole and the parts'. Especially in the religious poems, Thomas not only explores the secular in its *relation* to the sacred, but succeeds in re-contextualising the secular *within* the sacred. He is at pains in the poetry as a whole, but in particular in the religious poetry, to express the beauty and wholeness of the world as well as its brokenness and division, the redemption of humankind as well as its demise, belonging as well as alienation. Moreover, for Thomas, these opposites are often to be found within each other as elements in a larger whole. This idea of wholeness forms the foundation for A. M. Allchin's important book *Praise Above All: Discovering the Welsh Tradition* (1991). Like De Waal, Allchin (himself a Thomas scholar) also claims that at the heart of much Celtic poetry, both old and new, is

> a protest against a whole Christian culture, Latin and to some degree Greek, which rather sharply divides sacred from secular, priestly from poetic, grace from nature and God from humanity, on behalf of a world view which sees these things as very closely inter-related in ways which sometimes fascinate us and sometimes disconcert us. (10)

Such interrelation, although seemingly paradoxical, is rarely contradictory within this wider frame of reference to an ancient world-view in which the material and the spiritual were one. The creation of art, for Thomas, is nothing less than the fruit of this ancient impulse and struggle to knit two worlds together, to reconcile reality and the dream into a synthesis of wholeness.[4] Although that impulse and struggle may seem to form a quieter subtext in the poems, it is also foundational to them, a characterisitc which Thomas inherits more recently from Blake, and one which he shares with his contemporary Dylan Thomas.[5] All three poets depict the possibility of the physical and spiritual regeneration of the modern world through the realisation and application of a vision in which the dualities and divisions they perceive in contemporary urban or industrial life are re-incorporated through imagination and art into an original whole. R. S. Thomas is not only a poet who poses bleak dilemmas but one who, at times, offers 'answers' to those dilemmas which are characterised by an ancient simplicity, and which seek, ultimately, to reconstruct the world by 'crafting between the whole and parts'. In this, as well as in his continual affirmation of the practice of silence and waiting, Thomas makes his returns in poetry to a spiritual grounding which enables him, especially in the later poems, to voice an increasing resiliency and hope.[6]

The poem 'Groping' (*Frequencies*, 1978), which I have pointed to already as indicative of a shift towards interior explorations of deity as a 'ground of being', is a good example of the *via negativa* experience giving way to an experience of presence. In the poem's second stanza Thomas describes the inward search for divinity:

> For some
> it is all darkness; for me too,
> it is dark. (12)

While this is a classic description by Thomas of the *via negativa* experience, he goes on to complete the stanza, and the poem, with a qualification of the experience of darkness as punctuated by experiences of presence:

> But there are hands
> there I can take, voices to hear
> solider than the echoes
> without. And sometimes a strange light
> shines, purer than the moon,
> casting no shadow.

The images employed in these lines stand in direct contrast to the images we have already examined in the poem 'Via Negativa'. Here, absence is replaced by hands, silence by voices 'solider than the echoes / without', darkness by 'a strange light' which casts no shadow. In contrast to the *blocked* light, the paradoxically radiant dark, to take up Vaughan's image again, of the poem 'Shadows', here we find the light is pure, unimpeded, presence not as absence but as itself, as Thomas emerges from the mere inference of deity through absence to its actual realisation. We find this same kind of epiphanous presence depicted in 'The Answer', also from *Frequencies*:

> There have been times
> when, after long on my knees
> in a cold chancel, a stone has rolled
> from my mind, and I have looked

in and seen the old questions lie
folded and in a place
by themselves, like the piled
graveclothes of love's risen body. (46)

The phrase 'There have been times' clearly indicates that the experience of spiritual presence, of 'love's risen body' is recurring for the
poet. What I want to emphasise here, however, is not merely its repetitive nature, but that the experience of presence here, as in 'Groping',
comes 'after long on my knees', that is, as the culmination of a *via
negativa* experience. Like Thomas's experiences of deity in nature,
which I have examined in Chapter 4, these *affirmativa* experiences are
punctuations, recurring flashes of light in which, as Thomas describes
it in an allusion to Christ's resurrection in John 20.1–10, 'a stone has
rolled from [the] mind'. In this interiorisation of the resurrection experience it is the 'old questions' rather than the graveclothes of the risen
Christ which 'lie / folded and in a place / by themselves'. According
to this configuration, Thomas's philosophical dilemmas concerning
divinity have not ceased *per se* but, rather, have been punctured, effectively deflated in their significance by the poet's experience of 'love's
risen body'. The nature of that experience remains undisclosed, a mystical experience which, again, defies the expressive capacities of language rooted in sense experience.

Via affirmativa: Destinations and arrival

New directions are nearly always subtle and difficult to pinpoint in R.
S. Thomas's work. He was a poet who worked his field, constantly
making his returns, going slowly back over the old ground, relentlessly
working and reworking the new into the old, producing shades, echoes,
reflections. It is important to view Thomas's work less in terms of linear
stages of development and more in terms of a deepening and often paradoxical complexity in which seemingly separate 'categories' of poems
enjoy ongoing reciprocities of definition and meaning. Despite this, critics have sometimes sensed turning points in Thomas's work. For example, R. Gerallt Jones, in his review of the volume *Later Poems* (1983),
claims that the poems in the 'New Poems' section of that volume articulate a 'more positive consciousness of a purposeful Creator in the
observable phenomena of the universe as well as in the inner stirrings
of the spirit' (1983: 10). Jones writes that the poems 'record … a new
stage in a spiritual journey', and that 'a new dimension is being added

to the work of a major poet'. While Jones does not describe that 'new
stage' in any detail, he does cite the poem 'Suddenly' which clearly
expresses an intensity of affirmation largely absent from Thomas's work
up to this point:

> He addresses me from a myriad
> directions with the fluency
> of water, the articulateness
> of green leaves; and in the genes,
> too, the components
> of my existence. (201)

Thomas ends the poem, the cadence of which is breathless with presence, with a statement whose solidity of expression and lack of hesita-
tion challenge all preconceived notions of him as the poet merely of
bleak longing:

> I have no need
> to despair; as at
> some second Pentecost
> of a Gentile, I listen to the things
> round me: weeds, stones, instruments,
> the machine itself, all
> speaking to me in the vernacular
> of the purposes of One who is.

Similar evidence for the emergence of a more positive philosophical
stance in Thomas's work might be discerned from the poems 'Caller' and
'Arrival', also from *Later Poems*.

In contrast to Jones's emphasis on *Later Poems*, A. M. Allchin, in
his article 'Emerging: A Look at Some of R. S. Thomas' More Recent
Poems' (1992), argues that it is not *Later* Poems but the 1975 volume
Laboratories of the Spirit which represents a new strain of affirmation.
Allchin cites primarily the poems 'Emerging' and 'Good', while suggesting traces of affirmation as early as *H'm* (1972). But again, such
instances of affirmation in Thomas's work prior to 1985 remain rela-
tively isolated and largely uncharacteristic. What Allchin's reading does
re-affirm is that 'shifts' in Thomas's work are more often subtle and
gradual. Although *Later Poems* (1983) and *Laboratories of the Spirit*
(1975) do indicate the beginnings of a shift in Thomas's experience,
they primarily foreshadow an affirmation which finds its fullest expression in the 1985 collection *Destinations*. Gathered in *Destinations* is the

most substantial and explicit evidence of a gradual shift towards affirmation in Thomas's work. An exploration of that shift is vital to an
understanding of the sometimes complex development of Thomas's
poetic vision. In his 1993 article 'An Inexplicable Note of Hope',
Allchin rightly suggests that, while Thomas's work is commonly
renowned for pessimism and distress, such a view fails to realise the complexity of both the man and the work. He writes that

> bleak is one of the most frequently employed words to describe R.
> S. Thomas's vision of the world and our human situation in it …
> But here again we can be too absolute in our judgements. Much of
> what is commonly said about R. S. Thomas's work is true but is not
> the whole truth. (12)

Allchin concludes with the assertion that an

> inexplicable note of hope grows stronger in R. S. Thomas's latest
> poetry. It is never the dominant note, never pushed forward bla-
> tantly in terms of preaching or propaganda, yet it remains obsti-
> nately there. (14)

Such a note of hope, and perhaps more particularly of acceptance,
though it glimmers intermittently between *H'm* (1972) and *Later
Poems* (1983), finds its most unified and powerful expression in
Destinations. In the volumes which follow *Destinations* this expression
of hope and acceptance, though less obviously dominant, more incorporated or 'worked in' to the existing fabric, remains vitally present as
an *ingrained* characteristic. *Destinations* is the neglected mainspring of
this philosophical turning towards affirmation in R. S. Thomas.[7] The
probings that begin with *H'm* are undoubtedly continued in subsequent volumes, but with less urgency, with greater confidence in a presence which, if still at times elusive, is both benevolent and purposeful.
Thomas seems, by *Destinations*, to have evolved spiritually out of
unfathomable space and the predominating experience of absence, not
towards contentment or truce, but clearly into an expanded vision.
That vision creates a gentle lightening of tone in much of the later
poetry, a bleeding off of pressure, a calmness in waiting, out of which
the sometimes paradoxical complexity and richness of much of his later
work has been born.

'The Message', the first poem in *Destinations*, is similar in tone and
attitude to 'Suddenly', cited already as an early expression of a new *via
positiva* or *via affirmativa* approach for Thomas. One can hear the out-
breaking of joy so uncharacteristic of the poet's past work:

> A message from God
> delivered by a bird
> at my window, offering friendship.
> Listen. Such language!
> Who said God was without
> speech? Every word an injection
> to make me smile. (7)

As in 'Suddenly', after long silence God becomes voluble for the poet. It is, of course, Thomas himself who suggests in 'Via Negativa' that God is *without* speech, but here the unequivocal message from God is that life is joy, not momentary or fleeting, but promised and enduring. 'Meet me', the bird continues,

> tomorrow, here
> at the same time and you will remember
> how wonderful today
> was: no pain, no worry;
> irrelevant the mystery if
> unsolved.

Strangely, this is not one of Thomas's interior selves nor even nature speaking, but, indirectly, deity itself, teaching that 'the mystery' is irrelevant, that 'solving' is no longer of paramount importance. God goes on to tell Thomas that his gift as a poet, the 'X-ray eye', was given him not so much to search with but to search with and *to discover* 'the unmalignancy of love's / growth'. The poet is to see into the nature of things, under their surfaces, and find there not absence but love growing in place of disease. Here is a significant development in outlook when one considers that Thomas *is* a poet of search. Here he is instructed to turn aside from that search to vision and discovery.

The metaphor of the bird is central to the poem 'Vocabulary' as well:

> Ruminations, illuminations!
> Vocabulary, sing for me
> in your cage of time,
> restless on the bone's perch.
>
> You are dust; then a bird
> with new feathers, but always
> beating at the mind's bars. (11)

There is a conspicuous, almost alarming, absence of brooding here.
The tone is positive and excited, ruminations giving way to exclamated
illuminations. The poet remains undaunted by 'time's cage' even. The
command is to 'sing' in the face of time's restrictive nature. Like the
phoenix, vocabulary rises from its own dust and previous inadequacy
to a newly feathered bird, resurrected to new life and vigour. In the
conclusion to the poem Thomas calls himself a 'new Noah' and
despatches the bird to alight on 'steel branches'. But instead of using
the image of steel branches as an opening through which to introduce
the long shadow of modern technology or 'the machine', as one might
expect him to, Thomas, as the new Noah, calls the bird home to
himself,

> looking for the metallic
> gleam of a new poem in your bill.

There is no sarcasm in this, no bitter irony, but a surprising integration of the modern scientific world and the poet's visionary world. The
allusion to Noah underscores the death of the old for Thomas,
the 'flooding out' of an older order and, with it, the prospect of new
beginnings.

One of the most powerful poems in the collection, the sonnet titled
'The Other', recounts a less exaggerated though perhaps far deeper
rejoicing by Thomas.[8] The title is a reference to deity characteristic of
Thomas's *via negativa* stance of the 1970s: God is that which is not me
and beyond naming. The poem contains other threads from Thomas's
past work as well. There are the 'lean hours' in line 5 for example, the
monotony of the waves, the village 'without light / and companionless',
and, not least, God's ultimate silence (15). But despite all that, the whole
ethos of the poem is one of peace and presence. In the still night the poet
hears the small owl calling far off, and the miles-distant bark of the fox.
He lies awake listening

> to the swell born somewhere in the Atlantic
> rising and falling, rising and falling
> wave on wave on the long shore
> by the village, that is without light
> and companionless.

These distant voices, heard in the dark stillness, are the voices of a
presence which, for Thomas, are almost always apprehended in the
rhythms of the natural world. One notices the almost hypnotic repetition of present participial verbs in combination with the relentless

heave of the sea: calling, barking, listening, rising, falling, rising, falling, wave on wave. It is from out of these rhythms that Thomas arrives at the turning point, the *volta*, the epiphany of the poem in which he realises

> that other being who is awake, too,
> letting our prayers break on him,
> not like this for a few hours,
> but for days, years, for eternity.

Here, in the final four lines, the poem moves away from the natural to incorporate the divine and the human. Prayer becomes a part of the natural rhythm too, in league with the cry of the beasts and the crash of the surf, and endlessly acceptable to God. Thomas's sympathy for the song of nature becomes God's unsleeping sympathy for the song of nature, not the least part of which is now the prayer of humanity. Indeed, unity between Thomas, God, and nature has become a recurring motif in these poems. In 'The Message' God and Thomas 'connect' by way of the bird. In 'Vocabulary' the 'new Noah' emerges from floods of the spirit to receive poems from the bill of a vocabulary that was once dust, turned yet again into a feathered envoy from God. Now, in 'The Other', that unity comes to include God, nature, and not only Thomas himself but all humanity at prayer. It is '*our* prayers' that break on God in line 12.

In 'He and She' and 'Mother and Child' Thomas goes on to explore the more particular unity of human love. In 'He and She' the close physical proximity of the two characters develops quickly into a spiritual intimacy that is itself a reflection of something eternal. Thomas encapsulates that gradually deepening presence in the five lines which begin the poem:

> When he came in, she was there.
> When she looked at him,
> he smiled. There were lights
> in time's wave breaking
> on an eternal shore. (23)

Here is an image of the meeting of time and eternity similar to the endless breaking of 'our prayers' on God in 'The Other'. Again in these lines, time is giving way to eternity under the influence of love. Through a crafted metaphor in the second stanza the man and woman converse noiselessly:

> Thoughts mingling
> were lit up, gold
> particles in the mind's stream.

But perhaps most startling is stanza three, in which Thomas describes the nature of human love as contingent not only upon an aggressive initiative by one but, equally, upon a willing reception of those advances by the other. One finds in the final line that the lovers have previously known failure in their repeated attempts to cross the treacherous 'fathoms' of the heart. Thomas highlights by this image of dangerous depths the delicacy of the love relationship, but also, and most importantly here, the poignancy and power of its success:

> Were there currents between them?
> Why, when he thought darkly,
> would the nerves play
> at her lips' brim? What was the heart's depth?
> There were fathoms in her,
> too, and sometimes he crossed
> them and landed and was not repulsed.

'He and She' demonstrates not only a keen insight into the precarious nature of human love but an equally keen awareness of its heroic possibility. That same optimism is confirmed again in 'Mother and Child', a portrait of human love before

> that angled
> event that from beyond
> the horizon puts its roots
>
> down. (26)

Despite the potent threat of impending evil in the 'breast's apple' for which the child reaches, and in the sleeping snake, this is not indulgence in a dream of some mythical past prior to sin. Thomas claims in the poem that 'this is Eden / over again', allowing a reading of the poem as an instance of momentary innocence, of temporary purity and of the infinitely repeatable victory, even if fleeting, of love over division and of innocence over corruption. Each of these poems has, as its underlying theme, the nature of relationship, that is, the state of extensions and connections between humanity, nature, and God. This in itself is not new to Thomas's work. But where previously the state of those relations for

Thomas was predominantly elusive and broken, and the poetry a cry in desperation or anger emanating from that brokenness, the poems in *Destinations* reflect a definite healing of the wound. There is little desperation or anger here, little blindness and searching. These poems concern a wider vision of the connections between humanity, nature, and God which were once so acutely obscure, a return to wholeness, a 'crafting between the whole and the parts', a sanctification of the secular, a knitting together of worlds. More than that, they are expressions of the very invincibility of these relationships, making the collection as a whole strangely redolent of new hope.

Notes

1 Justin Wintle in his study of Thomas, *Furious Interiors* (1996), suggests not only that *Honest to God* is a 'useful introduction to contemporary Anglican thought' but that it also 'indicates the extent to which R. S. Thomas's "personal" search for God has been undertaken within a definable theological context' (415).

2 This in contrast to Buuren, who sees the mythic poems as Thomas's deliberate attempt to 'do away for ever with the theistic God, who simply cannot be the way people traditionally believe he is' (1993: 110). While clearly Thomas *is* expanding in a radical way more traditional images of deity, to see the mythic poems merely as a means of destroying the old to make way for the new seems to deny them, and the religious poems as a whole, a deeper complexity as multidimensional and paradoxical manifestations, simultaneously ironic and sincere, destroying and amalgamating.

3 Echoing this point, R. L. Brett, in his book *Faith and Doubt: Religion and Secularisation in Literature from Wordsworth to Larkin* (1997), indicates a similar shift in emphasis in contemporary religious sensibility from merely exterior forms of devotion to just such an interior and contemplative exploration, from spiritual stasis, as it were, to spiritual development, from religion as 'received' or even 'achieved' truth, to an emphasis on spiritual search characterised by uncertainty and even existential angst (157–8).

4 For a more detailed argument on this point see my article 'Reality and the Dream in the Recent Poetry of R. S. Thomas' *New Welsh Review* 44, (spring 1999).

5 This practice of subjective artistic unification was central to the so-called 'New Apocalypse' poets of the 1940s who took their name from D. H. Lawrence's *Apocalypse* (1939), a 'radical critique of cultural and religious orthodoxy', and whose principal practitioner was Dylan Thomas (Stringer 1996: 485).

6 Buuren discusses Thomas's religious poetry as reflective of ascending stages of prayer, from dialogue to monologue to, finally, silence and waiting as 'the ultimate alternative' (1993: 140–1).

7 Such neglect is due, at least in part, to the fact that *Destinations* was issued in a special, limited edition of only three hundred copies by the Celandine Press. The volume went, and continues to go, virtually unnoticed amongst critics, who have taken to the more obvious volumes of Thomas's Rhiw period, such as

    Experimenting with an Amen (1986) and *The Echoes Return Slow* (1988), and yet
    the exquisite production of the book and Thomas's republication of many of the
    poems in later collections both indicate *Destinations* to be a work of some impor-
    tance for the poet.
 8 'The Other', while perhaps most widely known by its later inclusion in Thomas's
    1988 collection *The Echoes Return Slow*, was originally published in *Destinations.*

Bibliography

Works by R. S. Thomas
Poetry collections

1946: *The Stones of the Field.* Carmarthen: The Druid Press Limited, 1946.
1952: *An Acre of Land.* Newtown: Montgomeryshire Printing Co. Ltd, 1952.
1955: *Song at the Year's Turning.* London: Rupert Hart-Davis, 1965.
1958: *Poetry for Supper.* London: Rupert Hart-Davis, 1967.
1961: *Tares.* London: Hart-Davis, 1961.
1963: *The Bread of Truth.* London: Rupert Hart-Davis, 1963.
1966: *Pieta.* London: Rupert Hart-Davis, 1966.
1968: *Not that He Brought Flowers.* London: Rupert Hart-Davis, 1969.
1972: *H'm.* London: Macmillan London Limited, 1972.
1972: *Young and Old.* London: Chatto & Windus Ltd, 1972.
1973: *Selected Poems 1946–1968.* London: Hart-Davis, 1973.
1974: *What Is a Welshman?* Llandybie: C. Davis, 1974.
1975: *Laboratories of the Spirit.* London: Macmillan London Limited, 1975.
1977: *The Way of It.* South Shields: Ceolfrith Press, 1977.
1978: *Frequencies.* London: Macmillan London Limited, 1978.
1981: *Between Here and Now.* London: Macmillan London Limited, 1981.
1983: *Later Poems.* London: Macmillan London Limited, 1983.
1985: *Destinations.* Shipston-on-Stour: The Celandine Press, 1985.
1985: *Ingrowing Thoughts.* Bridgend: Poetry Wales Press, 1985.
1986: *Experimenting with an Amen.* London: Papermac, 1986.
1987: *Welsh Airs.* Bridgend: Poetry Wales Press Ltd, 1987.
1988: *The Echoes Return Slow.* London: Macmillan London Limited, 1988.
1990: *Counterpoint.* Newcastle upon Tyne: Bloodaxe Books Ltd, 1990.
1992: *Frieze.* Schondorf am Ammersee: Babel, 1992.
1992: *Mass for Hard Times.* Newcastle-upon-Tyne: Bloodaxe Books Ltd, 1992.
1993: *Collected Poems 1945–1990.* London: J. M. Dent, 1993.
1995: *No Truce with the Furies.* Newcastle-upon-Tyne: Bloodaxe Books Ltd, 1995.
1997: *Six Poems.* Shipston-on-Stour: The Celandine Press, 1997.

Prose work and editorial

1945: 'The Depopulation of the Welsh Hill Country'. *R. S. Thomas Selected Prose*, ed. Sandra Anstey. Bridgend: Poetry Wales Press, 1986.

1961: *The Batsford Book of Country Verse*, ed. R. S. Thomas. London: B. T. Batsford Ltd, 1961.

1963: *The Penguin Book of Religious Verse*, ed. R. S. Thomas. Harmondsworth: Penguin Books Ltd, 1963.

1964: 'Words and the Poet'. *R. S. Thomas Selected Prose*, ed. Sandra Anstey. Bridgend: Poetry Wales Press, 1986.

1966: 'A Frame for Poetry'. *R. S. Thomas: Selected Prose*, ed. Sandra Anstey. Bridgend: Poetry Wales Press, 1986.

1968: 'The Mountains'. *R. S. Thomas: Selected Prose*, ed. Sandra Anstey. Bridgend: Poetry Wales Press, 1986.

1969: 'The Making of a Poem'. *R. S. Thomas: Selected Prose*, ed. Sandra Anstey. Bridgend: Poetry Wales Press, 1986.

1972: *Y Llwybrau Gynt (Former Paths)*, ed. and trans. Jason Walford Davies. *R. S. Thomas: Autobiographies*. London: J. M. Dent, 1997: 1–17.

1974: 'Where Do We Go from Here?'. *R. S. Thomas: Selected Prose*, ed. Sandra Anstey. Bridgend: Poetry Wales Press, 1986.

1976: 'Abercuawg'. *R. S. Thomas: Selected Prose*, ed. Sandra Anstey. Bridgend: Poetry Wales Press, 1986.

1978: 'The Creative Writer's Suicide'. *R. S. Thomas: Selected Prose*, ed. Sandra Anstey. Bridgend: Poetry Wales, 1986.

1984: 'A Thicket in Lleyn'. *Britain: A World by Itself.* London: Arum Press Limited, 1984.

1985: *Neb (No-one,* ed. and trans. Jason Walford Davies. *R. S. Thomas: Autobiographies.* London: J. M. Dent, 1997.

1986: 'Autobiographical Essay'. *Miraculous Simplicity: Essays on R. S. Thomas,* ed. William V. Davis. Fayetteville: University of Arkansas Press, 1993.

1988: 'Undod' (Unity). *Planet,* August/September 1988: 29–43.

1990a: *Blwyddyn yn Lleyn (A Year in Lleyn)*, ed. and trans. Jason Walford Davies. *R. S. Thomas: Autobiographies.* London: J. M. Dent, 1997.

1990b: 'Probings'. *Planet, The Welsh Internationalist* 80 (1990): 28–52.

1992: *Cymru or Wales?*, ed. Meic Stephens. Llandysul: Gomer Press, 1992.

1995: *ABC Neb*, ed. Jason Walford Davies. Caernarfon: Gwasg Gwynedd, 1995.

Selected poems, documentaries, and interviews

1949: 'Welsh Shepherd'. *The Dublin Magazine* 24 (1949): 5.

1972: Ormond, John. 'R. S. Thomas: Priest and Poet'. Film transcript. *Poetry Wales* 7 (1972): 49–57.

1983: *R. S. Thomas at Seventy.* BBC Radio 3 Broadcast, 7 December
    1983. See text in M. J. J. van Buuren, *Waiting: The Religious
    Poetry of Ronald Stuart Thomas.* University of Nijgmegen, 1993:
    172–81.
1991: *The South Bank Show Part Two: The Poetry and Life of R. S.
    Thomas.* HTV Wales, London, 17 February 1991.

Other works cited

Ackerman, John. 'Man & Nature in the Poetry of R. S. Thomas'. *Poetry
    Wales* 7 (1972): 15–26.
——. *Welsh Dylan: Dylan Thomas's Life, Writing and His Wales.* Bridgend:
    Poetry Wales Press Ltd, 1998.
Allchin, A. M. 'An Inexplicable Note of Hope'. *New Welsh Review* 20
    (1993): 10–14.
——. 'Emerging: A Look at Some of R. S. Thomas' More Recent Poems'.
    Critical Writings on R. S. Thomas, ed. Sandra Anstey. Bridgend: Seren,
    1992.
——. *Praise Above All: Discovering the Welsh Tradition.* Cardiff: University
    of Wales Press, 1991.
Anstey, Sandra. 'Some Uncollected Poems and Variant Readings from the
    Early Works of R. S. Thomas'. *The Page's Drift: R. S. Thomas at Eighty,*
    ed. M. Wynn Thomas. Bridgend: Poetry Wales Press, 1993.
Aquinas, St Thomas. *Summa Theologiae,* XLV 2a2ae 171–8. London:
    Blackfriars, 1970.
Astley, Ben. '"Somewhere Between Faith and Doubt": R. S. Thomas and
    the Poetry of Theology Deconstructed'. *Welsh Writing in English,* 4
    (1998): 74–93.
Barker, Simon. 'Revisiting the Sources: R. S. Thomas and the Redress of
    Poetry'. *Fire as Green as Grass,* ed. Belinda Humhprey, Landysul:
    Gomer Press, 1995.
Beam, Philip C. *Winslow Homer.* New York: McGraw Hill Inc., 1975.
Bentley, Paul. *The Poetry of Ted Hughes: Language, Illusion & Beyond.*
    London: Addison, Wesley Longman Limited, 1988.
Bowen, Euros. *Euros Bowen: Priest-Poet,* ed. Cynthia and Saunders Davies.
    trans. Euros Bowen and Cynthia Davies. Penarth: Church in Wales
    Publications, 1993.
Brett, R. L. *Faith and Doubt: Religion and Secularisation in Literature from
    Wordsworth to Larkin.* Cambridge: James Clarke & Co, 1997.
Brown, George Mackay. *Selected Poems 1954–1992.* London: John Murray,
    1996.
Brown, Tony. '"Over Seventy Thousand Fathoms": The Sea and Self-defi-
    nition in the Poetry of R. S. Thomas'. *The Page's Drift: R. S. Thomas
    at Eighty,* ed. M. Wynn Thomas, Bridgend: Poetry Wales Press Ltd,
    1993.
Buuren, M. J. J. van. *Waiting: The Religious Poetry of Ronald Stuart Thomas,
    Welsh Priest and Poet.* University of Nijmegen, 1993.

Castay, Marie-Thérèse. 'The Self and the Other: The Autobiographical Element in the Poetry of R. S. Thomas'. *The Page's Drift: R. S. Thomas at Eighty*, ed. M. Wynn Thomas, Bridgend: Poetry Wales Press Ltd, 93.

Christ, Carol T., *Victorian and Modern Poetics*. London: The University of Chicago Press, 1984.

Conran, Anthony. *The Cost of Strangeness: Essays on the English Poets of Wales*. Llandysul: Gomer Press, 1982.

——.'R. S. Thomas as a Mystical Poet'. *Poetry Wales* 4 (1979): 11–25.

Crotty, Patrick. '"Lean Parishes": Patrick Kavanagh's "The Great Hunger" and R. S. Thomas's "The Minister". *Dangerous Diversity: The Changing Faces of Wales*, ed. Katie Gramich and Andrew Hiscock. Cardiff: University of Wales Press, 1998: 131–49.

Darwin, Charles. *The Origin of Species*. Oxford: Oxford University Press, 1996.

Davies, Jason Walford. '"Thick Ambush of Shadows": Allusions to Welsh Literature in the Work of R. S. Thomas'. *Welsh Writing in English*. 1 (1995): 75–127.

Davies, John. *A History of Wales*. London: Penguin Books, 1990.

Davis, William V. '"At the Foot of the Precipice of Water ... Sea Shapes Coming to Celebration": R. S. Thomas and Kierkegaard'. *Welsh Writing in English* 4 (1998): 94–117.

De Waal, Esther. *Celtic Light: A Tradition Rediscovered*. London: Harper Collins, 1997.

Dunn, Douglas. 'Language and Liberty'. *The Faber Book of Twentieth Century Scottish Poetry*, ed. Douglas Dunn. London: Faber and Faber Limited, 1992: xvii–xlvi.

Eliot, T. S. *Collected Poems 1909–1962*. London: Faber and Faber Limited, 1974.

——.*Essays Ancient and Modern*. New York: Harcourt, Brace, 1936.

——.*The Varieties of Metaphysical Poetry*, ed. Ronald Schuchard. London: Faber and Faber, 1993.

Emerson, Ralph Waldo. *Essays and Lectures*. New York: Library of America, 1983.

Gregson, Ian. 'An Exhausted Tradition'. *New Welsh Review*, 27 (1994): 22–23.

Griffiths, Bryn. 'A Note for R. S. Thomas'. *Poetry Wales* 1 (1965): 23.

Gwenallt.'The Earth', trans. Dyfnallt Morgan. *The Oxford Book of Welsh Verse in English*, ed. Gwyn Jones. Oxford: Oxford University Press, 1977: 200–1.

Gwilym, Dafydd ap. *Poems*, ed. Rachel Bromwich. Llandysul: Gomer Press, 1982.

Heaney, Seamus. *Death of a Naturalist*. London: Faber and Faber, 1966.

——.*Door into the Dark*. London: Faber and Faber, 1969.

——.*Preoccupations: Selected Prose 1968–1978*. London: Faber and Faber, 1980.

——.*The Redress of Poetry Oxford Lectures*. London: Faber and Faber, 1995.

Herbert, George. *The Works of George Herbert*, ed. F. E. Hutchinson. Oxford: Clarendon Press, 1972.

Hooker, Jeremy. 'R. S. Thomas: Prytherch and After'. *The Presence of the Past: Essays on Modern British and American Poetry*. Bridgend: Poetry Wales Press, 1987.

Hopkins, Gerard Manley. *The Poetical Works of Gerard Manley Hopkins*, ed. Norman H. Mackenzie. Oxford: Clarendon Press, 1990.

Hughes, Ted. *Crow*. London: Faber and Faber, 1970

——. *The Hawk in the Rain*. London: Faber and Faber, 1957.

——. *Lupercal*. London: Faber and Faber, 1960.

——. hardcover jacket commentary for *Collected Poems 1945–1990* by R. S. Thomas. London: J. M. Dent, 1993.

Humfrey, Belinda. 'The Gap in the Hedge: R. S. Thomas's Emblem Poetry'. *Miraculous Simplicity: Essays on R. S. Thomas*, ed. William V. Davis. Fayetteville: University of Arkansas Press, 1993.

James, William. *The Varieties of Religious Experience*. London: Collier-Macmillan Ltd, 1961.

Jones, Ceri, and Rian Evans. 'Best Known Poems that Beat Dylan Thomas and Orwell'. *Western Mail*, 23 April 1999: 13.

Jones, Gwyn, ed. *The Oxford Book of Welsh Verse in English*. Oxford: Oxford University Press, 1977.

Jones, R. Gerallt. 'Later Poems'. *Book News / Llais Llyfrau* (autumn 1983): 9–10.

Jung, C. G. *Memories, Dreams, Reflections*, ed. Aniela Jaffe, trans. Richard and Clara Winston. London: Random House, Inc., 1963.

Keats, John. 'To George and Thomas Keats', 21 December 1817. Letter 32 of *Letters of John Keats*, ed. Frederick Page. London: Oxford University Press, 1954: 51–4.

Kierkegaard, Soren. *Either/Or: A Fragment of Life*. London: Penguin Books, 1992.

Langbaum, Robert. *The Poetry of Experience*. New York: W. W. Norton and Company Inc., 1957.

Lloyd, David. 'Through the Looking Glass: R. S. Thomas's *The Echoes Return Slow* as Poetic Autobiography'. *Twentieth Century Literature* 42 (1996): 438–51.

MacCaig, Norman. *The World's Room*. London: The Hogarth Press, 1974.

Macleod, Fiona. *The Winged Destiny: Studies in the Spiritual History of the Gael*. London: William Heinemann, 1913.

Mathias, Roland. 'Philosophy and Religion in the Poetry of R. S. Thomas'. *Poetry Wales* 7 (1972): 27–45.

Merchant, W. Moelwyn. *R. S. Thomas*. Fayetteville: University of Arkansas Press, 1990.

Montaigne, Michel de. *The Essays of Michel de Montaigne*, ed. and trans. M. A. Screech. London: The Penguin Press, 1991.

Morgan, J. Christopher. 'Destinations: Roots of Hope in R. S. Thomas'. *Welsh Writing in English* 4 (1998): 54–73.

——.'Reality and the dream in the Recent Poetry of R. S. Thomas'. *New Welsh Review* 44 (spring 1999): 56–60.

Nisbet, Robert. 'R. S. Thomas: The Landscape of Near-despair'. *Miraculous Simplicity: Essays on R. S. Thomas*, ed. William V. Davis. Fayetteville: University of Arkansas Press, 1993.

Olson, Charles. 'Projective Verse'. *Human Universe and Other Essays*, ed. Donald Allen. New York: Grove Press, Inc., 1967.

Peck, M. Scott. *Further Along the Road Less Travelled*. London: Simon and Schuster Ltd, 1993.

Phillips, D. Z. *R. S. Thomas: Poet of the Hidden God*. London: Macmillan, 1986.

Prys-Williams, Barbara. '"A Consciousness in Quest of its Own Truth": Some Aspects of R. S. Thomas's *The Echoes Return Slow* as Autobiography'. *Welsh Writing in English* 2 (1996): 98–126.

The Reader's Bible. London: Oxford University Press, 1951.

Robinson, John A. T. *Honest to God*. London: SCM Press Ltd, 1963.

Rolt, C. E. *Dionysus the Areopagite: The Divine Names and the Mystical Theology*. trans. C. E. Rolt. London: Lewis Reprints, 1975.

Savill, H. J. 'The Iago Prytherch Poems of R. S. Thomas'. *Critical Writings on R .S. Thomas*, ed. Sandra Anstey. Bridgend: Poetry Wales Press, 1992.

Scammell, William ed. *This Green Earth: A Celebration of Nature Poetry*. Maryport: Ellenback Press, 1992.

Shepherd, Elaine. *R. S. Thomas: Conceding an Absence*. London: Macmillan, 1996.

Smith, David. 'Confronting the Minotaur: Politics and Poetry in 20th Century Wales'. *Poetry Wales* 15 (1979): 4–23.

Stevens, Wallace. *The Collected Poems of Wallace Stevens*. New York: Alfred A. Knopf, 1955.

——.'The Noble Rider and the Sound of Words'. *The Necessary Angel: Essays on Reality and the Imagination*. London: Faber and Faber, 1951.

Stevenson, Anne. 'The Uses of Prytherch'. *The Page's Drift: R. S. Thomas at Eighty*, ed. M. Wynn Thomas. Bridgend: Poetry Wales Press, 1993.

Stringer, Jenny, ed. *The Oxford Companion to Twentieth Century Literature in English*. Oxford: Oxford University Press, 1996.

Tennyson, Alfred Lord. *In Memoriam*, ed. Robert H.Ross. New York: W.W Norton & Company, 1973.

Thomas, Dylan. *Collected Poems 1934–1953*, ed. Walford Davies and Ralph Maud. London: J. M. Dent, 1993.

Thomas, M. Wynn. 'Hidden Attachments: Aspects of the Relationship between the Two Literatures of Modern Wales'. *Welsh Writing in English*, 1 (1995): 145–63.

——.*Internal Difference: Twentieth Century Writing in Wales*. Cardiff: University of Wales Press, 1992.

——.'Introduction'. *The Page's Drift: R. S. Thomas at Eighty*, ed. M. Wynn Thomas. Bridgend: Poetry Wales Press, 1993.

Thomas, Ned. 'Introduction'. *R. S. Thomas Selected Prose,* ed. Sandra
    Anstey. Bridgend: Poetry Wales Press, 1986.
——. 'R. S. Thomas: The Question about Technology'. *Planet* (April/May
    1992), 54–60.
Thomas, R. G. 'Humanus Sum: A Second Look at R. S. Thomas'. *Critical
    Writings on R. S. Thomas,* ed. Sandra Anstey. Bridgend: Poetry Wales
    Press, 1992.
——. 'The Poetry of R. S. Thomas'. *A Review of English Literature* 3 (1962:
    85–95.
Thwaite, Anthony. 'Introduction'. *R. S. Thomas* by R. S. Thomas ed.
    Anthony Thwaite. London: Dent, 1996.
Tillich, Paul. *The Shaking of the Foundations.* Harmondsworth: Penguin
    Books Ltd, 1962.
Vaughan, Henry. *Poetry and Selected Prose,* ed. L. C. Martin. London:
    Oxford University Press, 1963.
——. *The Works of Henry Vaughan,* ed. L. C. Martin. London: Oxford
    University Press, 1957.
Walcott, Derek. *Collected Poems 1948–1984.* New York: Farrar, Straus &
    Giroux, 1986.
Ward, J. P. *The Poetry of R. S. Thomas.* Bridgend: Poetry Wales Press, 1987.
Wintle, Justin. *Furious Interiors: Wales, R. S. Thomas and God.* London:
    Harper Collins, 1996.
Wolters, Clifton, trans. *The Cloud of Unknowing.* Harmondsworth: Penguin
    Books Ltd, 1961.
Wordsworth, William. *Poems, Volume I,* ed. John O. Hayden.
    Harmondsworth: Penguin Books Ltd, 1977.
——. 'Preface to Lyrical Ballads'. *The Prose Work of William Wordsworth
    Volume I,* ed. W. J. B. Owen and J. W. Snyser. Oxford: Oxford
    University Press, 1974.
Yeats, W. B. 'Samhain:1905'. *Explorations,* ed. Mrs W. B. Yeats. London:
    Macmillan, 1962.

Further reading

Abse, Dannie, ed. *Twentieth Century Anglo-Welsh Poetry*. Bridgend: Seren, 1997.

Barnie, John. *No Hiding Place: Essays on the New Nature and Poetry*. Cardiff: University of Wales Press, 1996.

Conran, Tony, ed. *Frontiers in Anglo-Welsh Poetry*. Cardiff: University of Wales Press, 1997.

Garlick, Raymond. *An Introduction to Anglo-Welsh Literature*. Cardiff: University of Wales Press, 1970.

Hans-Werner, Ludwig and Lothar Fietz, ed. *Poetry in the British Isles: Non Metropolitan Perspectives*. Cardiff: University of Wales Press, 1995.

Humfrey, Belinda, ed. *Fire as Green as Grass: Studies of the Creative Impulse in Anglo-Welsh Poetry and Short Stories of the Twentieth Century*. Landysul: Gomer Press, 1995.

Jones, Glyn. *The Dragon Has Two Tongues: Essays on Anglo-Welsh Writers and Writing*. London: J. M. Dent & Sons Ltd, 1968.

Jones, Gwyn, ed. *The Oxford Book of Welsh Verse in English*. Oxford: Oxford University Press, 1977.

Lloyd, David, ed. *The Urgency of Identity: Contemporary English-language Poetry from Wales*. Evanston: Northwestern University Press, 1994.

Mathias, Roland. *Anglo-Welsh Literature: An Illustrated History*. Bridgend: Poetry Wales Press, 1986.

——. *A Ride Through the Wood: Essays on Anglo-Welsh Literature*. Bridgend: Poetry Wales Press, 1985.

Stephens, Meic, ed. *The Bright Field: An Anthology of Contemporary Poetry from Wales*. Manchester: Carcanet Press Limited, 1991.

Stephens, Meic and John Stuart Williams, ed. *The Lilting House: An Anthology of Anglo-Welsh Poetry 1917–1967*. London: Dent, 1969.

Wack, Amy, ed. *Burning the Bracken*. Bridgend: Seren Books, 1996.

Index

Notes: 'n.' after a page reference indicates the number of a note on that page.
R. S. Thomas's works are indexed under their title (followed by the collection in which they appear, where appropriate); other works are indexed under their poet's or author's name.